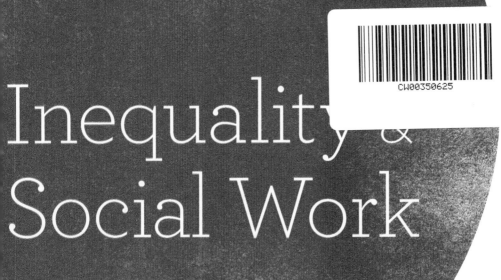

Inequality & Social Work

Rick Hood

S Sage

1 Oliver's Yard
55 City Road
London EC1Y 1SP

2455 Teller Road
Thousand Oaks, California 91320

Unit No 323-333, Third Floor, F-Block
International Trade Tower Nehru Place
New Delhi – 110 019

8 Marina View Suite 43-053
Asia Square Tower 1
Singapore 018960

Editor: Kate Keers
Editorial Assistant: Sahar Jamfar
Production Editor: Gourav Kumar
Copyeditor: Clare Weaver
Proofreader: Derek Markham
Indexer: KnowledgeWorks Global Ltd
Marketing Manager: Camille Richmond
Cover Design: Sheila Tong
Typeset by KnowledgeWorks Global Ltd
Printed in the UK

Library of Congress Control Number: 2023934302

British Library Cataloguing in Publication data

A catalogue record for this book is available from the British Library

ISBN 978-1-5297-6879-4
ISBN 978-1-5297-6878-7 (pbk)

At Sage we take sustainability seriously. Most of our products are printed in the UK using responsibly sourced papers and boards. When we print overseas we ensure sustainable papers are used as measured by the project paper chain grading system. We undertake an annual audit to monitor our sustainability.

Contents

For Vicki, Finn and William.

About the Author

Rick Hood is a registered social worker and Professor of Social Work in the Department of Social Work and Social Care at Kingston University. He studied modern languages at Cambridge University and spent a number of years doing youth and community work in Germany and France before training and practising as a social worker in South London. Most of his teaching and research has been in the field of children's social care, covering topics such as complexity, inequality, assessment and decision-making, reunification from care, interprofessional working, domestic abuse and child protection, and the inspection of services.

Introduction: Why Inequality Matters

Chapter overview

This introductory chapter will briefly introduce the concept of inequality and explain why it matters to social workers. Connections will be made to core values such as social justice, human rights, and respect for diversity, but also to questions of knowledge and power. A case will be made for adopting an inequalities lens in social work, which incorporates a broad definition of inequality that goes beyond income, poverty and class and incorporates various aspects of human identity and experience. The chapter concludes with an overview of the book and its contents.

Introduction

Why do you want to become a social worker? It is a question that applicants to social work courses are often asked. Usually they have an answer prepared! Although responses vary, two principal themes often emerge. The first is broadly about helping people, a desire to use professional knowledge, as well as the resources available to social workers, in order to support individuals to overcome challenges in their lives, achieve their personal goals, and improve their wellbeing. The second is more about social change, an awareness that private troubles are often linked to public issues such as poverty, racism and discrimination, and a belief that social work can contribute to efforts to address such problems. Some applicants mention inequality directly, but this is relatively rare; the concept is often implicit in the examples they give and the values they espouse. This book aims to make those connections more explicit. It will argue that understanding inequality is essential for contemporary social workers. This introductory chapter will consider why inequality matters so much, and why the concept acts as a kind of critical lens for examining the profession and indeed our own professional roles. The starting point, suitably enough, is social work's own self-definition.

Transforming Society

Among the professions, social work is arguably unique in its ambition to transform society. This idealistic outlook is captured in the global definition adopted by the International Federation of Social Workers (IFSW):

> Social work is a practice-based profession and an academic discipline
> that promotes social change and development, social cohesion, and
> the empowerment and liberation of people. Principles of social justice,
> human rights, collective responsibility and respect for diversities
> are central to social work. Underpinned by theories of social work,
> social sciences, humanities and indigenous knowledge, social work
> engages people and structures to address life challenges and enhance
> wellbeing. (IFSW, 2014)

Wisely, the IFSW's definition steers clear of saying what the endpoint of social change might be. However, it does say something about the direction of travel: towards a more just, humane and inclusive society, which places value on both individual freedom *and* collective responsibility. Similar statements are found in the values and standards promoted by national associations and professional bodies. In England, social workers are expected to 'challenge the impact of disadvantage and discrimination on people and their families and communities' and to 'promote social justice, helping to confront and resolve issues of inequality and inclusion' (Social Work England, 2020). These are just two professional standards (1.5 and 1.6) out of a total of fifty, which if nothing else shows that social workers have their work cut out! Such standards are intended to guide and inform practice rather than to make practitioners responsible for rectifying social ills. Nonetheless, they demonstrate that promoting social justice is still a core feature of contemporary social work. As we shall see in Chapter 1, the relationship between the concepts of (in)justice and (in)equality is quite complicated. We also need to acknowledge the tension in pursuing such ideals within the constraints of a professional project, which must also serve the interests – and values – of society in its current form. This means considering social work's legal status and its relationship to the state.

Social Work's Legal Status

In many countries, including the UK, social work is a regulated profession. This means that people cannot use the title of social worker, or its equivalent, unless they have done the required training and have registered with its professional body. Such measures are designed to protect members of the public who receive social work services and ensure that standards of practice are maintained. They also point to the relationship between social work and what might loosely be termed 'the state', meaning not just the national government and its policies, or the legal frameworks under which social workers operate, but also the organisations that recruit social workers to carry out various statutory remits. In England, many social workers are employed by local (municipal) governments, although they may also work in the private or voluntary sector. Moreover, frontline social workers tend to operate in a sensitive and contentious domain where social policy impinges directly on people's private and family life. Among other things, they contribute to assessments of people's mental capacity, the removal of children from their birth parents, and the need for compulsory admission to psychiatric hospital. In carrying out such tasks, they must be scrupulous about acting justly, ethically and legally, while also mindful that the need for intervention may itself reflect deeply entrenched social divisions.

When one looks more closely at what social workers do, as opposed to what the profession says about itself, there is little evidence of a utopian project of social change. Instead, the picture that emerges is a more familiar one of human beings grappling with the complexity of life, in all its messiness and contradiction (Howe, 2014). So, while a strong value base may be essential for social workers to discharge their duties in accordance with the expectations that society places on them, those expectations may also lead them to accommodate people as best as possible within existing social arrangements, no matter how unjust or unequal. This is highlighted by the figures cited in Chapter 2 and Chapter 4, for instance, about disparities in the care system or mental health services. To take the first example, since children from deprived backgrounds are much more likely to be taken into care than children from affluent backgrounds, does that mean that social workers are not doing their jobs properly? Most practitioners would probably say 'no' – it is unfair to blame social workers for such inequalities. Decisions to protect children from harm are not (or should not be) taken because of a child's poverty but because of various other factors including the standard of parental care. Such decisions are a last resort when other preventative measures have either failed or when the risks to a child's safety are so great that action must be taken. Moreover, there are other social workers, particularly in the voluntary sector, who are engaged in activities to address social problems and campaign for social change. Blaming the profession for inequalities in children's outcomes would do them a disservice; without their efforts, perhaps the gap would be even greater. A social worker's freedom to pursue social change depends on many things: her role and remit, organisational and institutional priorities, availability of resources, and the wider policy context, to name but a few. This book does not propose to make social workers responsible for social inequality. Instead, it will advocate an 'inequalities lens' – a way for all social workers (not just practitioners) to evaluate theory and practice in light of the profession's commitment to social justice.

An inequalities Lens

When I started work on this book, the Covid-19 pandemic was sweeping across the world. Among the many tragedies of this disease was (and still is) the spotlight it has thrown on inequality. In the UK, as well as in other countries, people have been more likely to become seriously ill or die from Covid if they are poor (Ahmed *et al.*, 2020; Patel *et al.*, 2020) and/or if they are from minority ethnic groups (Bentley, 2020; Hooper *et al.*, 2020). Furthermore, these groups are also more likely to suffer financial hardship because of measures taken by governments to slow the spread of the virus (Hu, 2020). These disparities are discussed further in Chapter 3. The main point for now is that such factors are social rather than individual in nature. They demonstrate the stark impact of social structures on people's health and life chances. Farmer *et al.* (2019) refer to the existence of health inequalities as a form of 'structural violence', a term coined by the Norwegian theologist Johann Galtung (1969). Unlike physical violence, structural violence can be hard for people to observe or understand:

> Structural violence is often embedded in longstanding 'ubiquitous social structures, normalized by stable institutions and regular experience' (Gilligan, 1996). Because they seem so ordinary in our ways of understanding the world, they appear almost invisible. Disparate access to resources, political power, education, health care, and legal standing are just a few examples. The idea of structural violence is linked very closely to social injustice and the social machinery of oppression. (Farmer *et al.*, 2019: 1686)

Since social structures help to shape our experiences and even our identities, we tend to see them as ordinary and innocuous. It requires a change of perspective to grasp that what is normal might also be harmful, or that it might disadvantage some people while benefiting others. This is often the subject of 'critical' analysis, which is discussed in Chapter 7, and is also fundamental to an inequalities lens. So, what does it mean to adopt an inequalities lens in social work? In some respects, this book is the long answer to that question! In short, it involves:

- a broad definition of inequality that incorporates various aspects of human identity and experience and emphasises the way these aspects overlap and intersect in people's lives;
- understanding the connection between the concept of (in)equality and core social work values such as social justice, human rights, and respect for diversity;
- examining inequalities in the production of knowledge and its implications for social work assessment and decision making;

- identifying the inequalities present in demand for, and provision of, social work services, and evaluating the extent to which social work practice may be contributing to them;
- orienting social work interventions as far as possible to the goal of reducing inequalities.

As noted already, this type of analysis is congruent with the profession's own self-definition and aligns with the national standards for social work in England as well as in other countries. However, adopting an inequalities lens also has a more pragmatic value for practitioners in the field. This book will argue at various points that social work interventions are more likely to succeed if they acknowledge and act on the basis that individual problems are linked to structural inequities. Elsewhere, I have suggested that social workers are professionally inclined to be system thinkers, trained to come to a holistic view of a situation before deciding how to proceed (Hood, 2018). By implication, this discourages an overly individualistic analysis, in which people's own behaviour and decisions are the only factors that are considered relevant. Of course, individual factors are hugely important and, in a crisis, inevitably become the focus for support and intervention. However, adopting an inequalities lens to understand the person in their social context can make a surprising difference to the outcome of an intervention. When it comes to planning and designing services, it also makes strategic sense to understand how inequalities impact on the welfare and wellbeing of different groups in the population.

Beyond the issue of effectiveness, employing an inequalities lens also means examining social work's credibility among the communities it serves. The profession's relationship with the state, particularly during a period of political polarisation, creates the risk that social workers are not seen as trustworthy partners by citizens who feel that their life challenges are rooted in forms of social injustice that are insufficiently acknowledged and even perpetuated by government policies. The problem is compounded by the fact that those citizens who have the most contact with social services also tend to be those who are most disadvantaged by the current distribution of power and resources in society. This presents a real problem for social workers, who rely on building relationships with people and working in partnership with them, even (or especially) if there is an element of coercion to the involvement of services, as in child protection or mental health settings. For this reason, maintaining a strategic focus on inequality makes sense as part of social work's long-term professional project, a necessary counterbalance to an institutional culture that seems to emphasise individual rather than collective responsibility for social ills.

Of course, the main reasons why inequalities matter have less to do with social work than with society in general. Over the past few decades, evidence has mounted that inequality is bad for us – not just for people who are most disadvantaged by it but for everyone else too. Much of this evidence was summarised by Wilkinson and Pickett (2010) in their book, *The Spirit Level*, which suggests that citizens of more equal societies tend to live longer and to lead healthier, happier lives (see Chapter 4). Equally, health and happiness cannot be boiled down to a simple formula. Recent decades have also shown that ecological and environmental concerns should be a fundamental part of such questions. Conflict and competition cannot be eliminated from society and have often spurred economic and political development. Nonetheless, there is good reason to think that fairness and reciprocity are just as important for human progress (Fehr and Schmidt, 2006; Flanagin *et al.*, 2021). Contemporary democratic societies are fundamentally based on the rule of law, under which all citizens are entitled to equal treatment. Many people would find it hard to envisage a prosperous, successful society that was also an unjust one (Rawls, 2001). As we shall see in the next chapter, the importance of equality, or the lack of it, is closely connected to the concept of justice.

My Position in this Work

Since inequality arises from power relations, some of which are to do with the control and production of knowledge, I want to say something here about my personal and professional biography – partly to explain how I came to write the book but also to reflect on my position in its writing. This is important because the usual caveats of an authorial viewpoint are particularly relevant to this book. While anyone writing on any subject necessarily does so from a partial perspective, writing about inequality is particularly problematic, not only because of the potential for bias, but also because of a limited understanding of issues that have not been personally experienced. In this section, I clarify my assumptions and values and how they are linked to my own life experiences, as well as acknowledging the insight and contribution of colleagues who have kindly supported this work.

Identity and social positioning are fundamental to social inequality. My own position relates to a combination of overlapping characteristics that are considered at various points in the book, including gender, ethnicity, sexuality, (dis)ability, class, age, and nationality. In these respects, I am positioned as: a cis-gender male, White British, straight, abled, middle-aged, middle-class and a British citizen. This is a privileged social position in pretty much every respect. For example, as a White man I benefit from both male privilege and White privilege. The latter has been memorably described as an 'invisible knapsack' by Peggy McIntosh (2020: 7–8): 'White privilege is like an invisible weightless, knapsack of special provisions, assurances, tools, maps, guides, code-books, passports, visas, clothes, compass, emergency gear, and blank checks.' My own knapsack is particularly full, since I benefit from the normative status of heterosexuality and 'able-bodiedness' in my culture and society, the social and economic capital that stems from a middle-class education, and the various advantages that come with

British citizenship, the UK being currently the eighth richest country in the world (and an imperial power). Such benefits are not only unearned, but they are also the flipside of structural inequalities, which mean that large swathes of humanity suffer from multiple forms of injustice: systemic racism, misogyny, class or caste oppression, homophobia, disablism, imperialism, colonialism, along with many other forms of discrimination and prejudice.

People's life stories are not entirely determined by the structural forces of privilege and oppression – if they were, there would be no need (or hope) for social workers. My interest in inequality stems from observations and encounters, both personal and professional, which have given me cause for reflection throughout my life. For example, growing up in the 1980s in a northern English mining town gave me some sense – without really understanding it – of the impact of de-industrialisation and neo-liberal ('Thatcherite') policies on working-class communities. My mother's experience of raising a family on her own meant that I noticed – again, without really understanding – some of the difficulties and barriers she faced as a woman living independently in a society still dominated by the male breadwinner model. Since we had moved to England from Germany, where I spent the first six years of my life as a German-speaker, I also learned something about having to adjust to a new homeland – although, being white-skinned, I had it much easier than some of my other classmates. Later on, when I left university to work – first, as a youth and community worker, and then as a social worker, I had plenty of opportunities to meet and learn from people whose backgrounds were both different and more disadvantaged than mine. Being a social worker taught me that evidence and expertise only become useful once you take the time to listen to people and understand what matters to them.

As an academic, the relationship between public issues and private troubles has continued to inform and shape my teaching and research, leading eventually to the decision to write this book. As suggested by the chapter summaries below, it was conceived partly as a textbook and partly as a commentary on social work and its social justice mission. While I have hopefully established some of the credentials for undertaking such a project, there is no getting away from the fact that many aspects of social inequality I have no way of relating to personally – or indeed, professionally, since much of my work has been in the field of child welfare. I am therefore very grateful to several people who agreed to act in an advisory capacity to the book, review chapter drafts, discuss key concepts, and make me aware of gaps in my understanding. The book is much improved as a result of their insights, although any remaining omissions and flaws are entirely my responsibility. I would particularly like to thank Paul Bywaters, Tam Cane, Peter Choates, Jahnine Davis, Brid Featherstone, Yvalia Febrer, Jacqueline Harry, and Rochelle Watson. As always, I welcome any feedback and suggestions from readers, who are sometimes kind enough to get in touch.

Structure of this Book

The book is divided into two sections to enable a range of theoretical concerns to be brought together in a critical dialogue with policy and practice. The first section will explore different aspects of inequality to help readers to understand its significance for society as a whole and for people receiving welfare services; the second will explore the role of social work in tackling inequality, drawing attention to some of the more innovative currents in social work that are closely attuned to the ideas of social justice and equality.

Chapter 1 will consider how to define and explain inequality, starting with the fundamental concepts of justice and fairness, as well as a contemporary focus on questions of power and intersectionality. There follows a discussion of equality of opportunity, which often underlies the notion of fairness in Western societies, along with related ideas about meritocracy, education and the significance of structural constraints. These ideas are then contrasted with equality of outcome, drawing on debates about freedom and the role of markets in organising human affairs. The chapter then moves to questions of measurement and operationalisation ('equality of what?'), in which the core values of health, welfare and happiness are linked to the idea of capability. The chapter concludes by drawing together the theoretical components of inequality as a foundation for considering its diverse forms in Chapter 2.

Chapter 2 examines some of the ways in which disparities in health, happiness and wellbeing are associated, systematically and unjustly, with human diversity and difference. The starting point is to consider how inequitable distribution of resources connects to social hierarchies and stratification, often in the form of class and caste systems. There is a discussion of poverty, income and deprivation, and the importance of geography and place. The chapter then turns to personal characteristics that are often the subject of equalities legislation but are nonetheless associated with significant inequalities: gender, race and ethnicity, age, sexuality and sexual orientation, and disability. Some theoretical concepts are introduced and a selection of empirical evidence is provided in each of these areas.

Chapter 3 examines the impact of inequality on people's health and wellbeing, starting with the social gradient, a fundamental concept in health inequalities research. The graded relationship between people's social position and health status is explored in relation to a range of outcomes, including life expectancy and serious illness. The social gradient interacts with other structural factors affecting people's health and wellbeing, as illustrated in numerous inequalities that have been exposed by the Covid-19 pandemic. The chapter proceeds to examine the social determinants of health and evidence that income inequality exacerbates many social problems including rates of imprisonment, obesity, mental illness, and addiction. The final section focuses on welfare inequalities and social care, showing how inequality manifests itself not only as unfair barriers to care and support, but also as the targeting of disadvantaged groups with surveillance and statutory intervention.

Chapter 4 focuses on the actions taken by governments to address social problems and improve the health and wellbeing of citizens. It begins with the concept of social welfare and establishment of the welfare state in the decades following the Second World War. Different types of welfare system are compared with reference to political value positions such as liberalism and conservatism. Common critiques of the welfare state are discussed alongside the increasing influence of neo-liberal policies in the 1980s and 1990s. The chapter proceeds to examine the unequal impact of austerity measures following the financial crisis of 2007/08, and to consider the effect of anti-discrimination and equalities legislation. It concludes with a discussion of populism and divisive approaches to inequality, which have become a key feature of the contemporary policy landscape.

Chapter 5 considers various aspects of global inequality, starting with the huge gaps in income and wealth that exist between countries and individuals in the world. It proceeds to examine the ambiguous role of globalisation in the production and perpetuation of inequalities, looking at the significance of global institutions such as the World Bank, the activities of transnational organisations, and the impact of environmental racism. The chapter then takes a closer look at the relationship between inequality and imperialism, including the enduring legacy of European colonial empires. One such legacy is the structuring of the global economy as a power hierarchy, with rich and powerful core nations seeking to dominate and exploit the weaker and poorer societies on the periphery. Another is the enduring impact of settler colonialism on Indigenous peoples, something with profound implications for social work and its role within the welfare state. The chapter concludes with a discussion of migration and its connection to inequalities both between and within countries.

Chapter 6 explores the role of social work in tackling inequality in its various forms. Its starting point is the professionalisation of social work, which has implications for power relations, the institutional context of practice, and constraints imposed on the pursuit of social justice goals. The chapter then turns to some of the core activities of social work within the welfare state, looking particularly at assessment, casework, and social regulation in areas such as child protection and mental health. The contrast between clinical and structural practice models brings out some of the tensions and ambiguities within social work, and the extent to which it may unwittingly reproduce or even exacerbate inequalities in wider society. The chapter concludes with a discussion of advocacy, empowerment, and anti-discriminatory practice, which pave the way for the more radical and transformational approaches considered in Chapter 7.

Chapter 7 examines the role of critical and radical social work in addressing inequality. These approaches use a structural analysis of social problems to understand how services can be aligned with emancipatory social justice aims.

The profession's radical core is traced from progressive elements of the 19th-century Settlement movement to social work's response to the social upheavals of the post-war period. The chapter then follows distinctive strands of radicalism, starting with Marxist and socialist perspectives and proceeding to examine a range of critical approaches to practice: feminist social work, anti-racist social work, Indigenous social work, the social model of disability, and LGBTQ+ affirmative social work. Intersectionality is highlighted as a key conceptual framework for placing the concerns of multiply marginalised groups and identities at the centre of an inequalities agenda. Possibilities for reform and transformation of services in the neo-liberal context of contemporary welfare systems are examined with reference to themes such as interest convergence, postcolonialism and allyship.

Chapter 8 focuses on community social work, which is broadly defined to encompass various types of community development, community organising and social action. Different understandings of community are considered and a brief history of community work provides some key reference points, including its origins in colonial projects and the settlement movement, the connections to trade unionism and the activity of radical organisers such as Saul Alinsky, and the later development of state-sponsored community work as part of urban policy and planning. The chapter continues with a discussion of skills in community practice, the benefits and pitfalls of professionalisation and voluntarism, and the pluralist approach adopted by social workers in locality-based settings. There is a brief introduction to approaches developed in the United States such as broad-based and asset-based community development. The chapter concludes with a discussion of radical community work, which in recent years has become increasingly concerned with intersecting inequalities.

The final chapter reviews some of the broad themes and implications of focusing on inequality in social work. The pitfalls of professionalisation and ties to the state are discussed, as well as the continuing relevance of national welfare systems in the era of global capitalism. It is argued that resistance to oppression is one of the hallmarks of unequal societies, yet also carries risks for those who resist. It is therefore imperative for the profession to maintain its critical and radical tradition, even as it comes under pressure from neo-liberal approaches and attitudes. The book concludes with a discussion of social work's mediating role, which requires practitioners to align themselves with the powerless at the same time as accommodating the interests of the powerful. Holding such dilemmas may prove untenable in contexts of very high inequality, but in a more equal society could enable the profession's renewal and transformation.

References

Ahmed, F., Ahmed, N.E., Pissarides, C. and Stiglitz, J. (2020) 'Why inequality could spread COVID-19', *The Lancet Public Health*, **5**(5), p. e240.

Bentley, G.R. (2020) 'Don't blame the BAME: Ethnic and structural inequalities in susceptibilities to COVID-19', *American Journal of Human Biology*, **32**(5), p. e23478.

Farmer, P.E., Nizeye, B., Stulac, S. and Keshavjee, S. (2019) 'Structural violence and clinical medicine', *The Social Medicine Reader*, **2**(3), pp. 156–169.

Fehr, E. and Schmidt, K.M. (2006) 'The economics of fairness, reciprocity and altruism–experimental evidence and new theories', *Handbook of the Economics of Giving, Altruism and Reciprocity*, **1**, pp. 615–691.

Flanagin, A., Frey, T., Christiansen, S.L. and Committee, A.M.o.S. (2021) 'Updated guidance on the reporting of race and ethnicity in medical and science journals', *Jama*, **326**(7), pp. 621–627.

Galtung, J. (1969) 'Violence, peace, and peace research', *Journal of Peace Research*, **6**(3), pp. 167–191.

Gilligan, J. (1996) *Violence: Reflections on a national epidemic*, New York, Vintage Books.

Hood, R. (2018) *Complexity in social work*, London, Sage.

Hooper, M.W., Nápoles, A.M. and Pérez-Stable, E.J. (2020) 'COVID-19 and racial/ethnic disparities', *Jama*, **323**(24), pp. 2466–2467.

Howe, D. (2014) *The compleat social worker*, Basingstoke, Palgrave Macmillan.

Hu, Y. (2020) 'Intersecting ethnic and native–migrant inequalities in the economic impact of the COVID-19 pandemic in the UK', *Research in Social Stratification and Mobility*, **68**, p. 100528.

International Federation of Social Work (IFSW) (2014) *Global Definition of the Social Work Profession*, Available online: http://ifsw.org/policies/definition-of-social-work/, Last Accessed: 01/05/2022.

McIntosh, P. (2020) 'White Privilege and Male Privilege: a personal account of coming to see correspondences through work in women's studies', in Weekes, K. (ed.), Privilege and prejudice: Twenty years with the invisible knapsack, Newcastle, Cambridge Scholars Publishing, pp. 7–19.

Patel, J.A., Nielsen, F.B.H., Badiani, A.A., Assi, S., Unadkat, V.A., Patel, B., Ravindrane, R. and Wardle, H. (2020) 'Poverty, inequality and COVID-19: The forgotten vulnerable', *Public Health*, **183**, pp. 110–111.

Rawls, J. (2001) *Justice as fairness: A restatement*, Cambridge, MA, Harvard University Press.

Social Work England (2020) *Professional Standards*, Available online: https://www.socialworkengland.org.uk/media/1640/1227_socialworkengland_standards_prof_standards_final-aw.pdf, Last Accessed: 26/02/2023.

Wilkinson, R. and Pickett, K. (2010) *The spirit level: Why equality is better for everyone*, Harmondsworth, Penguin.

1
What is Inequality?

Chapter overview
....

This chapter looks at how to define and explain inequality, starting with the fundamental concepts of justice and fairness, as well as a contemporary focus on questions
of power and intersectionality. There follows a discussion of equality of opportunity,
which often underlies the notion of fairness in western societies, along with related
ideas about meritocracy, education and the significance of structural constraints.
These ideas are then contrasted with equality of outcome, drawing on debates about
freedom and the role of markets in organising human affairs. The chapter then moves
to questions of measurement and operationalisation ('equality of what?'), in which
the core values of health, welfare and happiness are linked to the idea of capability.
The chapter concludes by drawing together the theoretical components of inequality
as a foundation for considering its diverse forms in the next chapter.

Introduction

In the introductory chapter, a case was made for adopting an 'inequalities lens' to
examine theory and practice in social work. The aim of this chapter is to examine
what is meant by inequality and discuss some of the debates and controversies
associated with this complex concept. A major reason for the complexity is the
relationship between inequality and difference. The former is associated with
unfairness and often perceived in negative terms, even though we often accen-
tuate and sometimes celebrate the latter. The connection is illustrated by the
question of how (or whether) to reward ability and effort. For example, think of
a cultural activity that you enjoy, e.g. watching a football match or going to the
theatre. Whatever the activity, you can expect to pay more to see or take part
in something that you consider to be higher quality. A season ticket to watch a
football team in the premier league, for example, will be much more expensive
(and may involve a long waiting list) than for a club in the lower leagues; likewise, the cost of admission to a major play headlined by a famous actor will
cost more than a local am-dram production. The corollary is that more talented

people – international footballers, say, or major Hollywood stars – earn more than those who are less talented. Such differences do not strike most people as particularly unfair. Yet, on aggregate, they contribute to types of inequality, such as large gaps in income levels or cultural participation, which do seem unfair to many people. Moreover, rewarding talent and effort often seems to reproduce rather than reduce structural disadvantages, as we shall see when we consider the concept of meritocracy later on.

Exercise 1.1

Consider the questions below. Think about the reasons for your responses. Are there any connections or contradictions between them?

1   Do you think that people's position in life is mainly down to them as individuals or mainly determined by social factors, such as family wealth?
2   Do you think there is enough opportunity for virtually everyone to get on in life if they really want to?
3   Do you think it is fair that women on average earn less than men and are less likely to be in senior positions?
4   Are you in favour of affirmative action to reduce inequalities, e.g. all-women shortlists or reserved places/posts for people from minority ethnic backgrounds?
5   Do you think that people with the greatest income and wealth should be taxed much more than they are now?
6   Should society reward people who work hard and make the most of their abilities?

The questions in Exercise 1.1 are designed to show that what we think about inequality might depend on how it is framed, and that the term can mean different things to different people. For example, some people will answer 'no' to question 3, considering it to be unfair that women earn more than men, while also answering 'no' to question 5, which is about taxation, even though higher earners are more likely to be men. In what follows, we will further explore some of those framings, including the distinction between equality of outcome and equality of opportunity, as well as the connection between equality and justice. However, our starting point is something that is more often implied than explicitly stated: namely, that inequality is fundamentally about power.

Inequality and Power

Power means different things to different people. Some might think of the coercive might of the state and its various incarnations: the army, police force, legal system, and so on. Some might see it more in terms of the capacity of individuals to influence others: charisma, expertise, authority, etc. Our focus in this book is on what Pratto *et al.* (2013) call 'group-based dominance hierarchies' – social structures based on arbitrary divisions, such as gender, race or class, which enable one group to secure privileges for itself and exploit others to its own advantage. Such divisions are arbitrary because they do not constitute a just basis for inequality; this is not to say that differences between people do not exist or don't matter. To take a less well-known example, hand preference (whether you prefer to use your right or left hand for everyday tasks such as writing) seems to be a natural predisposition – most people are right-handed but about ten percent of the population is left-handed. Because left-handers are in the minority, they live in a physical and social environment that is largely geared towards right-handedness (Masud and Ajmal, 2012). This could mean relatively minor things such as the design of door handles or the impracticality of fountain pens. However, in many cultures – historically but also today – left-handed people have been treated with disapproval and distrust, their hand preference viewed as abnormal and deficient, or even as a sign of evil[1], and have experienced discrimination, suppression and punishment (Smits, 2011). In other words, hand preference is an example of how a random and seemingly innocuous difference between people can be transformed into an arbitrary social division in which one group of people, sometimes but not necessarily in the majority, exerts power over others. This pattern of dominance becomes 'structural' when it persists over time, replicating itself through ideas, traditions, stories, laws, precedents, and so on.

The main social divisions with which this book is concerned are described in the next chapter. They include class, race, ethnicity, gender, sexuality, disability, and age. As the example of hand preference shows, there are many other differences that have formed the basis for discrimination against particular groups; it is necessary to acknowledge this diversity of experience when applying an inequalities lens to questions of social justice. Nonetheless, some social divisions assume particular significance because they serve as organising principles for the unequal distribution of goods and resources in society, leading to pronounced disparities in longevity, health, wellbeing and happiness (see Chapter 3). The structures of power, oppression and exclusion that underpin such social practices are often named after the divisions that they exploit: classism, racism, misogyny, heteronormativity, colonialism, disablism, ageism, and so on. Although these power structures focus on distinct axes of difference, they do not operate on their own. Instead, they function as a complex system of power and distinction, placing elites into positions of advantage and putting everyone else at a disadvantage. Another way of putting this is to say that inequalities are always intersectional.

---

1   I am left-handed myself. The Latin word, 'sinistra', meaning left, is also the root of the English word 'sinister'.

Intersectional Inequalities

Collins and Bilge (2020) define intersectionality as follows:

> Intersectionality investigates how intersecting power relations influence
> social relations across diverse societies as well as individual experiences in
> everyday life. As an analytic tool, intersectionality views categories of race,
> class, gender, sexuality, nation, ability, ethnicity and age – among others –
> as interrelated and mutually shaping one another. Intersectionality is a
> way of understanding and explaining complexity in the world, in people,
> and in human experiences. (Collins and Bilge, 2020: 2)

Intersectionality has its roots in Black feminism and critical race theory, drawing
on a long history of activism among diverse groups of women across the world
(McCall, 2005; Nash, 2008; Winker and Degele, 2011; Mattsson, 2014; Crenshaw,
2017; Almeida *et al.*, 2019; Collins and Bilge, 2020). Professor Kimberlé Crenshaw, an American legal scholar and critical race theorist, is usually credited
with coining the term and pioneering its use as a conceptual framework across
academic disciplines (Crenshaw, 1989, 1991). Crenshaw rejected the 'single axis
framework' that characterised much feminist and anti-racist politics at the time,
arguing instead for the need to recognise the 'multidimensionality' of marginalised people's lived experience. Intersectionality has therefore had a longstanding
concern with one particular intersection, that between race and gender, and with
one particular marginalised group, namely Black women (Nash, 2008). In the
intervening years, the scope of intersectional analysis has widened, reflecting a
critical dialogue with other theoretical traditions, including Latinx, Indigenous,
postcolonial, transnational and queer perspectives, in which the study of multiply
marginalised identities is a central concern (Mehrotra, 2010). As a result, intersectionality has emerged as the primary multi-disciplinary framework for examining the complexities of identity and oppression. Its importance is reflected in
an increasingly prominent role within social work theory, practice and education
(Yamada *et al.*, 2015; Nayak and Robbins, 2018; Almeida *et al.*, 2019; Bernard,
2021).

Inequality vs Equality

One of the lessons of intersectionality is to avoid overly essentialist readings
of identity and oppression, e.g. assuming that people's experience is the same
because they share a particular characteristic, or combination of characteristics.
Respect for internal differences, as well as the difference between the oppres-
sor and the oppressed, is also necessary in order to mobilise collective action
against injustice – otherwise, as scholars of intersectionality have observed, the

voices of multiply minoritised groups will be silenced within broader coalitions that cannot speak for them. This has implications for social movements, political activism, trade unions, advocacy groups and indeed any other efforts to bring people together for a common cause. Respect for difference means that equality is intersectional too; since people are not all the same, and do not aspire to be, it follows that equality cannot really be about sameness. Instead, since inequality arises from unjust social arrangements underpinned by oppressive power structures, equality is connected to our notions about what a just and fair society should look like. It is not a straightforward question, and the rest of this chapter will examine some of the different ways that people have tried to answer it.

Equality of Opportunity

Equality of opportunity is a common way of thinking about fairness in contemporary society. The metaphor often used to explore equality of opportunity is that of a race or competition. This reflects the fact that most societies are organised along hierarchical lines, so that power and resources are unevenly distributed. In pre-modern societies, people's place in the hierarchy was often fixed by birth, for example through rigid class or caste systems. Nowadays, the prevailing view is that social status should be determined by open and fair competition, usually in some sort of market, in which all citizens are eligible to take part on equal terms. Importantly, this approach does not rule out large differences in where people end up, as long as they start off on a more or less equal footing. The underlying principle is egalitarianism, which holds that all human beings are fundamentally equal in worth and moral status. This is closely related to the idea of basic rights and liberties, which are enshrined in international agreements such as the European Convention on Human Rights (Schabas, 2015). It follows that arbitrary distinctions that are not under people's control, such as who our parents are or the colour of our skin, should not be an impediment to achieving social success. The same applies to choices that reflect basic human liberties, such as religious belief. Such principles are enforced through anti-discrimination laws in many countries, an example of which is the 2010 Equality Act in the UK.

Equality of opportunity acknowledges that some individual traits, such as innate athleticism and intelligence, or aspects of personality such as conscientiousness, may confer an advantage in competition for prestigious roles and positions. Such advantages may be tolerated to the extent that assigning gifted people to such roles that make the most of their talents is to the benefit of society as a whole. A key test is whether two people, whose abilities are similar but whose initial social position is very different, have an equal chance of succeeding in a competitive process designed to select on the basis of those abilities. An example might be two women applying to an undergraduate course at Cambridge University, both of whom are hardworking and similarly equipped with the academic skills relevant to their course. One of the candidates is from an affluent family background and was privately educated, whereas the other is from a more deprived background and educated in a state school. If both women have the same chance of success, then the competitive procedure might satisfy what John Rawls calls 'fair equality of opportunity' (Rawls, 2009). On the other hand, if the chances of admission unduly favour the socially more advantaged candidate, then it would not be a fair process. To know whether this was the case we would need to know about the characteristics of successful vs unsuccessful applicants to universities. Strangely, such data is rarely made publicly available by elite universities! However, what information does exist suggests that the intake of students to the most prestigious universities in England is highly unrepresentative of the general population (Waller *et al.*, 2017). Applicants from Black British backgrounds and economically deprived areas seem to be at a particular disadvantage (Lammy, 2017; Montacute and Cullinane, 2018). Similar patterns have been observed in other countries, where overall access to higher education has increased over recent decades but opportunities to take up a place at a 'top' university remain unequal (Triventi, 2013b; Marginson, 2016). This matters because graduates from the most prestigious courses and institutions tend to have better employment prospects and higher future earnings than other graduates (Triventi, 2013a; De Vries, 2014).

Meritocracy

Advocates of equal opportunity insist that higher social status – and the power and wealth associated with it – should be based on merit rather than on birth or privilege. A society organised along these lines is sometimes called a 'meritocracy'. The term has found favour among politicians across the spectrum, who use it to frame their policies in what Sandel (2020) calls 'the rhetoric of rising'. The following quotes are from two former UK prime ministers:

> As a nation, we are wasting too much of the talent of too many of the people. The mission of any second term must be this: to break down the barriers that hold people back, to create real upward mobility, a society that is open and genuinely based on merit and the equal worth of all'. (Blair, 2001)

> 'I want Britain to be the world's great meritocracy – a country where everyone has a fair chance to go as far as their talent and their hard work will allow.' (May, 2016)

Although fifteen years apart and issued by the leaders of opposing political parties, the two statements espouse very similar visions of social progress towards a meritocratic ideal. Of course, such statements can encompass very different views about what is meant by equal opportunity and the policies necessary to achieve it. For example, governments may pursue policies of 'social investment' designed to increase social mobility and improve the life chances of children from disadvantaged backgrounds (Fawcett *et al.*, 2004; Parton, 2011), including measures aimed at educational access and attainment. Alternatively, there may be a geographical focus on 'regeneration' projects, designed to boost economic growth and social cohesion in deprived areas (Tallon, 2013; Pemberton, 2019). While government pledges to address such disparities might not always be perceived as sincere, the underlying idea of a society based on the promotion and recognition of merit has undeniable force.

Interestingly, despite the positive connotations it largely has now, the term meritocracy had a satirical and indeed pejorative meaning in the book where it was first popularised – Michael Young's *The Rise of the Meritocracy* (Young, 1958). Young thought that the rhetoric of merit would have unintended consequences once it became institutionalised. Rather than transforming power structures, all that would happen is that people who were ostensibly selected on the basis of merit would simply replace the ruling class that previously held sway. As we shall see below, educational credentials have assumed a critical role in this process. Another problem is that people who lose out in the race for distinction would have no-one to blame but themselves, since they obviously lacked merit! Moreover, those with a high social status would ascribe their position to their own efforts and talents rather than to good fortune, leading to what Sandel (2020) calls 'meritocratic hubris'. Needless to say, this is unhelpful for social cohesion; when people buy into the meritocratic ideal, there is little reason for the affluent and powerful to feel sympathy and solidarity for the poor and marginalised. At the same time, there will be anger and resentment towards a professional and intellectual 'elite', who are perceived as detached from and contemptuous of those left behind. Some commentators have argued that the resurgence of populist nationalism in many countries, often connected to antagonism towards and distrust of 'metropolitan elites', owes much to the failure of meritocracy as a political idea (Littler, 2017; Markovits, 2020; Sandel, 2020). Such analysis has troubling implications for what is traditionally seen as the key mechanism of equal opportunity: public education.

Pause and reflect: Is social work meritocratic?

There are various ways to approach this question. One is to consider whether the profession is successful in recruiting those with the talents and skills required to be a good social worker. For example, do social work courses admit the right candidates, do students' qualifications reflect their abilities, and do organisations employ the

Continued

best graduates? A related issue is whether social workers as a whole are sufficiently diverse in demographic terms, and knowledgeable in terms of life experience, to properly understand and serve the needs of people and communities who require social services.

Another approach is to consider how the profession itself is stratified. For example, it is sometimes said that social work is 'female-dominated' because a high proportion of frontline practitioners are women. Nonetheless, among practitioners there is a persistent pay gap in favour of men (ONS, 2020), while women have long been underrepresented in management positions (Davey, 2002). Does this sound meritocratic?

We might also want to consider whether social work itself contributes to a more meritocratic society. For example, by deploying resources and expertise to support people and their families during periods of crisis or difficulty, do social workers contribute to greater equality of opportunity?

Equally, we need to consider the role of social work in contributing to the more negative side of meritocracy, such as deciding which people or families 'deserve' help, or what it means for people to be responsible for their own welfare and that of others.

A final question is whether social work *should* aim to be meritocratic. If the goal is to transform society and/or empower people to achieve their full potential, social workers might seek to critique the idea of meritocracy rather than contribute to it.

What do you think?

Inequality and Education

Education plays a key role in modern societies concerned with ensuring equality of opportunity. The former UK prime minister cited above, Tony Blair, famously summarised his party's top three priorities for government as 'education, education, education', adding that such emphasis was needed to 'overcome decades of neglect and make Britain a learning society, developing the talents and raising the ambitions of all our young people' (Blair, 2001). During the 1990s and 2000s, political leaders often emphasised the need for a skilled workforce able to compete in global markets, with further training and education being seen as the default solution to workers who 'lost out' from globalisation, e.g. because companies had relocated their jobs to factories in countries with lower labour costs (Robertson, 2016). More broadly, universal access to school education for children has long been an important policy goal across the world (Spring, 2007), with a similar trend appearing in higher education over recent decades (Trow, 2007). In one sense, universal access is about the democratic or egalitarian principle of educational provision being open to all citizens regardless of their position in society (Mandler, 2020). However, education systems also aim to be meritocratic in the sense that they assess educational attainment with a view to reflecting individual differences in aptitude and understanding. For this reason, public education has been referred to as a 'sorting machine' (Spring, 1976), designed not only to give everyone a fair opportunity to develop their knowledge and skills but also to help institutions and employers select people on merit.

Nonetheless, it is worth noting that while state education might be egalitarian in principle, this is not the case for private education, which is mainly restricted to children from wealthy families. In the UK, only about 6% of the country's population attends a private school, but among families in the top 1% income bracket the proportion is more like 60% (Kynaston and Green, 2019). The expansion of higher education has also been accompanied by stratification, with entry to the most prestigious universities becoming simultaneously more selective and dominated by applicants from privileged backgrounds (Triventi, 2013a; Kynaston and Green, 2019). Inequalities are also apparent within state schools, with pupils from disadvantaged backgrounds achieving lower grades than their peers, which in turn affects their subsequent academic and vocational qualifications (Hutchinson *et al.*, 2020; Tuckett *et al.*, 2021). Such entrenched differences also contribute to what Sandel (2020) has called 'credentialism', or prejudicial attitudes towards people without higher qualifications. It has therefore been argued that the sorting machine of public education has unwittingly become an engine of inequality and so is failing in its civic purpose (Brink, 2018).

Opportunity, Difference, and Structural Constraints

The debate about education illustrates some of the issues raised by the concept of equal opportunity. One is how we know whether opportunities are in fact equal, i.e. whether differences in achievement and social status are due to differences in people's own preferences, talents and abilities, or whether they result from unfair disadvantages such as those incurred by discrimination. In practice, as we shall see shortly, trying to ascertain whether opportunities are equal often means examining outcomes even when equality of outcome is not the objective. A second question is how to specify equality of opportunity. The most minimal definition is that there should be no overt discrimination when it comes to accessing public resources or taking part in a selection process. A more comprehensive definition would acknowledge that even in the absence of explicit discrimination people may well be disadvantaged by factors outside of their control, such as variation in family assets and parental support, or the disguised operation of prejudice and unconscious bias. These are structural constraints in the sense that they are embedded in the social conditions that shape everyday life; they may include physical barriers, such as the accessibility of buildings and transportation to people with disabilities, but also widespread attitudes and perceptions that have a negative effect on people's ability to fulfil their potential.

Structural constraints are considered unjust because they operate on factors that are down to chance, which includes the social value attributed to personal characteristics such as gender and ethnicity but also the role of family in giving people their start in life. Of course, once we accept a concern with equalising opportunities to take account of 'luck', it can also be argued that people should not be unduly rewarded for their good fortune in possessing abilities or personal qualities that happen to be highly valued at a particular point in time. The best known exponent of this view is Rawls (2009), who thought that differences in people's 'natural assets' should lead to differential rewards only insofar as the overall gain to society would also benefit people whose endowments put them at a disadvantage. This 'difference principle' allows for a certain degree of inequality if it helps to incentivise socially valuable activity, but suggests that inequalities cannot be justified solely on the basis of merit.

Somewhat paradoxically, taking a strong position on equality of opportunity can lead to the conclusion that sometimes opportunities need to be unequal! This is because of the need to compensate for structural constraints, which continue to cause unfair differences in the distribution of resources and rewards even in the absence of overt discrimination. An example is the participation and representation of women in politics and public life. United Nations figures show that a quarter of all national parliamentarians and about a fifth of all government ministers are women (UN Women, 2020). In 2020, only four countries reported having 50% or more women representatives in their parliaments (see if you can guess which ones before looking at the footnote[2]). In the UK, where discrimination on the basis of gender is illegal, the proportion of women MPs reached an all-time high of 34% (at the time of writing) in the 2019 General Election (Uberoi *et al.*, 2021). Although many countries have seen an improvement in the political representation of women over recent decades, there is a persistent tendency for men to be over-represented, particularly in leadership positions. Studies have found a number of reasons for this, including implicit and explicit bias on the part of voters and party leaders, as well as institutional barriers that are a feature of certain electoral systems (Hessami and da Fonseca, 2020). Some countries have implemented measures to actively correct such institutional bias towards men, including quotas and other types of 'affirmative action' (Morgenroth and Ryan, 2018). While such measures are generally considered to be effective in tackling forms of group-based inequality, they are also quite controversial – particularly among privileged groups who believe themselves to be meritorious! Equality of opportunity can therefore mean a trade-off between fairness as perceived by the individual citizen, who might expect to be judged on their own merits, and broader social goals relevant to the purpose of a particular role or institution, such as addressing the under-representation of certain groups. Particularly for the latter, it may be necessary to consider, at least in principle, equality of outcome rather than opportunity.

---

2   They are: Rwanda (61%), Cuba (53%), Bolivia (53%) and the United Arab Emirates (50%). Source: UN Women, 2020.

Equality of Outcome

Equality of outcome requires that goods and resources be shared equitably among everyone in society. In theory, this differs quite radically from equality of opportunity, which only requires that individuals have a fair chance of obtaining the goods and resources they want. However, because people have different preferences it is difficult to establish which outcomes should be prioritised for equalisation. To take a simple example, since some people place a greater value on books than clothes, and vice versa, ensuring that everyone had equal amounts of books and clothes would mean the majority of people had either too many or too few of both. Money as the principal means of exchange in human societies is the obvious candidate for equality of outcome, but even on that basis, there are still various measures that could be used (e.g. income, savings, assets) at a range of time points (e.g. parental income, own income, earnings over a lifetime, earnings at the point of retirement, annual pension). Progressive tax regimes, where people on high incomes pay higher rates of taxation than people on low incomes, are one of the mechanisms through which net earnings are equalised to some degree – although never to the extent where everyone ends up with the same amount of money. Indeed, the concept of equality of outcome strikes many people as misguided. For instance, while it is customary to scrutinise educational attainment data for evidence of inequality, it would be difficult to imagine circumstances in which it would be either feasible or desirable to ensure that every schoolchild ended up with the same exam results. One of the arguments used by advocates of equality of opportunity, rather than outcome, is that competition and selection are part and parcel of life and so there will always be 'winners and losers'; what is important is that everyone has an equal chance to be on the winning side. The problem with this argument is that empirical evidence shows that the benefits of higher social status are mostly reserved for certain groups (see Chapter 2).

Fairness and Freedom

In some respects, equality of opportunity and outcome work in oppositive directions, since seeking the latter often means compromising the former. This trade-off was signalled in the earlier discussion of affirmative action, in the sense that addressing unfair structural constraints effectively means enhancing opportunities for some people while restricting them for others. Achieving 'true' equality of outcome would go even further by compensating for all individual differences, not just characteristics such as gender or ethnicity. This includes abilities and behaviour that are usually understood as deserving recognition and reward. After all, no-one actively chooses the things they are naturally good at, while the tendency to work hard and apply one's talents owes at least something to early socialisation and a supportive family environment, as well as aspects of person-ality that are inherited rather than learned. This line of thinking suggests that people's social status owes as much to luck as to merit, even if opportunities for people to better themselves are available to all. Egalitarian thinkers such as Rawls therefore insist that resources should be equally allocated, unless it can be shown that any inequities also benefit the less fortunate.

However, it has been argued that measures to ensure equality of outcome will impinge on people's freedom to the extent where they become oppressive. This concern is fictionalised in a satirical short story by Kurt Vonnegut, called *Harrison Bergemon*. Vonnegut imagines a dystopian future, in which the strict-est interpretation of equality has been constitutionally mandated. The central character, Harrison, is highly intelligent and so must wear a pair of earphones that emit electronic noises to disrupt his thinking. Dancers must wear masks if they are attractive and carry heavy weights to compensate for their natural grace, while newsreaders disguise their normally mellifluous voices to speak in a way that is 'absolutely uncompetitive'. The maintenance of absolute equal-ity is supervised by a government agency, which punishes any deviations. The story is deliberately absurd but is designed to highlight the risks to personal liberty when the power of the state is deployed to achieve social goals. These risks preoccupied writers such as Nozick (1974) and Hayek (1960), who argued that measures to curb inequality incur too high a cost in terms of individual freedom. Their view was that people should be free to engage in voluntary and consensual transactions, in which market forces determine the value attached to particular skills and attributes; the state should limit its activity to prohibiting overt discrimination, so that all careers are open to everyone, and enforcing the law of the land.

A different perspective on freedom and fairness comes from the tradition of libertarian socialism, also known as anarchism, which is characterised by radical opposition to structures of domination, authority and hierarchy (Guerin, 1970). Contrary to what is often assumed, anarchists advocate for a highly organised society – the difference being that anarchist societies are (or would be) organised on the principle of free and voluntary association rather individuals competing with each other to sell their labour for a wage. Instead, there is an assump-tion that resources are owned collectively and that decisions about distribution should be made democratically at every level. From an anarchist perspective, a capitalist society organised around markets is far from free, not least because it requires a powerful centralised state to regulate those markets and force people without capital to rent themselves out to people with capital. The only guarantee of freedom is to abolish any form of authority that cannot justify itself to those expected to submit to it. Anarchist ideas are fairly widespread in radical com-munity settings and anti-authoritarian movements, and have also been occasion-ally implemented in a wider social context – most famously in the 1871 Paris

Commune and anarchosyndicalist organisations during the 1936–39 Spanish Civil War. Yet this history also shows that workers' movements have often met with sustained and brutal suppression by the authorities, as well as frequent discrediting and distortion of their ideas by journalists, historians and intellectuals (Chomsky, 2013).

Freedom and Markets

In contrast to the treatment meted out to anarchists, the Hayekian story (or myth) about freedom and markets has been warmly received and generously retold by elites, particularly in the Global North, where it has exerted great influence on neo-liberal policymakers (see Chapters 4 and 5). In its strongest form, the doctrine of the market militates against any meritocratic efforts to create a level playing field. According to Hayek (1960), this is because economic rewards actually have very little to do with merit. Market value is simply a measure of the monetary value placed on a good or service by consumers, whereas merit is a moral judgement about what people deserve, usually based on some concept of virtue or their contribution to the common good. Sandel (2020) gives the example of a hedge fund manager, who earns much more than a schoolteacher even though the contribution of the latter may be more admirable as well as being more important to society. For Hayek, any perceived difference in the moral worth of fund management versus teaching (or the worthiness of fund managers versus teachers) is completely irrelevant to the question of what they are paid, which only reflects the economic value of the services they are offering. Of course, it is possible to use the same argument to justify redistributing wealth from those who are fortunate enough to be wealthy to those who are not. However, for Hayek and other advocates of neo-liberal markets, such efforts are bound to be coercive and may even turn out to be oppressive. Equality, except in the sense of formal equality before the law, is therefore seen as undesirable, and measures to achieve it as inimical to freedom.

Hayek's argument can be criticised on many grounds, not least because it relies on an unrealistic separation between market value and moral worth. After all, financial rewards bestowed by market forces are often accompanied by other benefits, such as status, recognition and influence over others, which explicitly convey social approbation and implicitly therefore some degree of moral worth. It hardly takes a great leap of imagination for people who are better-off to imagine themselves to be in some respects 'better' than their fellow citizens, particularly if they are encouraged to believe that their abilities mark them out as special or meritorious. In turn, such attitudes help to frame and restrict debates about inequality, for example about how much inequality people are prepared to tolerate in a society they perceive to be 'just'.

> ## Pause and reflect: A just society
>
> ....
>
> What comes to mind when you hear the term 'a just society'? What kind of society would this be? Are there any things you would change about the society you currently live in to make it more just? Would a more just society necessarily be a more equal one?

Health, Welfare, and Happiness

The notion of equality of outcome raises a key question: in what respect people should be equal, or made more equal, assuming that doing so does not unduly impinge on basic human liberties? There are many ways to tackle this question, as the next few chapters will show. One approach is to focus on people's health, using measures such as life expectancy, disease burden, health-related quality of life, or 'quality-adjusted life years' (Vergel and Sculpher, 2008). Much of the work on income inequalities and the social determinants of health has used these kinds of measures (Wilkinson and Marmot, 2003; Wilkinson, 2005). For example, a recent report on health inequalities in the UK confirmed that increasing social disadvantage was associated with both a shorter lifespan and earlier development of a health-related disability (Marmot *et al.*, 2020). During the past forty years male life expectancy has increased faster than female life expectancy, although women still tend to live longer than men on average. In the United States, people from First Nations and African American backgrounds are found to have a higher mortality rate than White Americans (Woolf *et al.*, 2018). Such findings illustrate the impact of overlapping structural (dis)advantages on people's health.

While the length of people's lifespans and their health-related quality of life are obviously important, it could be argued that they are not an end in themselves. Here we touch on matters of spiritual, moral and cultural significance that are largely beyond the scope of this book. What should we aim to maximise in a good life, beyond staying physically and mentally healthy for as long as possible? Among the many possible responses to this question, two concepts that are often discussed in relation to inequality are welfare and happiness. Both are deceptively complex. For example, Cohen (1993) argues that welfare has two principal meanings. The first is 'hedonic welfare', which is roughly equivalent to pleasure or enjoyment, 'a desirable or agreeable state of consciousness' (Cohen, 1993: 31). The second is 'preference satisfaction', which is the extent to which people's wants and wishes are fulfilled in the situation they find themselves in. The two do not necessarily have to align. For example, someone might prefer to maintain a grumpy disposition than a cheerful one or to undergo rigorous fasting in pursuit of a spiritual vocation. Economic models of welfare tend to use people's stated preferences, which are easier to measure and put in order than variations in someone's internal state of mind. A link could be made between preference satisfaction and humanist perspectives on need and 'self-actualisation', with which social workers tend to be more familiar (see Hood, 2018, for a discussion). Studies have tried to estimate how social welfare in a population changes according to income distribution, often concluding that a relatively low level of income inequality should in theory maximise welfare (Sadka, 1976; Sen and Foster, 1997).

The concept of happiness can also be approached in different ways. Broadly speaking, a distinction can be made between descriptive and evaluative theories. In the former, happiness is conceived in experiential terms, usually as an internal state of feeling or emotion, which can be described using psychological measures such as positive or negative 'affect', or life satisfaction. An evaluative concept of happiness goes beyond subjective experience to apply a normative judgement about people's actions and behaviour, usually from a moral or ethical point of view. In a purely descriptive sense, it would be possible for someone to be happy even while leading a life that most other people regard as morally reprehensible. However, from an evaluative position people can only really experience happiness if they lead a 'good life', in the sense of a virtuous life, as opposed to just feeling contented or satisfied. Some studies suggest that everyday notions of happiness tend to have an evaluative component, although there may be a number of reasons for this (Phillips *et al.*, 2017). Research into happiness mainly draws on descriptive methods such as surveys of people's self-reported life satisfaction (Diener *et al.*, 1985). While there is a relationship between income and life satisfaction, it is not as straightforward as might be expected; for example, Easterlin *et al.* (2010) report on the so-called 'happiness-income' paradox, finding that over the long term (usually ten years or more) people's self-reported life satisfaction does not increase as a country's income rises.

Capability

Our discussion so far has highlighted the link between the distribution of resources – or what Rawls would call 'primary goods' – and the distribution of outcomes, whether measured in terms of health, happiness or welfare. However, more consideration needs to be given to differences between people, both as individuals and as groups, which will be a key feature of the next chapter. The work of the Indian philosopher and economist Amartya Sen is particularly relevant in this respect. In his examination of inequality, Sen (1992) critiques and extends Rawls' theory in order to take into account the implications of human diversity. Sen points out that people vary greatly in their capability to transform goods and resources into what they need to achieve a certain standard of living or quality of life. This means that particular levels of income or other resources will disadvantage some people more than others. For example, a person with a high metabolic rate will need more calories to achieve the same level of nutrition as someone with a low metabolic rate; the health impact of urban pollution and poor-quality housing could be more severe for an asthmatic than for someone with no respiratory condition. Sen gives the example of someone whose physical disability means they require more resources (than a person without a disability) to accomplish what matters to them:

> Such disparities in personal characteristics and circumstances are not just 'exceptional cases', as they are sometimes made out to be. On the contrary, interpersonal variations are pervasive, and relate both to disparities in 'personal' characteristics such as gender, age, and proneness to illness, as well as 'social' features such as epidemiological surroundings and other environmental determinants that influence the conversion of personal resources into the freedom to lead lives without unacceptable deprivations. (Sen, 1994: 334)

Sen builds on this insight to argue that measures to address inequality should not just focus on the distribution of resources, or indeed welfare, but rather on the space in-between, which he defines through the idea of 'capability'. In Sen's usage, capability is a complex concept. In one sense, it retains its everyday meaning of 'basic capabilities', i.e. what people are able to do, and the extent to which allocation of goods and resources enables people to undertake desirable activities, achieve their goals, and improve their quality of life. However, capability also refers to a broader sense of potential that may not be immediately realised in people's own efforts and aspirations. In this sense, it is about the conditions for freedom, or the entitlements that make it possible for people to truly exercise choice and participate in society on an equal basis. Cohen (1993) cites Sen as stating that 'freedom is concerned with what one *can* do' but also 'with what one can *do*' (Sen, 1985). Elsewhere, Sen has acknowledged the links between this broader meaning of capability and the concept of human rights, while maintaining that the two are distinct and should not be subsumed in one another (Sen, 2005). In the field of social work, some readers may also see parallels with the social model of disability (see Chapter 2), which emphasises the social, economic and environmental barriers to participation in society (Burchardt, 2004). How society understands and treats difference is fundamental not only to how we see other people's capabilities, but also to what we imagine to be our own.

Theoretical Components of Inequality

Having considered various theoretical approaches to inequality, we are now in a position to think about how they fit together. Figure 1.1 illustrates three principal themes explored in this chapter, and indeed in the book as a whole. The first is difference, which refers to differences that exist between people. This can mean differences in resources such as income, assets or social capital, or the characteristics of places such as neighbourhoods, cities or countries, or individual characteristics such as gender and ethnicity, or groups such as those defined by culture and religion. The second component is outcome, which refers to the indicators commonly used to assess the impact of inequality on people's health, welfare and happiness. The third component is distribution, emphasising the point that differences and outcomes vary in systematic ways that are both unfair and avoidable. For example, societies allocate fewer resources to some groups of people and more resources to others, while at the same time some groups of people consistently experience higher levels of health, welfare and happiness than others. This point becomes more obvious when we think about personal characteristics such as gender, race and ethnicity. Evidence of inequalities often emerges in the comparison between population distributions and outcome distributions for oppressed groups, as seen, for example, in disproportionate rates of early mortality, anxiety and depression, arrest and imprisonment, and so on. This evidence will be considered at greater length in the next chapter.

Three further thematic elements are illustrated in Figure 1.1. The first is capability, which concerns what people are able to do with the resources they have, as well as their freedom to choose among the same range of options as others. The second is about the intersection between different personal characteristics and social identities, which is an important theoretical lens for inequality as for social

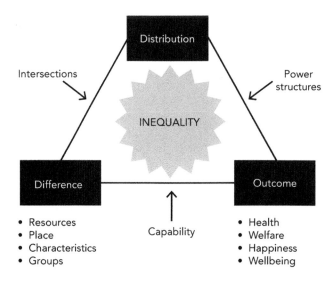

Figure 1.1 Theoretical components of inequality

work practice (see Chapter 7). Intersectionality teaches us that difference is not tied to a particular category, such as age or (dis)ability, but is a multi-dimensional construct mediated by power structures that interact to shape the experiences of people in different circumstances. The third unit of analysis is therefore power, the starting point for our understanding of inequality and a recurring theme in all the chapters of this book.

Conclusion

This chapter has explored inequality from a theoretical point of view, in order to establish a foundation for the issues considered in later chapters. Equality of opportunity is probably the dominant way of thinking about inequality in affluent western societies, influenced in recent decades by the idea of meritocracy and belief in the education system as a way of equalising opportunities and selecting for merit. However, studies of outcomes have exposed flaws in the concept of meritocracy and shown that structural constraints persist in spite of the rhetoric of opportunity. An alternative approach is to focus on equality of outcome, bearing in mind that state intervention to achieve equal outcomes might impinge on people's individual freedom and autonomy. Studying the impact of inequality, or evaluating the impact of interventions designed to promote greater equality, also raises the question of which outcomes should be measured. As Amartya Sen puts it: equality of what? Commonly used indicators include measures of health, welfare and happiness. However, Sen's capabilities approach reminds us that people will differ widely in the choices available to them, in their ability to make use of particular resources, and in the support needed for them to participate fully in society. The intersection between different structural constraints will shape people's lived experience of inequality, but also how the distribution of power between different groups in society assist or hinder their efforts to achieve a good life.

References

Almeida, R.V., Werkmeister Rozas, L.M., Cross-Denny, B., Lee, K.K. and Yamada, A.-M. (2019) 'Coloniality and intersectionality in social work education and practice', *Journal of Progressive Human Services*, **30**(2), pp. 148–164.

Bernard, C. (2021) Intersectionality for social workers: A practical introduction to theory and practice, Abingdon, Routledge.

Blair, T. (2001) I want a meritocracy, not survival of the fittest, Available online: www.independent.co.uk/voices/commentators/i-want-meritocracy-not-survival-fittest-5365602.html, Last Accessed: 09 April 2021.

Brink, C. (2018) *The soul of a university: Why excellence is not enough*, Bristol, Policy Press.

Burchardt, T. (2004) 'Capabilities and disability: The capabilities framework and the social model of disability', *Disability & Society*, **19**(7), pp. 735–751.

Chomsky, N. (2013) *On anarchism*, London, Penguin.

Cohen, G.A. (1993) 'Equality of what? On welfare, goods, and capabilities', in Nussbaum, M. and Sen, A. (eds), *The quality of life*, Oxford, Oxford University Press, pp. 9–29.

Collins, P.H. and Bilge, S. (2020) *Intersectionality* (2nd Edition), Cambridge, Polity Press.

Crenshaw, K. (1989) 'Demarginalizing the intersection of race and sex: A Black feminist critique of antidiscrimination doctrine, feminist theory, and antiracist politics', *University of Chicago Legal Forum*, **140**, pp. 139–167.

Crenshaw, K. (1991) 'Mapping the margins: Identity politics, intersectionality, and violence against women', *Stanford Law Review*, **43**(6), pp. 1241–1299.

Crenshaw, K.W. (2017) *On intersectionality: Essential writings*, New York, The New Press.

Davey, B. (2002) 'Management progression and ambition: Women and men in social work', *Research Policy and Planning*, **20**(2), pp. 21–34.

De Vries, R. (2014) 'Earning by Degrees: Differences in the career outcomes of UK graduates', London, Sutton Trust.

Diener, E., Emmons, R.A., Larsen, R.J. and Griffin, S. (1985) 'The satisfaction with life scale', *Journal of Personality Assessment*, **49**(1), pp. 71–75.

Easterlin, R.A., McVey, L.A., Switek, M., Sawangfa, O. and Zweig, J.S. (2010) 'The happiness–income paradox revisited', *Proceedings of the National Academy of Sciences*, **107**(52), pp. 22463–22468.

Fawcett, B., Featherstone, B. and Goddard, J. (2004) *Contemporary child care policy and practice*, Basingstoke, Palgrave Macmillan.

Guerin, D. (1970) *Anarchism: From theory to practice*, New York, NYU Press.

Hayek, F. (1960) *The constitution of liberty*, Chicago, University of Chicago Press.

Hessami, Z. and da Fonseca, M.L. (2020) 'Female political representation and substantive effects on policies: A literature review', *European Journal of Political Economy*, **63**, p. 101896.

Hood, R. (2018) *Complexity in social work*, London, Sage.

Hutchinson, J., Reader, M. and Akhal, A. (2020) 'Education in England: Annual report 2020', London, Education Policy Institute.

Kynaston, D. and Green, F. (2019) Engines of privilege: Britain's private school problem, London, Bloomsbury.

Lammy, D. (2017) Seven years have changed nothing at Oxbridge. In fact, diversity is even worse, Available online: www.theguardian.com/commentisfree/2017/oct/20/oxford-cambridge-not-changed-diversity-even-worse-admissions?CMP=Share_iOSApp_Other, Last Accessed: 09 April 2021.

Littler, J. (2017) Against meritocracy: Culture, power and myths of mobility, Abingdon, Routledge.

Mandler, P. (2020) The crisis of the meritocracy: Britain's transition to mass education since the Second World War, Oxford, Oxford University Press.

Marginson, S. (2016) 'The worldwide trend to high participation higher education: Dynamics of social stratification in inclusive systems', *Higher Education*, **72**(4), pp. 413–434.

Markovits, D. (2020) *The meritocracy trap*, London, Allen Lane.

Marmot, M., Allen, J., Boyce, T., Goldblatt, P. and Morrison, J. (2020) *Health equity in England: The Marmot Review 10 years on*, London, Institute of Health Equity.

Masud, Y. and Ajmal, M.A. (2012) 'Left-handed people in a right-handed world: A phenomenological study', *Pakistan Journal of Social and Clinical Psychology*, **10**(1), pp. 49–60.

Mattsson, T. (2014) 'Intersectionality as a useful tool: Anti-oppressive social work and critical reflection', *Affilia*, **29**(1), pp. 8–17.

May, T. (2016) Britain, the great meritocracy: Prime Minister's speech, Available online: www.gov.uk/government/speeches/britain-the-great-meritocracy-prime-ministers-speech, Last Accessed: 09 April 2021.

McCall, L. (2005) 'The complexity of intersectionality', *Signs: Journal of Women in Culture and Society*, **30**(3), pp. 1771–1800.

Mehrotra, G. (2010) 'Toward a continuum of intersectionality theorizing for feminist social work scholarship', *Affilia*, **25**(4), pp. 417–430.

Montacute, R. and Cullinane, C. (2018) 'Access to advantage: The influence of schools and place on admissions to top universities', London, Sutton Trust.

Morgenroth, T. and Ryan, M.K. (2018) 'Quotas and affirmative action: Understanding group-based outcomes and attitudes', *Social and Personality Psychology Compass*, **12**(3), p. e12374.

Nash, J.C. (2008) 'Re-thinking intersectionality', *Feminist Review*, **89**(1), pp. 1–15.

Nayak, S. and Robbins, R. (2018) Intersectionality in social work: Activism and practice in context, Abingdon, Routledge.

Nozick, R. (1974) *Anarchy, state and utopia*, New York, Basic Books.

Office for National Statistics (ONS) (2020) Gender pay gap in the UK: 2020, Available online: www.ons.gov.uk/employmentandlabourmarket/peopleinwork/earningsand workinghours/bulletins/genderpaygapintheuk/2020, Last Accessed: 22/03/2021.

Parton, N. (2011) 'Child protection and safeguarding in England: Changing and competing conceptions of risk and their implications for social work', *British Journal of Social Work*, **41**(5), pp. 854–875.

Pemberton, S. (2019) *Rural regeneration in the UK*, Abingdon, Routledge.

Phillips, J., De Freitas, J., Mott, C., Gruber, J. and Knobe, J. (2017) 'True happiness: The role of morality in the folk concept of happiness', *Journal of Experimental Psychology: General*, **146**(2), p. 165.

Pratto, F., Stewart, A.L. and Bou Zeineddine, F. (2013) 'When inequality fails: Power, group dominance, and societal change', *Journal of Social and Political Psychology*, 1(1).

Rawls, J. (2009) *A theory of justice: revised edition*, Cambridge, MA, Harvard University Press.

Robertson, S.L. (2016) 'Piketty, capital and education: A solution to, or problem in, rising social inequalities?', *British Journal of Sociology of Education*, **37**(6), pp. 823–835.

Sadka, E. (1976) 'Social welfare and income distribution', *Econometrica*, **44**(6), pp. 1239–1251.

Sandel, M. (2020) *The tyranny of merit: What's become of the common good?*, New York, Farrar, Straus and Giroux.

Schabas, W.A. (2015) The European Convention on Human Rights: A commentary, Oxford, Oxford University Press.

Sen, A. (1985) 'Rights and capabilities', in Honderich, T. (ed.), *Morality and objectivity: A tribute to J. L. Mackie*, London, Routledge, pp. 130–148.

Sen, A. (1992) *Inequality reexamined*, Oxford, Oxford University Press.

Sen, A. (2005) 'Human rights and capabilities', *Journal of Human Development*, **6**(2), pp. 151–166.

Sen, A. and Foster, J. (1997) *On economic inequality*, Oxford, Oxford University Press.

Smits, R. (2011) *The puzzle of left-handedness*, London, Reaktion Books.

Spring, J.H. (1976) The sorting machine: National educational policy since 1945, New York: McKay.

Spring, J.H. (2007) A new paradigm for global school systems: Education for a long and happy life, Mahwah, NJ, Lawrence Erlbaum.

Tallon, A. (2013) Urban regeneration in the UK, Abingdon, Routledge.

Triventi, M. (2013a) 'The role of higher education stratification in the reproduction of social inequality in the labor market', *Research in Social Stratification and Mobility*, **32**, pp. 45–63.

Triventi, M. (2013b) 'Stratification in higher education and its relationship with social inequality: A comparative study of 11 European countries', *European Sociological Review*, **29**(3), pp. 489–502.

Trow, M. (2007) 'Reflections on the transition from elite to mass to universal access: Forms and phases of higher education in modern societies since WWII', in Forest, J. and Altbach, P. (eds), *International handbook of higher education*, New York, Springer, pp. 243–280.

Tuckett, S., Robinson, D. and Bunting, F. (2021) *Measuring the disadvantage gap in 16-19 education*, London, Education Policy Institute.

Uberoi, E., Watson, C., Mutebi, N., Danechi, S. and Bolton, P. (2021) 'Women in politics and public life', London, House of Commons Library.

UN Women (2020) *Facts and figures: Women's leadership and political participation*, Available online: www.unwomen.org/en/what-we-do/leadership-and-political-participation/facts-and-figures#_edn1, Last Accessed: 22/04/2021.

Vergel, Y.B. and Sculpher, M. (2008) 'Quality-adjusted life years', *Practical Neurology*, **8**(3), pp. 175–182.

Waller, R., Ingram, N. and Ward, M. (2017) Higher education and social inequalities: University admissions, experiences, and outcomes, Abingdon, Routledge.

Wilkinson, R. (2005) The impact of inequality: How to make sick societies healthier, Abingdon, Routledge.

Wilkinson, R.G. and Marmot, M. (2003) *Social determinants of health: The solid facts*, World Health Organization.

Winker, G. and Degele, N. (2011) 'Intersectionality as multi-level analysis: Dealing with social inequality', *European Journal of Women's Studies*, **18**(1), pp. 51–66.

Woolf, S.H., Chapman, D.A., Buchanich, J.M., Bobby, K.J., Zimmerman, E.B. and Blackburn, S.M. (2018) 'Changes in midlife death rates across racial and ethnic groups in the United States: Systematic analysis of vital statistics', *BMJ*, **362**.

Yamada, A.M., Rozas, L.M.W. and Cross-Denny, B. (2015) 'Intersectionality and social work', *Encyclopedia of Social Work*, Available online, https://doi.org/10.1093/acrefore/9780199975839.013.961

Young, M.D. (1958) *The rise of the meritocracy*, London, Thames and Hudson.

2

The Many Faces
of Inequality

Chapter overview

....

This chapter examines some of the ways in which disparities in health, happiness and
wellbeing are associated, systematically and unjustly, with human diversity and difference. Our starting point is to consider how inequitable distribution of resources
connects to social hierarchies and stratification, often in the form of class and caste systems. There is a discussion of poverty, income and deprivation, and the importance of
geography and place. The chapter then turns to personal characteristics that are often
the subject of equalities legislation but are nonetheless associated with significant
inequalities: gender, race and ethnicity, age, sexuality and sexual orientation, and (dis)
ability. Some theoretical concepts are introduced and a selection of empirical evidence
is provided in each of these areas.

Introduction

Chapter 1 highlighted the way in which inequality is linked to difference. Through
the operation of power structures in society, both on a global and national scale,
human diversity becomes linked to inequitable allocation of resources and a skewed
distribution of outcomes. This is not to assume an over-deterministic position. It is
inevitable that some people will lead healthier, happier or more fulfilled lives than
others. It is also important to acknowledge the role played by luck as well as the consequences of our own choices and actions. Some degree of inequality is implied by
human autonomy and free will, which includes the right to make 'bad' decisions and
act in ways that might seem contrary to our own interests. However, when we talk
about social inequality, we do not mean the natural variation in developmental outcomes – we mean unfair and systematic disparities. In this chapter, we will consider
the evidence for these disparities in relation to the differences that exist between
people. Drawing on the model outlined in Figure 1.1, the main categories of difference discussed here are resources and personal characteristics, which incorporate

factors such as class, poverty, and income as well as ethnicity, gender and (dis)ability. The significance of intersectional inequalities for people's lived experience will be highlighted, drawing on key frameworks such as Critical Race Theory.

Resources

In Rawls' theory of justice, the main site of inequality lies in the 'primary goods', which constitute all the resources that people need or find useful to achieve their goals and participate freely in society. This includes natural goods such as athleticism, creativity, intelligence and conscientiousness, but also social goods such as rights, liberties, income and wealth. While the distribution of natural goods could be regarded as fairly random, albeit subject to some degree of heritability, the distribution of social goods is bound up with issues of fairness, merit and capability, as discussed in the previous chapter. In most (if not all) modern societies, access to these goods varies according to people's status and their position in the social hierarchy. Class differences and their relationship to poverty and deprivation are therefore one of the key features of inequality. Equally important are personal characteristics such as race, gender, (dis)ability, and sexuality, which will be introduced in the second half of this chapter.

Social Class

Giddens (2009, p. 437) defines class as 'a large-scale grouping of people who share common economic resources, which strongly influence the type of lifestyle they are able to lead'. Class is a type of social stratification, in which individuals are ranked according to a culturally imposed set of characteristics and their ranking determines the opportunities they have and the resources they are allocated. Historically, there have been many types of stratification across the world, such as caste systems in many parts of Asia, the feudal estates of Europe, and the slave-owning societies of colonial America. The modern understanding of class is distinguished by the shift away from traditional social markers such as birth, religion and race, and towards economic markers such as education, work, and income. Classes are more fluid and impersonal than older systems of stratification, permitting a degree of mobility as people move up and down the rankings. However, the political rhetoric of meritocracy is often hostile towards class distinctions, seeing them as a barrier to equal opportunity. For example, the former UK prime minister John Major once declared his intention to create a 'classless society', characterised by 'the equal treatment of all citizens by the state, and the chance of advancement for all' (Major, 1993).

Despite such pronouncements, class divisions continue to shape the life experiences of people in the UK and other countries. They encode differences in education, occupation, earnings, language and lifestyle in ways that are immediately recognisable for people who grow up in that society (Bourdieu, 1987). Some markers of status are obvious, such as the distinction between living in a crowded tenement block or a spacious suburb, or relying on the local food bank versus shopping in the food hall at Harrods. Others are more subtle. For example, Anantharaman (2017) discusses how middle-class cyclists in India distinguish themselves from the poorer sections of the population, for whom cycling is an essential form of transport, by marking their status through expensive imported bikes, specialist clothing and accessories, or T-Shirts with ecological slogans. The everyday practice of class distinction, which in modern societies is often patterned as particular forms of consumption, not only serves to mark power, prestige and success. Such practices also enable privilege to be consolidated and reproduced, for example by facilitating networks of influence through participation in particular activities or membership of exclusive clubs. Alongside transfers of wealth and access to elite education, inculcating social and cultural capital is another way for middle- or upper-class parents to pass their own status on to their children.

Socio-cultural markers of distinction are quite context-specific and can change over time, so may not be a reliable way of measuring class. In many countries, categories based on people's occupation are used for this purpose. For example, in the UK the Office for National Statistics has constructed a Socio-Economic Classification (NS-SEC), which allocates people to eight social class rankings ranging from 'higher managerial and professional occupations' to 'those who have never had paid work and the long-term unemployed' (ONS, 2011). The classification is conceptually based on employment relations in modern industrialised economies, in which occupations are differentiated in terms of reward structures, opportunities for promotion, autonomy and job security (Scambler, 2012). Under this scheme, people in higher managerial and professional jobs have an advantage over people in routine manual jobs – not just because they tend to earn more money but also because they have more opportunities for advancement, more autonomy within their jobs (e.g. in terms of making decisions and allocating their time), and more job security. The Covid-19 pandemic highlighted these advantages, with managerial/professional jobs less affected in terms of loss of earnings and redundancy as well as conferring less risk of infection on those able to work from home. Of course, there are also problems with this way of defining class. People's occupation may not align with other aspects of their identity or standard of living[1]. Socio-cultural aspects of class distinction are underplayed by occupational typologies, as well as the role of stigma and labelling in perpetuating social divisions (Dorling, 2015) – all important structural effects of what might be termed 'classism' (see Chapter 1).

---

1   As illustrated by a news story about a university lecturer who slept in a tent for two years while completing her PhD (Fazackerley, 2021).

Notwithstanding these limitations, measures such as the NS-SEC enable researchers to track 'social mobility', which means the extent to which people are able to move from a lower social class to a higher one. This research shows that class membership is not random but is largely hereditary, i.e. parents often manage to pass on their social and economic advantages to their offspring (Nunn *et al.*, 2007; Hecht *et al.*, 2020). This is particularly the case for people in so-called 'elite' professions, such as law, medicine and finance, which are dominated by the children of higher managers and professionals (Friedman *et al.*, 2015). Even when people from working-class backgrounds do manage to enter elite occupations, they tend to earn less than colleagues from middle-class backgrounds, evidence of what Friedman and Laurison (2020) call the 'class ceiling'. Moreover, these class differences intersect with inequalities around race and gender. Membership of elites, particularly in rich Western countries, is dominated by White men (Atkinson *et al.*, 2018; Cousin *et al.*, 2018) with huge under-representation of women and people from racialised and minoritised groups. Sexist and racist power structures are therefore crucial for the production and reproduction of class privilege across generations.

Exercise 2.1: Social work and class position

There are various ways to think about our social class position vis-à-vis other people. Most of the time, we do not do this consciously, but research suggests that such comparisons are a fundamental part of social interaction. It is therefore an important part of critical reflection in social work. To explore this issue, have a think about the following questions:

1 How would you describe your own class background? Relevant to this question might be what your parents did for a job, how much money they earned, what area you grew up in, what kind of home you lived in (e.g. flat, house, rented, owned), what expectations were placed on you in terms of your education, or what attitudes your family had (e.g. about work, saving, means-tested benefits).
2 How would you describe your current class position? Is it the same as your class background or different? What has changed (if anything)?
3 How much importance do you ascribe to your class background and position, relative to other aspects of identity, e.g. ethnicity, religion, gender, sexuality, (dis)ability?
4 What do you assume (or know) to be the class background and position of people using social work services? Is it often different from your own?
5 How and why does this matter? How do class differences affect the way professionals go about their work?

Poverty and Income

Inequality is often discussed in relation to poverty, although the link is a complex one (Grusky *et al.*, 2006; Jenkins and Micklewright, 2007). One approach to poverty is to distinguish between absolute and relative poverty. The former refers to a set of essential human needs that have to be met for people to subsist in a basic physiological and psychological sense. Such needs include food, shelter, and warmth but also clothes, transport and education. Relative poverty, on the other hand, refers to the conditions that make it possible for people to fully participate in society and lead a good and valued life (Townsend, 1979). This means that poverty is understood in relation to the standards and expectations of society at a particular point in time, i.e. as society changes, so does the nature of poverty (Spicker, 2007). Relative poverty is explicitly connected to inequality as it is affected by changes to the standard and quality of life enjoyed by people who are not poor. Economic growth may eventually 'float' a large number of people out of absolute poverty, but if the rewards of growth are unequally distributed then the resources required to live a good and valued life will remain beyond the means of many. Relative approaches are also better at recognising the multi-dimensional nature of poverty, which includes the experience of shame and stigma that results from people being unable to realise their basic capabilities (Sen, 1999; Lister, 2004). The most sophisticated measures of poverty seek to capture this complexity through detailed statistical analysis of underlying factors such as material deprivation, financial strain, social isolation, psycho-social strain, and civic participation (Tomlinson *et al.*, 2008; Webb, 2019). In the UK, the Social Metrics Commission's approach to measurement encompasses all material resources and assets possessed by families, 'inescapable costs' such as housing and childcare, as well as factors such as overcrowding, 'deep poverty', and people's lived experience (Social Metrics Commission, 2020).

Despite such advances in conceptualisation, official measures of poverty continue to focus heavily on income. The World Bank, for example, calculates poverty lines using an internationally comparable measure of purchasing power parity, with 'extreme poverty' currently defined as an income below $1.90 a day (World Bank, 2020). The UK's poverty statistics draw on the Households Below Average Income (HBIA) poverty line, which is calculated both as a relative measure (income below 60% of median household income) and absolute measure (income below 60% median household income in some base year, usually 2010/11). Government figures for 2019/20 show that 18% of the UK population were living in relative poverty and 14% in absolute poverty (Francis-Devine, 2021), although these figures are higher (22% and 18% respectively) after housing costs are included. Rates of poverty differ widely among different groups in the population, based on personal characteristics such as age and ethnicity, as well as between different parts of the country. These differences are illustrated in Table 2.1. showing the intrinsic connection between poverty and other forms of social inequality.

Table 2.1 Relative poverty in the UK population (*Source*: Francis-Devine, 2021)

Measure	%
Whole population living in relative low income — before housing costs[1]	18%
Whole population living in relative low income — after housing costs[1]	22%
Relative low income among children[1,2]	31%
Relative low income among pensioners[1,2]	18%
Population living on persistent low income[3]	13%
Children in workless families on relative low income[1,2]	53%
Children living in the social rented sector on relative low income[1,2]	56%
Relative low income among families where someone is disabled[2]	27%
Percentage of children in relative low income among White families[2,4,5]	26%
Percentage of children in relative low income among Bangladeshi families[2,4,5]	68%
Percentage of people in relative low income in South East England[2,5]	14%
Percentage of people in relative low income in North East England[2,5]	25%

Notes:
[1] *2019/20*
[2] *After housing costs*
[3] *People on a low income continuously from 2015/16 to 2018/19*
[4] *By ethnic group of the head of household*
[5] *2017/18 to 2019/20*

Pause and reflect

....

Take a few minutes to examine the figures presented in Table 2.1. What differences do you observe in the rates of poverty depending on how it is measured and for whom? What do you think might explain those differences?

There are various drawbacks to poverty lines based on HBAI. The 60% threshold is essentially arbitrary and does not take account of fluctuations in the cost of living that may disproportionately affect poorer families, such as higher food prices. Other income-based approaches try to compensate for some of these disadvantages. For example, the Minimum Income Standards (MIS) are annual estimates of the budget that families in the UK need to achieve an acceptable standard of living (Davis *et al.*, 2021). Weekly MIS budgets are calculated for four household types, such as a single working age adult or a couple with two children, based on typical expenditure on items such as food, clothing, fuel, social/cultural participation, and either including or excluding childcare and housing costs. The results show that for most households the MIS is well above the poverty line, which has particular implications for families on means-tested benefits. For example, Davis *et al.* (2021) reported that out-of-work families with children on universal credit[2] fell about 40% short of the income they needed, while those without children fell 60% short. Overall, 30% of the UK population were estimated to have had an income below the MIS in 2020–21.

From an inequalities perspective, the distribution of income in a population can be measured in various ways. The most common method is a statistic known as the Gini coefficient, which is generally given as either a percentage or a decimal between zero and one. A Gini coefficient of one (or 100%) indicates the maximum possible inequality, e.g. a population where just one person earns all the income while everyone else has nothing. In contrast, a Gini coefficient of zero would indicate complete equality, e.g. everyone in the population earns the same income. On this measure, household income inequality in the UK was reported to be 36.3% during 2019–20, its highest level for 10 years (Office for National Statistics, 2021). Longitudinal analysis has shown that the Gini coefficient remained roughly unchanged between 1961 and 1979, before undergoing a sharp increase during the 1980s and then broadly stabilising after 1991 (Cribb *et al.*, 2018). However, this picture masks the increasing share of total income among the top echelon of earners over the past 30 years (Atkinson and Jenkins, 2020; Hecht *et al.*, 2020). It is therefore helpful to combine the Gini coefficient with other measures of income inequality. For example, the P90/P10 ratio compares the ratio of the income of the person at the bottom of the top 10% with that of the person at the top of the bottom 10%. The P90/P10 ratio was reported to be 4.5 in 2020, compared with 4.1 in 2011, while the amount of income accounted for by the richest 1% increased by 1.3 percentage points to 8.3% between 2011 and 2020 (Office for National Statistics, 2021).

As well as enabling researchers to track (and dispute) trends within countries, measures of income inequality also allow for international comparisons (see Chapter 5). Again, the Gini coefficient is the most commonly cited statistic for this purpose. The OECD (2021) reports that among the countries reporting data on income inequality in 2020, the highest Gini coefficient was found in South Africa (62%) and the lowest in the Slovak Republic (22%). The UK ranked 33rd (out of 40), making it one of the most unequal countries in the developed world. Gini coefficients and other measures of income distribution have also been used to analyse health inequalities (see Chapter 3 and Chapter 5).

Deprivation and Place

Deprivation is closely related to poverty, although they are not synonymous. Poverty is a broader concept, whereas deprivation often has a more technical meaning. For example, the term 'material deprivation' is used to refer to people

---

2   A means-tested monthly payment to help with living costs, paid by UK central government to people who are unemployed or on a low income.

or households who lack the ability to access key goods or services. These might include keeping up to date with bills, replacing broken electrical goods, or being able to take a week's holiday, which the UK government estimates is experienced as unaffordable for 30% of children and 36% of pensioners (Francis-Devine, 2021: 55). In this sense, deprivation can be seen as an indicator of low living standards, to be considered alongside low income and other aspects of poverty. Deprivation is also used to characterise the social and economic circumstances of geographical areas. For example, the English Indices of Multiple Deprivation (IMD) are a summary measure of area-level deprivation in England (MHCLG, 2019). They combine weighted scores in seven domains: income, employment, education, health, crime, barriers to housing and services, and living environment. Indicators in the 'crime' domain measure the risk of personal and material victimisation at local level, education indicators measure the level of attainment and skills in the local population, and so on. Deprivation scores are calculated for 32,844 small neighbourhoods in England, which are then ranked according to their level of deprivation relative to other areas. The most recent release (MHCLG, 2019) reported that 61% of local authority (LA) districts contained at least one of the most deprived neighbourhoods in England, although LAs with the highest proportion of neighbourhoods in the 10% most deprived nationally were all in the north of the country (e.g. Middlesbrough, Liverpool and Knowsley). There has been some debate about the extent to which IMD actually captures area-level effects as opposed to simply aggregating household data, or its ability to adequately identify need in both urban and rural contexts (Deas et al., 2003). Nonetheless, development of the IMD has been important for the study of inequalities in social care provision, as we shall see in the next chapter.

In relation to inequality, deprivation points to the importance of geography and place as a unit of analysis. Returning to the idea of social mobility examined earlier, there is evidence that geographical factors play a key part in the formation of elites. Hecht et al. (2020) show that households in England with very high incomes are extremely concentrated in London, and particularly in West London. Living in the capital acts as a 'regional escalator' offering much faster career progression than elsewhere in the country. However, this escalator is largely reserved for people from privileged backgrounds, who are disproportionately able to move to London to pursue an elite career. International migrants, or 'ordinary' Londoners who already live there, actually have lower prospects for social mobility compared with their peers in other (more deprived) regions such as Merseyside or Tyne and Wear (Friedman and Macmillan, 2017). Somewhat counter-intuitively, geographical mobility is therefore not a common feature for those who achieve upward social mobility. However, it does seem to be a crucial feature of social class advantage when it comes to the reproduction of elites at the economic and political epicentre, where the highest rewards are to be found.

Personal Characteristics

Having considered some of the ways in which inequality manifests itself in terms of class, poverty and deprivation, we turn now to other social divisions that expose people to the structural impact of discrimination, exclusion and oppression (see Chapter 1). Unlike socio-economic categories, the characteristics discussed below are recognised by equality and human rights legislation in several countries. In the UK, for example, the 2010 Equality Act legally protects people from discrimination, both in the workplace and in wider society, on the basis of nine protected characteristics, including gender, race, age and disability (see Chapter 4). Nonetheless, there is ample evidence that societies generate inequitable opportunities and outcomes for people with these characteristics. Moreover, people's progress through life is affected by multiple forms of advantage and disadvantage. It is problematic to use a single lens, such as gender or ethnicity, to define someone's lived experience. The theoretical concepts we use to explore and analyse our complex social existence are limited approximations – as social workers well know, to try and understand another human being (or indeed ourselves) is a unique endeavour that is never complete. With this in mind, five personal characteristics that are particularly associated with social stratification are discussed below.

Gender

Many sociologists argue that gender is socially constructed, meaning that the characteristics of men, women and various gendered identities are not really about biological difference but the result of a complex web of human beliefs and practices (Thompson and Armato, 2012). In other words, gender is not innate but is collectively produced by society and 'performed' by people via norms, roles and relationships (Butler, 1990). For example, the clothes we wear help to define our perceived gender, but expectations on how males and females should dress vary greatly between societies and over time. Individuals 'do' gender in that they choose to represent or challenge accepted gender arrangements around behaviour and self-presentation. However, it is not an equal choice; gender nonconformity carries the risk of social discomfort and being forced to deal with aggression and violence from conforming individuals. In addition, gender – like class – serves as a system of social stratification, in that it plays an important role in shaping people's health, welfare and life chances.

Gender has traditionally been a binary concept in that most societies expect people to identify as either male or female (and behave accordingly). In turn, gender inequality is mostly understood in terms of patriarchal social structures, which perpetuate the domination of one gender (males) and subordinate the other (females). However, there is increasing recognition of non-binary, genderfluid or genderqueer understandings of gender (Richards *et al.*, 2016). These approaches deconstruct the distinction between gender and biological sex, which is conventionally seen as being 'assigned' to a person on the basis of primary sex characteristics (genitalia) and reproductive functions. Transgender people experience a 'discordance between their personal sense of their own gender and the sex assigned to them at birth' (Winter *et al.*, 2016: 390). They are affected by many types of inequality, including social stigma and non-acceptance, workplace discrimination, barriers to healthcare, inadequate access to goods and services, and bullying and harassment in public spaces (Whittle *et al.*, 2007). Minoritised gender and sexual identities share some commonalities, including a history of oppression and marginalisation within mainstream society, and are sometimes considered together (see below).

At the same time, it is important to remember that these are not homogenous groups, nor should they be perceived through a deficit lens only focusing on discrimination, disparities and negative health outcomes. Calls to highlight the euphoria and joy of embracing authentic gender and sexual identities, notwithstanding the real problems caused by oppressive social environments, are becoming more prominent in the sociological and health inequalities literature (Shuster and Westbrook, 2022; Holloway, 2023). The same consideration applies to all minoritised groups whose lived experience may be misrepresented and distorted by a mainstream discourse concerned exclusively with dysphoria and suffering.

Historically, feminist analysis of gender inequality has focused on the social system of patriarchy, which allocates disproportionate power and status to men in both public and private spheres. Central to gendered power relations are the socialisation processes through which different norms, behaviours, objects and values come to constitute masculinity and femininity in particular cultures. What has been termed 'hegemonic masculinity' (Connell, 1987) emerges when being male is associated with authority in various ways, e.g. through cultural representations of leadership, assertiveness and power, whereas femininity is defined in ways that suggest a subordinate status, e.g. representations that emphasise physical attractiveness (to men), caring for others, and undertaking emotional labour. Such assumptions serve to underpin inequitable (heteronormative) social arrangements, such as the under-representation of women in leadership roles and over-representation in caring roles, making such arrangements seem natural and resistant to change. It follows that addressing inequalities will often entail challenging and undermining traditional notions of masculinity and femininity.

Sen (2001) discusses seven types of gender inequality that are commonly found across the world:

- *Mortality* – in some regions, such as North Africa and South Asia, women have higher mortality rates than men.
- *Natality* – a cultural preference for boys over girls in male-dominated societies, combined with greater access to medical technology that can

determine the gender of a foetus, has led to sex-selective abortion becoming common in some countries, including China and India.

- *Basic facility* – girls have less opportunity for schooling in some countries, and other social and institutional barriers may discourage the development of their natural talents or their participation and contribution to social life.
- *Special opportunity* – inequitable access to specialist resources such as higher education and professional training is a feature of even rich countries.
- *Professional* – women often face greater barriers than men in terms of employment and promotion, particularly in high status professions, and are disproportionately employed in low-paid occupations.
- *Ownership* – property rights are unequally shared in many societies, if shared at all, making it harder for women to flourish in socio-economic terms.
- *Household* – gender relations within families are often unequal, so that women do the bulk of childcare and household duties whereas men are able to concentrate on paid work outside the home.

Gender inequality has a huge impact on health and socio-economic outcomes. Women are more likely to be poor, to earn less than men, and to hold responsibility for children, elderly relatives and other dependents (Christensen, 2019). Women often suffer disproportionately during famines and other natural disasters, particularly in poorer parts of the population (Neumayer and Plümper, 2007). Women are excluded from political power, both in terms of their minority representation in government and leadership roles but also because of the prevalence of sexism, harassment and abuse even when they do gain access to such roles. Women are disproportionately exposed to sexual violence, the majority of which is perpetrated by men (Kearns *et al.*, 2020). Likewise, they are often deprived of power to negotiate safe sex and cohabiting relationships, which makes them vulnerable to sexually transmitted illnesses such as HIV/Aids (Madiba and Ngwenya, 2017). Challenging such inequalities and taking action to address them has been central to feminist movements and has also played an important role in social work, as we shall see in Chapter 7.

Gender inequality resulting from patriarchy benefits men and disadvantages women. However, there are some ways in which men do worse than women, despite (or because of) living in a patriarchal society. For example, men have a shorter life expectancy than women almost everywhere in the world (Barford *et al.*, 2006). Moreover, there is evidence that high levels of gender inequality have a negative effect on men's health as well as women's health (Kolip and Lange, 2018). Although depression is more common in women, men are more likely to commit suicide and less likely to seek help for emotional and psychological problems (Rosenfield and Mouzon, 2013). Cultural norms around 'hegemonic masculinity' also contribute to the discrimination and exclusion experienced by gay men, intersex and transgender people, and can make it harder for men to enter traditionally female-dominated professions, including social work (Nentwich *et al.*, 2013).

Exercise 2.2: Social work and women

Orme (2003, p. 132) states that 'social work as a profession came about and developed because of women'. The early pioneers of social work were mainly women, and the profession's role in the emerging welfare state not only offered women a route to employment but also directly affected women's lives. Nowadays, the large majority of qualified social workers are women. They are also more likely to work with women, e.g. as parents, carers and family members.

Why do you think that social work is a female majority profession? Do gender inequalities play a part?

It may be helpful to think about:

1   Gendered attitudes to caring, e.g. social work seen as a 'caring profession' and the large majority of paid and unpaid care work undertaken by women.
2   Ideologies about masculinity, e.g. men not 'seeing themselves' in social work, or considering it to be 'women's work'.
3   Lower pay and status of female majority professions compared to traditionally male majority professions, such as medicine.
4   Male student experiences in female majority professional education and training, e.g. feeling isolated or excluded.
5   The 'glass elevator' (Williams, 1992) – a phenomenon in which men entering female majority professions find it easier than their female peers to be promoted to managerial and leadership positions.

Race and Ethnicity

Race and ethnicity are socially constructed categories that have no biological meaning, since human beings are almost identical genetically (Collins and Mansoura, 2001). Ethnicity may be defined as a process of group identification that produces a sense of belonging to a distinctive cultural group, including language, customs and traditions that provide a common heritage for people across generations (Bhavnani *et al.*, 2005). In contrast, race is a social construct based on the arbitrary classification of human features – 'broad categories of people that are divided arbitrarily but based on ancestral origin and physical characteristics' (Flanagin *et al.*, 2021). In some contexts, ethnicity may be deployed as a proxy or 'code' for race, which carries a risk of promoting essentialist stereotypes – the 'conviction that category membership is constant, unchangeable and permanent' rather than fluid and contingent (Tedam, 2020: 108). There are important distinctions between how people might self-identify in terms of race and ethnicity and the labels that are ascribed to them, including in the administrative data collected by the state or by services (Jones, 2002). Shared cultural traditions are important in understanding ethnicity, which also means that significant differences exist between people who might be grouped together within broad categories such as 'Black British' or 'Asian American'.

From an inequalities perspective, race and ethnicity are connected to the social processes of racialisation and minoritisation, underpinned by the fundamental problem of racism. As Singh and Masocha (2019) point out, the concept of race has been severely criticised for its role in the construction of racial hierarchies, and yet it remains relevant to many people's lived experience. The concept of racialisation, defined by Omi and Winant (2014: 111) as 'the extension of racial meaning to a previously racially unclassified social relationship, social practice or group', conveys the complex political and socio-economic processes through which racial hierarchies are created and maintained. Racialisation is often targeted at Black, Indigenous and 'minority' ethnic groups in order to legitimatise their marginalisation and exclusion; however, the minoritisation of these groups is not a given but is actively pursued by systems of oppression that create and perpetuate racial hierarchies (Selvarajah et al., 2020). The politics of minoritisation creates further difficulties for 'minorities within minorities', for example when the dominant liberal regime attempts to frame people's choices about how to live as a supposed conflict between individual rights (conferred by the regime) and their community's cultural values (Eisenberg and Spinner-Halev, 2005).

The history of many countries has been marked by violent conflict related to race and ethnicity, in some cases giving rise to genocide and so-called 'ethnic cleansing', a racist project to create an ethnically homogenous state through large-scale persecution, removals and mass murder. Some countries, such as the USA and South Africa, have historically had laws that enforced physical and social segregation of people based on racial categories and notions of White supremacy. Although such laws no longer exist there, it can be argued that de-facto segregation does persist, on the basis of the neighbourhoods where people live, the schools and universities they attend, the services they use, the jobs they do and the life chances they have (Carr and Kutty, 2008; Butler, 2017). Similar arguments could be made about other countries, including the UK, where an ostensible commitment to pluralism is contradicted by deep-rooted inequalities reinforced by the everyday experience of racism and discrimination (Byrne et al., 2020).

Critical Race Theory (CRT) is a valuable framework for trying to understand some of these complexities. CRT emerged from the American radical tradition exemplified by figures such as Sojourner Truth and W.E.B. Du Bois, but was further developed in the 1970s through the work of Derrick Bell, an African American civil rights lawyer and legal scholar (e.g. Bell, 1980, 1992). Bell took issue with the incremental legalism of traditional civil rights discourse, instead mounting a challenge to the normative standards of White liberalism from the distinctive perspective of Black Americans in the United States. CRT nowadays is a broad movement of 'activists and scholars engaged in studying and transforming the relationship among race, racism, and power' (Delgado and Stefancic, 2023: 3), and encompasses a diverse body of work from writers of Black, Asian, Indigenous, Latinx, LGBTQ+, Muslim and Arab origin.

With a focus on anti-oppressive social work practice (see Chapter 6), Tedam (2020: 98–99) uses CRT to examine approaches to racism and draws attention to the following points:

1 *Racism is endemic*, i.e. a daily occurrence for Black and minoritised groups, and because it is systemic often goes unnoticed by White people. Reid (2020) puts this another way: 'When you're accustomed to privilege, equality feels like oppression'.

2 *Marginalised people are better placed to tell their own stories*, as opposed to people from dominant groups who take it upon themselves to do so, which puts the onus on promoting and advancing the voices of people who are seldom or never heard from directly.

3 *Differential racialisation* occurs when dominant groups arrogate to themselves the power to decide which racialised groups are considered to be relatively more deserving or meritorious than others. This contributes to unfair treatment and stereotyping of people from different Black backgrounds but also has a bearing on discrimination against some minoritised White groups, such as Traveller and Roma people (see Case Study 2.1).

4 *Interest convergence*, sometimes also called 'racial realism', derives from Bell's insight, based on his analysis of American civil rights jurisprudence, that '[t]he interest of blacks in achieving racial equality will be accommodated only when it converges with the interests of whites' (Bell, 1980: 523). Interest convergence has important implications for anti-racist practice, as discussed in Chapter 7.

5 *Intersectionality* of identity and oppression means that although race is the main concern of CRT it is almost always considered alongside other characteristics and structural inequalities, such as class, gender, sexuality, (dis)ability, and age.

Evidence of racial and ethnic inequalities comes in many forms, including disparities in health and welfare outcomes (see Chapter 3), educational access and achievement, involvement in and treatment by the criminal justice system, vulnerability to crime, patterns of employment and barriers to professional advancement (Byrne *et al.*, 2020). Such systematic effects are well documented but only rarely receive widespread attention. International outrage was expressed when George Floyd was murdered by a police officer in Minneapolis in 2020, yet this was part of a long history of acts of deadly violence by American police against black citizens. Such patterns cannot be explained by the actions of a few racist individuals. The concept of institutional racism (Better, 2008) is sometimes used to explain how racism operates on a structural level throughout society, including in powerful agencies such as the police and military. In the UK, awareness of institutional racism rose in the wake of a public inquiry into the bungled police investigation into the murder in 1993 of a black teenager, Stephen Lawrence, by a gang of white youths (McLaughlin and Murji, 1999). However, over the next two decades the need to address institutional racism received less attention and was largely ignored by policymakers, at least until the Black Lives Matter movement forced it back into the public arena (see Chapter 7).

Contributing to institutional racism are aspects of political discourse, popular culture and media reporting that – whether deliberately or unwittingly – perpetuate negative stereotypes and prejudicial attitudes towards ethnically minoritised groups. An example is the subject of migration and refugees, which is often discussed by politicians and the media in antagonistic terms designed to raise concerns about illegality, criminality and dependency, while ignoring the positive contributions made by migrants (Capdevila and Callaghan, 2008). Another example is the way in which Islamophobia, or anti-Muslim racism, has become normalised in media news reporting as well as in government statements and policies (Elahi and Khan, 2018). Linked to such tendencies is the rise of nationalism and political populism in many countries, as demonstrated by the 2016 Brexit referendum in the UK and the US presidential election in the same year, both of which were marked by divisive and often explicitly racist rhetoric from right-wing politicians. Arguably more subtle, although just as divisive, are statements designed to deflect attention and legitimacy away from inequalities experienced by ethnically minoritised groups; a typical strategy is to focus on socio-economic inequalities among the majority group, e.g. in relation to the 'white working class' (Begum *et al.*, 2021).

As the last point goes to show, racial and ethnic inequalities are highly relevant to other forms of structural disadvantage including poverty and deprivation – and vice versa. Spatial factors are also important, particularly where there are distinct communities living in particular areas and neighbourhoods or where geographical mobility may differ between different ethnic groups. The intersection between race and gender has been foundational to the field of intersectionality, which has assumed increasing importance within social work (Bernard, 2021). Similar concerns are applicable to other minoritised groups, such as people with disabilities, for whom the lived experience of inequality interacts in complex ways with other aspects of identity.

Case Study 2.1: Social work and the Roma community (Valero *et al.*, 2021)

Roma refers to diverse groups, including Romany, Gypsies, Travellers, Manouche, Ashkali, Sinti and Boyash, who vary considerably in terms of language, religion,

Continued

culture, location and lifestyle. Roma constitute the largest minority ethnic group in Europe, with around 10–12 million living in all European countries and particularly in Central and Eastern Europe. Roma communities are exposed to significant inequalities, such as poverty, discrimination, hate crime, poor health, barriers to education and other forms of social exclusion. Negative attitudes and prejudices towards Roma are a significant barrier to professional support. Social workers may be perceived as a source of surveillance and control rather than as providing culturally appropriate forms of support and assistance. Focusing on social work with the Roma community in Spain, Valero et al. (2021) review some examples of practice from a critical social work perspective. They examine three key elements: evidence-based actions, solidarity and respect, and recognition of the Roma identity. They argue that for social work to be effective in marginalised communities, sensitivity to cultural beliefs is not enough – interventions should ideally emerge from, and be led by, people from those communities. As an example, they discuss *Drom Kotar Mestipen*, a Roma women's association founded by a group of Roma women to fight against discrimination and exclusion, and for equality and solidarity.

Age

Age as a social construct is different from – although obviously linked to – biological ageing. Perceptions and expectations of people at different stages of life can vary widely between societies and over time. For example, the modern concept of childhood is bound up with the transformation wrought by industrialisation and mass education to traditional agrarian societies. In recent decades, demographic changes stemming from falling birth rates and increasing life expectancy may have contributed to more negative attitudes towards older adults, including in Eastern cultures in which old age has traditionally been held in high esteem (North and Fiske, 2015). Ageing has many social consequences for individuals, including their rights and responsibilities, chances of employment, norms around appearance and lifestyle, and the opportunity to contribute and feel valued by society. The impact of other social divisions, such as gender and class, are often exacerbated over time, which is why social policy often concentrates on early life as a strategy to invest in people's life chances (see Chapter 5).

Childhood and old age are the life stages most commonly associated with concerns about inequality. As noted above, children are more likely than adults to live in poverty, while childhood disadvantage has been found to lead to poorer health outcomes in later life (Ferraro *et al.*, 2016; Morton, 2022). Children are more dependent on adults to look after them and correspondingly more vulnerable to neglect, abuse and exploitation. Adolescence and the associated developmental challenges around identity formation are a common site of psycho-social strain as well as intergenerational tension and conflict, e.g. around culture, gender and sexuality, which can be exacerbated for young people in minoritised groups. Moral panics about youth subcultures are also a perennial feature of political discourse and media reporting, in the process contributing to longstanding forms of prejudicial stereotyping, e.g. the criminalisation of black musical subcultures in the UK (Fatsis, 2019). Even before the Covid-19 pandemic, there was increasing concern about the prevalence of mental health problems among adolescents, which far exceeded the capacity of specialist provision (Deighton *et al.*, 2019). There is also a global dimension to childhood inequality, with huge disparities in rates of child mortality, nutrition, education, and the use of child labour (UNICEF, 2021).

At the other end of the lifecourse, there are many inequalities that affect people in later life. Poverty and material deprivation affect many older people; in the UK, for example, pensioners are more likely than working-age people to have a persistent low income (Francis-Devine, 2021). Negative attitudes towards older people exist in many societies and contribute to age discrimination in various parts of society, including the workplace (Shore and Goldberg, 2012). Life expectancy differs widely between countries (see Chapter 4) but also within countries, with stark differences in the health and quality of life of people living in the richest and poorest areas (see Chapter 3). The phenomenon of ageing populations seen almost everywhere in the industrialised world is subject to widespread misconceptions and media scaremongering, with terms such as 'demographic timebomb' used to present older people as a threat to social cohesion and a drain on public resources. Rationing and cuts to social care provision disproportionately affect older people (Hood *et al.*, 2022), leading to chronic underfunding of services and reinforcing inequalities in end of life care (Payne, 2010).

Sexuality and Sexual Orientation

Sexuality as a social construct is linked to gender through the 'normative practice' of heterosexuality (Jackson, 2006), which reinforces gender identity as a binary distinction between males and females while defining sexual identity in terms of desires, practices and relationships that occur between men and women. Through its association with traditional ideas about masculinity and femininity, as well as family and marriage, heterosexuality also underpins the gendered division of labour and resources. What has been termed 'heteronormativity' is therefore 'not only a normative sexual practice but also a normal way of life' (Jackson, 2006: 107). Heteronormative discourses and practices are inherently unequal, for example because they exclude the possibility of non-binary gender identities, or promote the view that homosexual relationships are socially less acceptable than heterosexual ones. A notable challenge to heteronormativity has come from queer theory, a diverse body of work that has questioned the nature of identity and subjectivity and deconstructed the fields of knowledge and power that make heterosexuality seem both coherent and privileged (Hicks and Jeyasingham, 2016). More generally, heteronormative assumptions have been challenged by diverse groups and communities that have produced (and are still creating) new definitions, identities and understandings of gender and sexuality. Some of these are encapsulated in the acronym LGBTQ+ (Lesbian, Gay, Bi, Trans, Questioning plus other sexual and gender minority identities).

Table 2.2 Selected LGBTQ+ terms (Source: Stonewall[3])

Term	Definition
Aro/Ace	Umbrella terms describing a wide group of people who experience a lack of, varying or occasional experiences of romantic and/or sexual attraction.
Bi	An umbrella term used to describe a romantic and/or sexual orientation towards more than one gender.
Cisgender/Cis	Someone whose gender identity is the same as the sex they were assigned at birth.
Gay	Refers to a man who has a romantic and/or sexual orientation towards men. Also a generic term for lesbian and gay sexuality.
Intersex	A term used to describe a person who may have the biological attributes of both sexes or whose biological attributes do not fit with societal assumptions about what constitutes male or female.
Lesbian	Refers to a woman who has a romantic and/or sexual orientation towards women. Some non-binary people may also identify with this term.
Non-binary	An umbrella term for people whose gender identity does not sit comfortably with 'man' or 'woman'. Non-binary identities are varied.
Questioning	The process of exploring your own sexual orientation and/or gender identity.
Trans	An umbrella term to describe people whose gender is not the same as, or does not sit comfortably with, the sex they were assigned at birth.

In large part due to the activism, campaigning and advocacy of LGBTQ+ movements, the past few decades have seen increasing acceptance of diverse forms of human sexuality, particularly in the Global North (see Chapter 5). Nonetheless, there continues to be widespread intolerance and discrimination towards people whose sexual orientation and activity does not conform to heteronormative ideas. Homosexuality remains illegal in some countries, while in others the authorities ignore or even support overt discrimination, hostility and violence towards LGBTQ+ people (Weiss and Bosia, 2013). Even in countries with relatively progressive policies and legal protections against homophobic discrimination, basic equalities have been hard won and only recently achieved. In the UK, for example, legislation enabling same-sex couples to marry was only passed in 2013. Homophobic attitudes remain prevalent in countries where such liberalisation has occurred, while opportunities for people with diverse

---

3   See stonewall.org.uk for a comprehensive and up-to-date list of terms and definitions.

sexual identities to live freely and without stigma are experienced unequally by people of different class, gender, ethnicity, age and geographical backgrounds (McDermott, 2011).

Disability

There are various contemporary frameworks for understanding disability. Arguably, the most familiar to social workers is the social model of disability, which was developed to oppose and go beyond individualised understandings of disability as being mainly about deviation from biomedical norms. The social model distinguishes between impairment, which can be defined in biological or functional terms (e.g. living with chronic pain, limited mobility, or a learning difficulty), and the disabling barriers that prevent people from fulfilling their potential (Oliver and Sapey, 2018). The focus on barriers counters a professional tendency to view disability through the lens of individual deficits and interventions, which leads (sometimes unwittingly) to discriminatory and paternalistic practices. Within a social model, disabled people are not seen as passive recipients of care and support but rather as experts on their own lives and as equal partners in the creation of a more just society. This paradigm shift in thinking has contributed to efforts by disabled activists and allies in the disability rights movement to build an agenda for political change, both in the UK (where the model originated) and internationally. Over the years, the social model has evolved to address the diversity of the disabled population, the importance of intersectional inequalities, and the psycho-emotional aspects of what Thomas (2007) terms 'disablism'.

An alternative framework is the interactional model of disability, which seeks to integrate the medical and social models into a more universal, health-based approach (WHO, 2001). Interactional approaches place emphasis on the lived experience of impairment, regarding disability as 'a complex interaction between the traits inherent to a person (or one's impairment) and how these traits manifest themselves in the environment they find themselves in (the disabling facts of one's impairment)' (Riddle, 2013: 378). All people are considered to be at risk of disability, whether through inherited traits, illness, ageing or accidental injury, with this risk being mediated by the social determinants of health (see Chapter 3). Some interactional theorists have criticised the social model's focus on exclusionary barriers, arguing that disability cannot be defined wholly in terms of oppressive social structures since even if barriers are removed as far as possible, many people will still experience disadvantages to having an impairment (Shakespeare, 2006). In turn, proponents of the social model have expressed concerns that a renewed focus on impairment can be (and has been) used to justify government policies to reduce support and provision for disabled people (Oliver, 2013).

UK government figures indicate that there were roughly 14.1 million disabled people living in the UK in 2020. They also show that outcomes for this substantial group reflect 'stark differences between the experience of disabled and non-disabled people' (Office for National Statistics, 2020):

- *Education* – disabled people are less likely to have a degree than their non-disabled peers and nearly three times more likely to have no qualifications.
- *Employment* – disabled people have lower chances of employment than non-disabled working age people.
- *Housing* – disabled people are less likely to own their own home and more likely to live in rented social housing.
- *Wellbeing* – disabled people tend to report lower average wellbeing, happiness and life satisfaction, and higher levels of anxiety and loneliness.
- *Violence* – disabled people are more likely to have experienced domestic abuse in the last 12 months.

Research similarly shows multiple inequities in outcomes for disabled people, including the impact of the Covid-19 pandemic (see Chapter 3). In their overview of evidence on inequality and disability, Simcock and Castle (2016) discuss findings relating to the exploitation of disabled people's labour, their marginalisation from education and employment, disproportionate exposure to poverty, debt and financial hardship, relative powerlessness in their interactions with professionals and service providers, and the risk of suffering violence and abuse. Reeve (2014) discusses the psycho-emotional consequences of exclusion and discrimination, which operate not only on a structural level, e.g. as barriers to participation, but are also experienced on a private level as 'internalised oppression'. For example, government processes for receiving statutory support may lead some disabled people to emphasise their deficits rather than capabilities when applying for means-tested benefits. Conversely, negative cultural attitudes towards disability may lead some people to conceal their impairment (if not immediately visible to others) so as to 'pass as normal'. The distress and psychological strain associated with such processes can have significant consequences for people's physical and mental health.

The size and diversity of the disabled population makes it important to examine the complexity of lived experience. Disability may not be central to how people who fall under institutional or legal categories of disability see themselves. For example, someone from the Deaf community might consider themselves to be part of a cultural and linguistic minority and the notion that they have an impairment to be offensive. Other aspects of identity, such as ethnicity or sexuality, may be more important to someone's self-concept than disability. At the same time, disability intersects in important ways with personal and social characteristics. For example, there is some evidence of what Maroto *et al.* (2019) call 'hierarchies of categorical disadvantage', in that poverty levels are highest among women and ethnically minoritised groups with disabilities. Purdam *et al.* (2008) found that older Asian and Black Caribbean people (aged 50–64) generally had considerably higher disability rates than the White population in the same age group.

Exercise 2.3: Inequality and positionality

Building on your reflection on class and social position in Exercise 2.1, consider your relationship to the different types of structural inequality that have been outlined here (as well as any others you can relate to). While they may be analysed on a broad social scale, these concepts also speak to the multi-faceted nature of personal identity. Human beings are complex and how we perceive someone will often differ from how they see themselves. Such misunderstandings are likely to happen if we use a single lens, such as class or disability, to think about people and their circumstances. In reflecting on our own position with regard to inequalities, it can therefore help to think about questions such as:

- What aspects of social identity are important to me, e.g. how do I usually choose to define myself (e.g. in relation to class, ethnicity, gender, religion, sexuality, disability, age, and so on)? Are there situations in which I emphasise some aspects of my identity but not others?
- What aspects of my social identity do other people, especially those who do not know me well, tend to focus on? Is this sometimes problematic, e.g. because I have to explain myself when other people don't, or because I experience prejudice or discrimination? If it is rarely or never problematic – why might that be the case?
- Am I disadvantaged or privileged by any of the social inequalities outlined in this chapter? How do these disadvantages and/or privileges manifest themselves in my personal experience?
- What are the main characteristics of my social group, e.g. family, friends, colleagues – are there things they mostly have in common, or are they all different? Who do I think of as 'people like me'? Who do I think of (perhaps unconsciously) as 'not like me'? Are these categories connected to inequalities?
- How might my positionality affect my professional practice as a social worker (or social work student), e.g. when meeting people for the first time, understanding and assessing their needs, or putting together a care plan. What might be easier, or harder, for me? Under which circumstances?

Conclusion

This chapter has explored the many faces of inequality, highlighting its relationship to human diversity and difference, hierarchical social structures and the struggle for power and resources. Empirical evidence has been presented to justify a central claim, which is that structural inequalities operate to the advantage of some people and to the detriment of everyone else. Of course, there are pitfalls to this kind of analysis. For example, focusing too much on the social determinants of health and welfare risks downplaying the importance of individual agency. The tension between individual and structural explanations – and interventions – is a core issue in social work practice and will be a key theme in later chapters. Examining the evidence for inequalities in separate domains might also make it harder to maintain an intersectional perspective and respect the unique constellation of attributes and differences that contribute to our personal identities. In some ways, an inequalities lens should operate like a kaleidoscope as well as a magnifying glass – bringing together aspects of difference into closer view, in order to study the effects of interlocking patterns of injustice in a particular form, before shifting the pieces to a different perspective. In the next chapter, this kind of approach will be applied to consider the fundamental impact of inequality on people's health and welfare.

References

Anantharaman, M. (2017) 'Elite and ethical: The defensive distinctions of middle-class bicycling in Bangalore, India', *Journal of Consumer Culture*, **17**(3), pp. 864–886.

Atkinson, A.B., Casarico, A. and Voitchovsky, S. (2018) 'Top incomes and the gender divide', *The Journal of Economic Inequality*, **16**(2), pp. 225–256.

Atkinson, A.B. and Jenkins, S.P. (2020) 'A different perspective on the evolution of UK income inequality', *Review of Income and Wealth*, **66**(2), pp. 253–266.

Barford, A., Dorling, D., Smith, G.D. and Shaw, M. (2006) 'Life expectancy: Women now on top everywhere', **332**(7545), p. 808.

Begum, N., Mondon, A. and Winter, A. (2021) 'Between the "left behind" and "the people": Racism, populism and the construction of the "white working class" in the context of Brexit', *Routledge Handbook of Critical Studies in Whiteness*, Abingdon, Routledge, pp. 220–231.

Bell, D. (1980) 'Brown v. Board of Education and the interest-convergence dilemma', *Harvard Law Review*, **93**(3), pp. 518–533.

Bell, D. (1992) Faces at the bottom of the well: The permanence of racism, New York, Basic Books.

Bernard, C. (2021) Intersectionality for Social Workers: A Practical Introduction to Theory and Practice Paperback, Abingdon, Routledge.

Better, S. (2008) Institutional racism: A primer on theory and strategies for social change (2nd Edition), Plymouth, Rowman & Littlefield.

Bhavnani, R., Mirza, H.S. and Meetoo, V. (2005) *Tackling the roots of racism: Lessons for success*, Bristol, Policy Press.

Bourdieu, P. (1987) *Distinction: A social critique of the judgement of taste*, Boston, MA, Harvard University Press.

Butler, A. (2017) *Contemporary South Africa* (3rd Edition), London, Palgrave.

Butler, J. (1990) *Gender trouble*, New York, Routledge.

Byrne, B., Alexander, C., Khan, O., Nazroo, J. and Shankley, W. (2020) *Ethnicity, race and inequality in the UK: State of the nation*, Bristol, Policy Press.

Capdevila, R. and Callaghan, J.E. (2008) '"It's not racist. It's common sense". A critical analysis of political discourse around asylum and immigration in the UK', *Journal of Community & Applied Social Psychology*, **18**(1), pp. 1–16.

Carr, J.H. and Kutty, N.K. (eds) (2008) *Segregation: The rising costs for America*, London, Routledge.

Christensen, M.A. (2019) 'Feminization of poverty: Causes and implications', in Leal Filho, W., Azul, A.M., Brandli, L., Özuyar, P.G. and Wall, T. (eds), *Gender Equality*, Cham, Springer International Publishing, pp. 1–10.

Collins, F.S. and Mansoura, M.K. (2001) 'The Human Genome Project: Revealing the shared inheritance of all humankind', *Cancer: Interdisciplinary International Journal of the American Cancer Society*, **91**(S1), pp. 221–225.

Connell, R. (1987) Gender and power: Society, the person and sexual politics, Cambridge, Polity Press.

Cousin, B., Khan, S. and Mears, A. (2018) *Theoretical and methodological pathways for research on elites*, Oxford, Oxford University Press.

Cribb, J., Norris Keiller, A. and Waters, T. (2018) *Living standards, poverty and inequality in the UK: 2018*. IFS Report, No. R145, London, Institute for Fiscal Studies.

Davis, A., Hirsch, D., Padley, M. and Shepherd, C. (2021) *A minimum income standard for the United Kingdom in 2021*, York, Joseph Rowntree Foundation.

Deas, I., Robson, B., Wong, C. and Bradford, M. (2003) 'Measuring neighbourhood deprivation: A critique of the Index of Multiple Deprivation', *Environment and Planning C: Government and Policy*, **21**(6), pp. 883–903.

Deighton, J., Lereya, S.T., Casey, P., Patalay, P., Humphrey, N. and Wolpert, M. (2019) 'Prevalence of mental health problems in schools: Poverty and other risk factors among 28 000 adolescents in England', *British Journal of Psychiatry*, **215**(3), pp. 565–567.

Delgado, R. and Stefancic, J. (2023) *Critical race theory: An introduction*, New York, New York University Press.

Dorling, D. (2015) *Injustice (revised edition): Why social inequality still persists*, Bristol, Policy Press.

Eisenberg, A. and Spinner-Halev, J. (2005) *Minorities within minorities: Equality, rights and diversity*, Cambridge, Cambridge University Press.

Elahi, F. and Khan, O. (eds) (2018) *Islamophobia: Still a challenge for us all*, London, Runnymede.

Fatsis, L. (2019) 'Grime: Criminal subculture or public counterculture? A critical investigation into the criminalization of Black musical subcultures in the UK', *Crime, Media, Culture*, **15**(3), pp. 447–461.

Fazackerley, A. (2021) '"My students never knew": The lecturer who lived in a tent', Available online: www.theguardian.com/education/2021/oct/30/my-students-never-knew-the-lecturer-who-lived-in-a-tent, Last Accessed: 25 February 2019.

Ferraro, K.F., Schafer, M.H. and Wilkinson, L.R. (2016) 'Childhood disadvantage and health problems in middle and later life: Early imprints on physical health?', *American Sociological Review*, **81**(1), pp. 107–133.

Flanagin, A., Frey, T., Christiansen, S.L. and Committee, A.M.o.S. (2021) 'Updated guidance on the reporting of race and ethnicity in medical and science journals', *Jama*, **326**(7), pp. 621–627.

Francis-Devine, B. (2021) *Poverty in the UK: Statistics*, London, House of Commons Library.

Friedman, S. and Laurison, D. (2020) *The Class Ceiling: Why it pays to be privileged*, Bristol, Policy Press.

Friedman, S., Laurison, D. and Miles, A. (2015) 'Breaking the "class" ceiling? Social mobility into Britain's elite occupations', *The Sociological Review*, **63**(2), pp. 259–289.

Friedman, S. and Macmillan, L. (2017) 'Is London really the engine-room? Migration, opportunity hoarding and regional social mobility in the UK', *National Institute Economic Review*, **240**, pp. R58–R72.

Giddens, A. (2009) *Sociology* (6th Edition), Cambridge, Polity Press.

Grusky, D.B., Kanbur, S.R. and Sen, A.K. (2006) *Poverty and inequality*, Stanford, CA, Stanford University Press.

Hecht, K., McArthur, D., Savage, M. and Friedman, S. (2020) 'Elites in the UK: Pulling Away? Social mobility, geographic mobility and elite occupations', London, The Sutton Trust.

Hicks, S. and Jeyasingham, D. (2016) 'Social work, queer theory and after: A genealogy of sexuality theory in neo-liberal times', *The British Journal of Social Work*, **46**(8), pp. 2357–2373.

Holloway, B.T. (2023) 'Highlighting trans joy: A call to practitioners, researchers, and educators', *Health Promotion Practice*, Available online, https://doi.org/10.1177/15248399231152468

Hood, R., Goldacre, A., Abbott, S. and Jones, R. (2022) 'Patterns of demand and provision in English adult social care services', *British Journal of Social Work*, **52**(7), pp. 3858–3880.

Jackson, S. (2006) 'Interchanges: Gender, sexuality and heterosexuality: The complexity (and limits) of heteronormativity', *Feminist Theory*, 7(1), pp. 105–121.

Jenkins, S.P. and Micklewright, J. (2007) *Inequality and poverty re-examined*, Oxford, Oxford University Press.

Jones, C.P. (2002) 'Confronting institutionalized racism', *Phylon (1960-)*, pp. 7–22.

Kearns, M.C., D'Inverno, A.S. and Reidy, D.E. (2020) 'The association between gender inequality and sexual violence in the US', *American Journal of Preventive Medicine*, **58**(1), pp. 12–20.

Kolip, P. and Lange, C. (2018) 'Gender inequality and the gender gap in life expectancy in the European Union', *European Journal of Public Health*, **28**(5), pp. 869–872.

Lister, R. (2004) *Poverty*, Cambridge, Polity Press.

Madiba, S. and Ngwenya, N. (2017) 'Cultural practices, gender inequality and inconsistent condom use increase vulnerability to HIV infection: Narratives from married and cohabiting women in rural communities in Mpumalanga province, South Africa', *Global Health Action*, **10**(sup2), p. 1341597.

Major, J. (1993) *Speech to the Carlton Club – 3 February 1993*, Available online: https://johnmajorarchive.org.uk/1993/02/03/mr-majors-speech-to-the-carlton-club-3-february-1993/, Last Accessed: 24 June 2021.

Maroto, M., Pettinicchio, D. and Patterson, A.C. (2019) 'Hierarchies of categorical disadvantage: Economic insecurity at the intersection of disability, gender, and race', *Gender & Society*, **33**(1), pp. 64–93.

McDermott, E. (2011) 'The world some have won: Sexuality, class and inequality', *Sexualities*, **14**(1), pp. 63–78.

McLaughlin, E. and Murji, K. (1999) 'After the Stephen Lawrence Report', *Critical Social Policy*, **19**(3), pp. 371–385.

Ministry of Housing Communities & Local Government (MHCLG) (2019) *English indices of deprivation 2019*, Available online: www.gov.uk/government/ statistics/english-indices-of-deprivation-2019, Last Accessed: 19 June 2021.

Morton, P.M. (2022) 'Childhood disadvantage and adult functional status: Do early-life exposures jeopardize healthy aging?', *Journal of Aging and Health*, p. 08982643211064723.

Nentwich, J.C., Poppen, W., Schälin, S. and Vogt, F. (2013) 'The same and the other: Male childcare workers managing identity dissonance', *International Review of Sociology*, **23**(2), pp. 326–345.

Neumayer, E. and Plümper, T. (2007) 'The gendered nature of natural disasters: The impact of catastrophic events on the gender gap in life expectancy, 1981–2002', *Annals of the Association of American Geographers*, **97**(3), pp. 551–566.

North, M.S. and Fiske, S.T. (2015) 'Modern attitudes toward older adults in the aging world: A cross-cultural meta-analysis', *Psychological Bulletin*, **141**(5), p. 993.

Nunn, A., Johnson, S., Monro, S., Bickerstaffe, T. and Kelsey, S. (2007) *Factors influencing social mobility*, London, Department for Work and Pensions.

OECD (2021) *Income inequality (indicator)*, Available online: doi: 10.1787/459aa7f1-en, Last Accessed: 06 January 2022.

Office for National Statistics (ONS) (2011) *The National Statistics Socio-economic classification (NS-SEC)*, Available online: www.ons.gov.uk/methodology/ classificationsandstandards/otherclassifications/thenationalstatisticssocio economicclassificationnssecrebasedonsoc2010, Last Accessed: 25 July 2021.

Office for National Statistics (ONS) (2020) *Outcomes for disabled people in the UK: 2020*, Available online: www.ons.gov.uk/peoplepopulationandcommunity/ healthandsocialcare/disability/articles/outcomesfordisabledpeopleintheuk/2020, Last Accessed 19/04/2023.

Office for National Statistics (ONS) (2021) *Household income inequality, UK: financial year ending 2020*, Available online: www.ons.gov.uk/ peoplepopulationandcommunity/personalandhouseholdfinances/ incomeandwealth/bulletins/householdincomeinequalityfinancial/ financialyearending2020, Last Accessed: 22/03/2021.

Oliver, M. (2013) 'The social model of disability: Thirty years on', *Disability & Society*, **28**(7), pp. 1024–1026.

Oliver, M. and Sapey, B. (2018) *Social work with disabled people* (3rd Edition), Basingstoke, Palgrave Macmillan.

Omi, M. and Winant, H. (2014) *Racial formation in the United States*, New York, Routledge.

Orme, J. (2003) '"It's feminist because I say so!" Feminism, social work and critical practice in the UKZ', *Qualitative Social Work*, **2**(2), pp. 131–153.

Payne, M. (2010) 'Inequalities, end-of-life care and social work', *Progress in Palliative Care*, **18**(4), pp. 221–227.

Purdam, K., Afkhami, R., Olsen, W. and Thornton, P. (2008) 'Disability in the UK: Measuring equality', *Disability & Society*, **23**(1), pp. 53–65.

Reeve, D. (2014) 'Psycho-emotional disablism and internalised oppression', in Swain, J., French, S., Barnes, C. and Thomas, C. (eds), *Disabling barriers – Enabling environments*, London, Sage, pp. 92–98.

Reid, W. (2020) *When you're accustomed to privilege, equality feels like oppression*, Available online: www.basw.co.uk/resources/psw-magazine/psw-online/%E2%80%98when-you%E2%80%99re-accustomed-privilege-equality-feels-oppression%E2%80%99, Last Accessed: 28 February 2023.

Richards, C., Bouman, W.P., Seal, L., Barker, M.J., Nieder, T.O. and T'Sjoen, G. (2016) 'Non-binary or genderqueer genders', *International Review of Psychiatry*, **28**(1), pp. 95–102.

Riddle, C.A. (2013) 'Defining disability: Metaphysical not political', *Medicine, Health Care and Philosophy*, **16**(3), pp. 377–384.

Rosenfield, S. and Mouzon, D. (2013) 'Gender and mental health', in Aneshensel, C.S., Phelan, J.C. and Bierman, A. (eds), *Handbook of the Sociology of Mental Health*, Dordrecht, Springer Netherlands, pp. 277–296.

Scambler, G. (2012) 'Health inequalities', *Sociology of Health & Illness*, **34**(1), pp. 130–146.

Selvarajah, S., Abi Deivanayagam, T., Lasco, G., Scafe, S., White, A., Zembe-Mkabile, W. and Devakumar, D. (2020) 'Categorisation and minoritisation', *BMJ Global Health*, **5**(12), p. e004508.

Sen, A. (1999) *Development as freedom*, Oxford, Oxford University Press.

Sen, A. (2001) 'The many faces of gender inequality', *New Republic*, **18**, pp. 35–39.

Shakespeare, T. (2006) *Disability rights and wrongs*, Abingdon, Routledge.

Shore, L.M. and Goldberg, C.B. (2012) 'Age discrimination in the workplace', in Dipboye, R.L. and Colella, A. (eds), *Discrimination at work: The psychological and organizational bases*, New York, Psychology Press, pp. 231–254.

Shuster, S.M. and Westbrook, L. (2022) 'Reducing the joy deficit in sociology: A study of transgender joy', *Social Problems*, Available online, https://doi.org/10.1093/socpro/spac034

Simcock, P. and Castle, R. (2016) *Social work and disability*, Cambridge, Polity Press.

Singh, G. and Masocha, S. (2019) 'Introduction', in Singh, G. and Masocha, S. (eds), *Anti-racist social work: International perspectives*, London, Bloomsbury, pp. 1–12.

Social Metrics Commission (2020) 'Measuring Poverty 2020: A report of the Social Metrics Commission', London, Legatum Institute.

Spicker, P. (2007) *The idea of poverty*, Bristol, Policy Press.

Tedam, P. (2020) Anti-oppressive social work practice, London, Sage.

Thomas, C. (2007) Sociologies of disability and illness: Contested ideas in disability studies and medical sociology, Basingstoke, Palgrave Macmillan.

Thompson, M.E. and Armato, M. (2012) *Investigating gender*, Cambridge, Polity Press.

Tomlinson, M., Walker, R. and Williams, G. (2008) 'Measuring poverty in Britain as a multi-dimensional concept, 1991 to 2003', *Journal of Social Policy*, **37**(4), pp. 597–620.

Townsend, P. (1979) *Poverty in the United Kingdom*, Harmondsworth, Allen Lane.

UNICEF (2021) 'Child labour: Global estimates 2020, trends and the road forward', New York, International Labour Office and United Nations Children's Fund.

Valero, D., Elboj, C., Plaja, T. and Munté Pascual, A. (2021) 'Social work and the Roma community: Elements to improve current practices', *European Journal of Social Work*, **24**(6), pp. 978–989.

Webb, C.J. (2019) Constructing a reliable and valid measure of multidimensional poverty. PhD Thesis. Sheffield, University of Sheffield.

Weiss, M. and Bosia, M. (eds) (2013) *Global homophobia: States, movements, and the politics of oppression*, Chicago, University of Illinois Press.

Whittle, S., Turner, L., Al-Alami, M., Rundall, E. and Thom, B. (2007) 'Engendered penalties: Transgender and transsexual people's experiences of inequality and discrimination', London, The Equalities Review.

WHO (2001) The international classification of functioning, disability and health, Geneva, World Health Organisation.

Williams, C.L. (1992) 'The glass escalator: Hidden advantages for men in the "female" professions', *Social Problems*, **39**(3), pp. 253–267.

Winter, S., Diamond, M., Green, J., Karasic, D., Reed, T., Whittle, S. and Wylie, K. (2016) 'Transgender people: Health at the margins of society', *The Lancet*, **388**(10042), pp. 390–400.

World Bank (2020) 'Monitoring global poverty', in World Bank (ed.), *Poverty and Shared Prosperity 2020: Reversals of Fortune*, https://elibrary.worldbank.org/doi/abs/10.1596/978-1-4648-1602-4_ch1, pp. 27–80.

3
Health and Welfare Inequalities

Chapter overview

··

This chapter examines the impact of inequality on people's health and wellbeing, starting with the social gradient, a fundamental concept in health inequalities research. The graded relationship between people's social position and health status is explored in relation to a range of outcomes, including life expectancy and serious illness. The social gradient interacts with other structural factors affecting people's health and wellbeing, as illustrated in numerous inequalities that have been exposed by the Covid-19 pandemic. The chapter proceeds to examine the social determinants of health and the evidence that income inequality exacerbates many social problems including rates of imprisonment, obesity, mental illness, and addiction. The final section focuses on welfare inequalities and social care, showing how inequality manifests itself not only as unfair barriers to care and support, but also as the targeting of disadvantaged groups with surveillance and statutory intervention.

Introduction

Health inequalities may be defined as 'avoidable, unfair and systematic differences in health between different groups of people' (Williams *et al.*, 2020). They mean that our health and wellbeing depend to a large extent on our social status and the social context in which we lead our lives. Health differences can be measured in various ways, including life expectancy, levels of illness and poor health, access to medical treatment, and the quality of care. A broader definition of health inequalities can also cover aspects of people's behaviour that present a risk to health, such as smoking and drug misuse, as well as contextual factors such as the quality of housing or access to clean water. Unfair differences in health status or risks to health will be experienced by people in a range of social groups, as explored in Chapter 2. People may experience health inequalities based on socio-economic factors, such as class, income, poverty and deprivation, as well as personal characteristics such as gender, ethnicity and disability. Interactions between these dimensions contribute to the type and extent of differences in health outcomes and how they are experienced. Underlying many forms of health inequality is a pervasive relationship between socio-economic status and health, sometimes known as the 'social gradient'.

The Social Gradient

The social gradient in health means that 'the higher one's social position, the better one's health is likely to be' (Marmot *et al.*, 2010: 16). The idea of a gradient is important because health inequalities are not just about big differences between the poorest and most affluent people, although these certainly exist. For example, men living in the 10% least deprived areas in England in 2020 could expect to live 9.5 years longer than men living in the 10% most deprived areas, while the equivalent gap for women was 7.7 years (Marmot *et al.*, 2020a: 16). These gaps in life expectancy have been widening over the past decade; shockingly, life expectancy for women has fallen in the country's most deprived neighbourhoods, and in some regions for men too (Marmot *et al.*, 2020a). However, the graded relationship between health and social circumstances means that everyone in the population is affected, not just those at the bottom and top of the scale. In other words, inequality is not just about the gap between rich and poor because even people who are well-off will have worse outcomes than the very richest. The gradient is also responsive to social and economic change. Marmot *et al.* (2020a) found that growth in average life expectancy (which had been increasing steadily since the beginning of the 20th century) had stalled in England, while the time people could expect to spend in good health was decreasing. Most long-term health conditions are both more prevalent and more severe among people from lower socio-economic groups, while inequalities in healthy life expectancy are higher than inequalities in overall life expectancy (Williams *et al.*, 2020). This means that people from more deprived areas not only have shorter lives compared to people from less deprived areas but also spend a greater part of their lives in poor health.

Oppression and Health Inequalities

The social gradient interacts with other structural factors affecting people's health and wellbeing, such as the impact of racism, misogyny, disablism, homophobia, and other forms of oppression. In England, analysis of life expectancy shows that people from Black, Asian and Mixed ethnic backgrounds have significantly lower healthy life expectancy than White British men or women (Marmot, 2020a: 24), while older people from these groups are more likely to report poor health and life-limiting conditions (Toleikyte and Salway, 2018). In the United States, Black Americans have substantially worse health and shorter life expectancies than their White counterparts (Hardeman and Karbeah, 2020). The social gradient is relevant to such inequalities because differences in socio-economic status are ethnically stratified. There is a causal connection between racism and ethnic-racial inequalities in socio-economic status, which contributes to systematic differences in health outcomes via the social gradient of health. However, this is not the full picture. Research in the United States has established that significant inequities in health status exist between Black and White Americans even *after* controlling for socio-economic factors (Franks *et al.*, 2006), while Phelan and Link (2015) present evidence that systemic racism is a fundamental cause of health inequalities independently of socio-economic status.

Similar findings obtain for gender and other personal characteristics. Although women tend to live longer than men, they spend more years in poor health (Read and Gorman, 2010). The former is generally attributed to biological advantages and a positive behavioural profile, e.g. women tend to smoke less than men and are more likely to attend preventative health visits. The latter is usually explained by socio-economic inequalities, which disadvantage women by limiting their access to the resources needed to prevent and treat illness, for example through lower paid, lower status and more insecure work, as well as imposing higher levels of psychosocial strain over the course of their lifetimes (Marmot *et al.*, 2010). This points to the stratification of socio-economic status by sex and gender, which in turn leads to inequalities in health outcomes via the social gradient of health. However, the effects of racial-ethnic, gender and socio-economic stratification interact with each other to produce steeper health inequalities for particular groups of people. For example, Brown *et al.* (2016) studied differences in self-reported health among White, Black and Mexican Americans. They found that the greatest racial-ethnic inequalities were found among women, i.e. Black and Mexican American women had the worst self-rated health and White American men had the best. They also found that racial-ethnic gaps in self-rated health tended to decline between middle and late adulthood, but this was not the case with highly educated Black and White Americans, whose health gap increased with age. Their study demonstrates the importance of a lifecourse approach as well as studying the intersections between various structural factors associated with health inequalities.

Exercise 3.1: Identifying health inequalities

Think about the structural factors which might impact people's health in the following cases.

1   A 35-year-old cisgender heterosexual White British woman, from a working-class background, who lives with her two children in rented accommodation in a prosperous village in rural England, and has recently separated from an abusive partner.

Continued

2   A 20-year-old cisgender heterosexual Black British man living in a deprived area of Birmingham (a large city in central England), whose income from warehouse work does not cover his food and fuel bills during the winter.

3   A 70-year-old gay cisgender Asian man, from a middle-class background and living in an affluent suburb of west London, who is estranged from his family and whose long-term partner has recently died unexpectedly.

4   An 18-year-old transgender heterosexual Black African woman, who came to the UK as an unaccompanied asylum-seeking child at the age of 15 and whose visa status and leave to remain has not yet been decided by the Home Office.

5   A 65-year-old cisgender lesbian woman living in Glasgow, Scotland, who is of mixed Black Caribbean and White British heritage and has been targeted by racist and homophobic abuse by a group of young people in her area, and has been afraid to leave her flat for several weeks.

Health Inequalities and Covid-19

The Covid-19 pandemic threw a spotlight onto health inequalities across the world, drawing public attention to the social gradient of health and the increased risk borne by minoritised and vulnerable groups in the population. Throughout the pandemic, higher Covid-19 mortality rates were reported for older age groups, among men, in more deprived areas, and for minority ethnic groups (Mishra *et al.*, 2021). In England, government statistics for Covid-19 in 2021 (Public Health England, 2021) showed that:

- The cumulative health age-standardised mortality rate for the most deprived areas was 2.4 times the rate for the least deprived areas.
- Cumulative Covid-19 mortality rates in Black and Asian ethnic groups were more than double the rate in the White population.
- After controlling for age, deprivation and pre-existing health conditions, survival rates among many ethnic minority groups remained lower than the White group, particularly for people from Bangladeshi, Pakistani, Chinese and Black Other ethnic groups.
- Disproportionately high rates of infection and mortality were experienced by socially excluded groups, such as homeless people, migrants, sex workers, Gypsy, Roma and Traveller communities, people in prison, and people in contact with the justice system.
- Covid-19 death rates for adults with learning disabilities were significantly higher than for the general population.

As these figures show, being already subject to longstanding health inequalities meant that many disadvantaged groups were exposed to a higher level of risk right from the start of the pandemic. This includes LGBTQ+ people, although worryingly little research has been carried out in this area (McGowan *et al.*, 2021).

The experience of disabled people shows how pre-existing inequalities became exacerbated during the public health crisis caused by Covid-19. For example, when the virus first began to spread there were widespread concerns about the danger it posed to disabled people (Lund *et al.*, 2020). This was partly because some individuals, such as those with severe respiratory conditions, were more susceptible to illness. However, it was also recognised that living and care arrangements for many disabled people meant not only an increased risk of transmission (e.g. because of the proximity and turnover of carers) but also a risk that their support needs would not be met (e.g. because of carers being absent with illness). Other risks followed from the compounding effects of multiple inequalities. Disabled people are more likely to live in poverty (Hughes, 2013) and have been greatly affected by government austerity policies over the past decade (Rummery, 2019). As a result, even before Covid-19 many disabled people were struggling to obtain adequate support from an overstretched and underfunded adult social care system (Kings Fund, 2020). In such circumstances, the effect of the pandemic on disabled people's mental and physical health has been described as 'catastrophic' (Shakespeare *et al.*, 2022).

Pause and reflect: The Covid-19 pandemic

Take a moment to reflect on your experience of the Covid-19 pandemic. What factors affected your ability to keep safe, and to protect people close to you, in the period before vaccines became available? Were you affected by the knock-on effects of national lockdowns on people's jobs, relationships, and mental health? What kinds of health inequalities were you aware of during this time?

Income Inequality and Health

Alongside deprivation and other structural factors, there is evidence that large income differences within populations have damaging effects on people's health. Much of this evidence comes from comparisons between countries, or between large areas (e.g. states) within countries, using measures such as the Gini coefficient (described in Chapter 2). Wilkinson and Pickett (2010) show that for countries who reach an advanced stage of economic development, further increases in average income do nothing to improve average life expectancy. In other words, economic growth can be expected to improve people's overall health in poor countries but not in rich countries. Instead, a large majority of studies have concluded that population health is better in societies where income differences are smaller (Wilkinson and Pickett, 2006). For example, societies where there is greater income inequality tend to have shorter life expectancy and higher infant mortality than more equal societies with the same average GDP per head

(Wilkinson and Pickett, 2010). The tendency for health and social problems to be worse in more unequal countries has been documented for a range of indicators, including homicides, imprisonment, teenage births, obesity, mental illness, drug and alcohol addiction (Wilkinson and Pickett, 2010).

At the same time, more equal societies tend to experience higher levels of social mobility, social cohesion and trust. This is thought to be a crucial reason why greater equality brings health benefits (Pickett and Wilkinson, 2015). Countries and cultures with greater income differences tend to be more hierarchical and socially stratified, with a steep social gradient in indicators of welfare, wellbeing and happiness. Living in such a society produces high levels of distrust and anxiety relating to social evaluation, i.e. how we perceive ourselves, our dignity and self-worth, in relation to others. This leads to the type of chronic stress that is known to have severe biological and psychological effects, including faster ageing and higher levels of morbidity, i.e. suffering from a disease or medical condition. Over the course of a lifetime, the psycho-social strain of living in an unequal society has adverse health effects that are experienced by everyone in society. These effects also cause a steep social gradient in outcomes, meaning that the worst health and most visible social problems are found among those at the bottom of the socio-economic scale.

The Social Determinants of Health

The literature on income inequality demonstrates that people's health, as well as the wider risk factors that impact on their health, are socially determined. This is an important point, which relates to the insights of the social model of disability (see Chapter 2) as well as the debates around meritocracy (see Chapter 1). For example, some people might argue that the social gradient of health is an unintended consequence of the 'sorting' mechanism of outcomes in a meritocratic society, so that people with poorer health are less likely to gain good qualifications or highly paid jobs. Higher levels of income inequality might therefore be caused by higher levels of poor health in a population, rather than the other way round. However, this interpretation has been disproved by studies that show a substantial time-lag between increases in inequality and deterioration in population health, as well as an association between inequality and indicators of children's health, including birth weight and infant mortality (Pickett and Wilkinson, 2015). An alternative argument is that health differences are down to individual choices around lifestyle and behaviour, rather than being determined by structural factors such as poverty and inequality. Of course, this would be an unconvincing explanation for inequalities in the physical and mental health of children. However, such arguments are often deployed by right-wing politicians seeking to promote an individualist explanation for social problems that mainly affect adults, such as unemployment or drug addiction (see Chapter 5). When it comes to behavioural risk factors with a steep social gradient, such as obesity or drug and alcohol misuse, it must be remembered that while individuals certainly do have a choice about how to lead their lives, patterns that are identified within or between populations must necessarily have a social explanation. For example, it has often been observed that in poor (as in economically undeveloped) countries, it is richer people who tend to be overweight while poorer people tend to be thin (or malnourished). In affluent countries, it is the other way round: rich people tend to be thin while obesity has become a problem of people living in poverty (Wilkinson and Pickett, 2010). In other words, individual choices must be understood within the wider social and historical context in which they are made.

The World Health Organisation's Commission on the Social Determinants of Health (WHO, 2008) explicitly stated the connection between poor health, the social conditions in which people lived, and the economic and social policies pursued by governments:

> The poor health of the poor, the social gradient in health within countries, and the marked health inequities between countries are caused by the unequal distribution of power, income, goods, and services, globally and nationally, the consequent unfairness in the immediate, visible circumstances of people's lives – their access to health care, schools, and education, their conditions of work and leisure, their homes, communities, towns, or cities – and their chances of leading a flourishing life. This unequal distribution of health-damaging experiences is not in any sense a 'natural' phenomenon but is the result of a toxic combination of poor social policies and programmes, unfair economic arrangements, and bad politics. (WHO, 2008)

This statement is as much a call for action as it is an empirical statement of fact and so has direct implications for government policy. In the UK, similar calls to reduce health inequities have been made regularly over the past four decades, starting with the Black report in 1980 – which was 'virtually disowned' by the government at the time (Gray, 1982) – and most recently continuing with an exhortation to 'build back fairer' in light of the huge disparities exposed by the Covid-19 pandemic (Marmot et al., 2020b). Marshalling the evidence on the social determinants of health, Marmot et al. (2010) produced a comprehensive set of policy recommendations, which are summarised below in Table 3.1. The report emphasises the importance of a whole-systems approach to implementing these recommendations, so as to avoid over-simplification, unintended consequences and other pitfalls when designing policies for complex social problems (see Hood, 2018).

The Marmot Review report adopts a holistic approach to improving public health by tackling social inequalities. It arguably represents an entire programme for government, which means it needs to be considered against the broader policy context (see Chapter 5). It is also notable for focusing on ill health prevention rather than on acute and clinical care, which is where most public funding of health services ends up. Both points – the focus on social issues and the emphasis

Table 3.1 Policy objectives and recommendations in the Marmot Review (Marmot *et al.*, 2010)

Policy objective	Recommendations
Give every child the best start in life	• Increased investment in early years • Supporting families to develop children's skills • Quality early years education and childcare
Enable all children, young people and adults to maximise their capabilities and have control over their lives	• Reduce the social gradient in educational outcomes • Reduce the social gradient in life-skills • Ongoing skills development through lifelong learning
Create fair employment and good work for all	• Active labour market programmes • The development of good quality work • Reducing physical and chemical hazards and injuries at work • Shift work and other work-time factors • Improving the psychosocial work environment
Ensure healthy standard of living for all	• Implement a minimum income for health living • Remove 'cliff edges' for those moving in and out of work and improve flexibility of employment • Review and implement systems of taxation, benefits, pensions and tax credits
Create and develop health and sustainable places and communities	• Prioritise policies and interventions that reduce both health inequalities and mitigate climate change • Integrate planning, transport, housing and health policies to address the social determinants of health • Create and develop communities
Strengthen the role and impact of ill health prevention	• Increased investment in prevention • Implement evidence-based ill health preventative interventions • Public health to focus interventions to reduce the social gradient

on prevention – are highly relevant to the role of social work in addressing inequality, which will be taken up in Chapter 6. Equally, it is important to note that the health inequalities approach taken by Marmot and others, such as Pickett and Wilkinson, has been criticised for overlooking the political and structural causes of social gradients in favour of a psycho-social analysis of stress, stigma and shame (Coburn, 2004; Scambler, 2012). This critique is relevant to how inequalities are treated within radical social work perspectives (see Chapter 7). It has also been pointed out that analysis of health inequalities often takes for granted the existence of legal environments that support the development of publicly funded health systems, which may be a Eurocentric perspective since in many countries the rule of law is regarded as a significant social determinant of health (Dingake, 2017).

Inequalities in Access to Healthcare

While Marmot *et al.* (2010) acknowledged inequalities in access to healthcare, this issue was not directly addressed by their review, which focused on the social determinants of health. Yet it is important to recognise that substantial inequalities in access exist even in countries with advanced healthcare systems, while they are a vital concern in countries where such systems are still developing (see Chapter 4). In the UK, the publicly funded National Health Service (NHS) is based on the principle of free universal health coverage. However, the history of the NHS itself demonstrates the persistent nature of inequalities even when health services are available to everyone free at the point of access. This is partly because of the interaction of demand and provision in societies with a steep social gradient of health. Since the burden of poor health and illness is experienced disproportionately in more deprived areas, the need for healthcare is much higher in those areas. However, the availability of services tends not to match the level of demand; instead, it is often lower in areas where need is higher. This has been termed the 'inverse care law', defined by Tudor Hart (1971) as the tendency for the availability of medical care 'to vary inversely with the need for it in the population served'. Tudor Hart ascribed this tendency to various factors, including variations in quality of care (e.g. length of consultations with doctors) and the distribution of resources (e.g. upgrading of buildings and equipment), but also the ability of higher income groups to ensure they receive a better standard of service. Similar problems have been experienced in other developed countries. In their review of inequalities in access to healthcare across Europe, Baeten *et al.* (2018) identified the following challenges for policymakers:

- Inadequate funding and resources invested in the health system.
- Fragmented population coverage and inadequate availability of services, particularly affecting rural areas and disadvantaged groups.
- Gaps in the range of benefits covered by insurance schemes.
- Prohibitive charges, particularly for pharmaceutical products, with vulnerable groups often unprotected from such charges.
- Use of waiting lists to manage demand, with lack of transparency on how priorities are set.
- Problems with attracting and retaining health professionals.

Inequalities in access to healthcare affect many marginalised groups and communities, including sections of the population that are likely to have higher health needs. For example, Sakellariou and Rotarou (2017) found that people with a severe disability had higher odds of facing unmet needs and disabled people generally reported worse access to healthcare, with transportation, cost and long waiting lists being the main barriers. Racial disparities have been found in access to healthcare services, especially when insurance coverage is not universal (Brown *et al.*, 2000), while people from ethnically minoritised groups are less likely to access mental health services, putting them at greater risk of illness such as depression (Cooper *et al.*, 2013; Cook *et al.*, 2019). There is also evidence of health disparities among LGBTQ+ groups (Zeeman *et al.*, 2018), although there is a need for better data and more research in this area.

Welfare Inequalities and Social Care

'Inverse care' patterns – where levels of provision vary systematically and in the opposite direction to the social gradient of demand – have been observed in other sectors, including housing (Blane, Mitchell and Bartley, 2000), adult social care (Chinn, Levitan and Murrells, 2017), and children's social care (see Case Study 3.1). Such inequalities bear closer scrutiny. This is partly because of the close connection to social work, which is the main professional group responsible for coordinating and delivering social care. It is also because social care services can differ in important ways from health services, particularly in the way that 'need' is perceived and determined. For example, some forms of social care provision are arguably more like regulatory interventions than services directly requested by the recipient (see Chapter 6, and Hood, 2019). Examples include compulsory admissions to a psychiatric ward, adult safeguarding procedures, and out-of-home care for children experiencing abuse and neglect. Social workers play a crucial role in these processes, which may involve intervening without people's consent or against their wishes. Such decisions involve balancing people's rights and responsibilities, autonomy and best interests, while also providing them with the right support and assistance. Having to reconcile the resulting dilemmas – between care and control, prevention and policing, support and intervention – has long been recognised as a core part of social work (Howe, 2014; Hood, 2018). However, similar imperatives are arguably present in many services that seek to 'help' people at the same time as subjecting them to surveillance and control. The obvious example is the administration of benefits claims by unemployed or disabled adults, in which financial support is underpinned by a strict compliance regime. Another example is educational provision for children assessed with emotional and behavioural difficulties, as discussed below.

Applying a health inequalities lens to social care can lead to ambiguities in interpretation. For example, researchers in several countries have found a social gradient in demand for child welfare services (Sedlak *et al.*, 2010; Cancian *et al.*, 2013; Lefebvre *et al.*, 2017). In the UK, deprivation is recognised to be a key driver of referrals to children's social care as well as protective interventions and admissions to state care (Hood *et al.*, 2019). In many respects, this is another consequence of the social inequalities highlighted in the UK by Marmot *et al.* (2010) and internationally by Wilkinson and Pickett (2010). Children's health and wellbeing are adversely affected by the material and developmental consequences of living in poverty, while the greater prevalence of social problems among poorer parts of the population also exposes them to risks such as domestic violence, substance misuse and mental illness. Children from disadvantaged backgrounds are more likely to report experiences of abuse and neglect (Radford *et al.*, 2011) and to be subject to interventions from child protection agencies (Bywaters, 2020).

However, welfare inequalities are not 'only' about the problems that are caused by poverty and deprivation. They also reflect the policies, attitudes and assumptions that prevail in society as a whole, are embedded in the institutions set up to identify and respond to social problems, and are acted on by managers, professionals and other frontline workers in their interactions with families. The existence of an 'inverse intervention law' in child protection interventions in countries such as England (see Case Study 3.1) illustrates the way supply-side factors shape the response to need and risk. This is particularly important when it comes to neglect, for which there seems to be a steeper social gradient than for other categories of maltreatment (Goldacre and Hood, 2022). As well as children's services, welfare inequalities have been identified in many other sectors and are not limited to socio-economic differences. For example, studies in England have highlighted the difficulties experienced by older people and disabled people in obtaining adequate care and support, exacerbated by over a decade of austerity policies and cuts to services (Kings Fund, 2020; Glasby *et al.*, 2021). Hood *et al.* (2022) found evidence of inverse care effects in adult social care relating to both age and disability, which they attribute partly to rationing mechanisms designed to control expenditure on long-term residential care. As always, such inequalities intersect in ways that create specific problems for specific groups; for example, ageing with a learning disability carries particular risks in an era of declining statutory care (Power and Bartlett, 2019).

Case Study 3.1: Child welfare inequalities and the 'inverse intervention law' (Bywaters, 2020)

The Child Welfare Inequalities Project (CWIP) conducted research from 2014–19 to examine inequalities in rates of statutory child welfare interventions in the four UK countries. It sought to identify the scale of inequalities and understand how they were produced by the interaction between different factors in family lives and service responses. A steep social gradient was found in children's chances of a coercive intervention. For example, children in the most deprived 10% of small neighbourhoods in the UK were over 10 times more likely to be in foster or residential care or on protection plans than children in the least deprived 10%. In England, the study also found evidence that local authorities in more affluent areas tended to intervene more readily 'using high end, expensive, more coercive forms of intervention' (Bywaters, 2020: 6) such as child protection plans and admissions to care. This was a systematic pattern that had nothing to do with random variation in rates of provision, or differences in leadership styles, or models of social work practice. Instead, the pattern was to do with deprivation: when comparing families in similar socio-economic circumstances, the least deprived local authorities intervened more frequently in family life

Continued

than the most deprived authorities. The researchers called this statistical relationship the 'inverse intervention law' (IIL), with reference to the inverse care law observed by Tudor Hart (1971). The relationship was not found to obtain in Wales and could not be studied in Scotland or Northern Ireland due to insufficient data. A later study by Goldacre and Hood (2022), using a national dataset for England, indicated that the IIL was linked to the tendency for the social gradient of intervention to be steeper in more affluent local authorities. Rationing decisions are one plausible explanation, since more deprived local authorities have suffered disproportionate funding cuts from central government and so have fewer resources relative to need. Webb *et al.* (2020b) found that income inequality played an important role, since the steepest social gradients were found in local authorities that were both less deprived and more unequal. Ethnicity is also a key factor in unequal rates of intervention, although disentangling ethnicity from socio-economic factors is often challenging due to limitations in the data (Webb *et al.*, 2020a).

In the field of mental health, while people from minority ethnic groups face barriers to accessing mental health services, they are comparatively more likely to experience compulsory admission to psychiatric hospital, although it is important to recognise the variation between different minority groups (Audini and Lelliott, 2002; Barnett *et al.*, 2019). Indeed, the tendency for ethnically minoritised groups to receive less in the way of care but more in the way of policing can be observed in many sectors, including drug and alcohol services, youth justice, and special educational needs and disabilities (SEND). For example, Strand and Lindsay (2009) found that school children from Black Caribbean and Mixed White and Black Caribbean backgrounds were more likely to be identified as having behavioural, emotional and social difficulties than White British pupils (after adjusting for gender and socio-economic status), and were more likely to be excluded from school, while Gillborn (2015) reports the difficulties that Black parents can have in overcoming racist stereotypes about their children in order to get appropriate SEND support.

Overall, the literature on welfare inequalities suggests a set of mutually reinforcing processes:

- Greater prevalence of poor health, social problems and associated risks to people's welfare in disadvantaged areas, communities and groups.
- The tendency for services providing assistance and support to be under-resourced in disadvantaged areas, communities and groups.
- The tendency for services involving surveillance, compliance and coercion to be disproportionately targeted at disadvantaged areas, communities and groups.

Conclusion

In the previous chapter, inequalities were discussed in relation to the inequitable distribution of resources and how this was linked to social divisions and categories of difference. In this chapter, attention was turned to the outcomes of inequality for people's health, wellbeing and welfare. A foundational concept is the social gradient of health, which leads to two essential insights: first, inequality is bad for everyone in society except for the few people right at the top of the scale; and second, the fundamental determinants of health are social, not individual. After a certain level of affluence, societies do not get healthier or happier by getting richer; instead, it is the quality and nature of relationships between people that are most vital to improving our collective wellbeing. However, the social gradient and income inequality are only part of the picture. Institutional racism and other forms of structural oppression create a double bind for public services, which may reinforce systematic inequalities in access to care and support while targeting disadvantaged groups with coercive and punitive interventions. We shall return to these issues in later chapters, which discuss the potential for social work to contribute to policies and institutions that will address rather than reproduce inequalities.

References

Audini, B. and Lelliott, P. (2002) 'Age, gender and ethnicity of those detained under Part II of the Mental Health Act 1983', *The British Journal of Psychiatry*, **180**(3), pp. 222–226.

Baeten, R., Spasova, S., Vanhercke, B. and Coster, S. (2018) 'Inequalities in access to healthcare: A study of national policies', Brussels, European Commission.

Barnett, P., Mackay, E., Matthews, H., Gate, R., Greenwood, H., Ariyo, K., Bhui, K., Halvorsrud, K., Pilling, S. and Smith, S. (2019) 'Ethnic variations in compulsory detention under the Mental Health Act: A systematic review and meta-analysis of international data', *The Lancet Psychiatry*, **6**(4), pp. 305–317.

Blane, D., Mitchell, R. and Bartley, M. (2000) 'The "inverse housing law" and respiratory health', *Journal of Epidemiology and Community Health*, **54**(10), pp. 745–749.

Brown, E.R., Ojeda, V.D., Wyn, R. and Levan, R. (2000) 'Racial and ethnic disparities in access to health insurance and health care', Los Angeles, UCLA: Center for Health Policy Research.

Brown, T.H., Richardson, L.J., Hargrove, T.W. and Thomas, C.S. (2016) 'Using multiple-hierarchy stratification and life course approaches to understand health inequalities: The intersecting consequences of race, gender, SES, and age', *Journal of Health and Social Behavior*, **57**(2), pp. 200–222.

Bywaters, P. (2020) *The Child Welfare Inequalities Project: Final Report*, Coventry, Child Welfare Inequalities Project and Nuffield Foundation.

Cancian, M., Yang, M.-Y. and Slack, K.S. (2013) 'The effect of additional child support income on the risk of child maltreatment', *Social Service Review*, **87**(3), pp. 417–437.

Chinn, D., Levitan, T. and Murrells, T. (2017) 'Equity in social care for people with intellectual disabilities? A cross-sectional study examining the distribution of social care funding across local authorities in England', *Health and Social Care in the Community*, **25**(3), pp. 901–911.

Coburn, D. (2004) 'Beyond the income inequality hypothesis: Class, neo-liberalism, and health inequalities', *Social Science & Medicine*, **58**(1), pp. 41–56.

Cook, B.L., Hou, S.S.-Y., Lee-Tauler, S.Y., Progovac, A.M., Samson, F. and Sanchez, M.J. (2019) 'A review of mental health and mental health care disparities research: 2011–2014', *Medical Care Research and Review*, **76**(6), pp. 683–710.

Cooper, C., Spiers, N., Livingston, G., Jenkins, R., Meltzer, H., Brugha, T., McManus, S., Weich, S. and Bebbington, P. (2013) 'Ethnic inequalities in the use of health services for common mental disorders in England', *Social Psychiatry and Psychiatric Epidemiology*, **48**(5), pp. 685–692.

Dingake, O.B.K. (2017) 'The rule of law as a social determinant of health', *Health Human Rights*, **19**(2), pp. 295–298.

Franks, P., Muennig, P., Lubetkin, E. and Jia, H. (2006) 'The burden of disease associated with being African-American in the United States and the contribution of socio-economic status', *Social Science & Medicine*, **62**(10), pp. 2469–2478.

Gillborn, D. (2015) 'Intersectionality, critical race theory, and the primacy of racism: Race, class, gender, and disability in education', *Qualitative Inquiry*, **21**(3), pp. 277–287.

Glasby, J., Zhang, Y., Bennett, M.R. and Hall, P. (2021) 'A lost decade? A renewed case for adult social care reform in England', *Journal of Social Policy*, **50**(2), pp. 406–437.

Goldacre, A. and Hood, R. (2022) 'Factors affecting the social gradient in children's social care', *The British Journal of Social Work*, Available online, https://doi.org/10.1093/bjsw/bcab255

Gray, A.M. (1982) 'Inequalities in health. The Black Report: A summary and comment', *International Journal of Health Services*, **12**(3), pp. 349–380.

Hardeman, R.R. and Karbeah, J.M. (2020) 'Examining racism in health services research: A disciplinary self-critique', *Health Services Research*, **55**(Suppl 2), pp. 777–780.

Hood, R. (2018) *Complexity in social work*, London, Sage.

Hood, R. (2019) 'What to measure in child protection?', *The British Journal of Social Work*, **49**(2), pp. 466–484.

Hood, R., Goldacre, A., Abbott, S. and Jones, R. (2022) 'Patterns of demand and provision in English adult social care services', *The British Journal of Social Work*, Available online, https://doi.org/10.1093/bjsw/bcac011

Hood, R., Goldacre, A., Gorin, S. and Bywaters, P. (2019) 'Screen, ration and churn: Demand management and the crisis in children's social care', *The British Journal of Social Work*, **50**(3), pp. 868–889.

Howe, D. (2014) *The compleat social worker*, Basingstoke, Palgrave Macmillan.

Hughes, C. (2013) 'Poverty and disability: Addressing the challenge of inequality', *Career Development and Transition for Exceptional Individuals*, **36**(1), pp. 37–42.

Kings Fund (2020) *Social Care 360*, London, Kings Fund.

Lefebvre, R., Fallon, B., Van Wert, M. and Filippelli, J. (2017) 'Examining the relationship between economic hardship and child maltreatment using data from the Ontario Incidence Study of Reported Child Abuse and Neglect-2013 (OIS-2013)', *Behavioral Sciences*, **7**(1), p. 6.

Lund, E.M., Forber-Pratt, A.J., Wilson, C. and Mona, L.R. (2020) 'The COVID-19 pandemic, stress, and trauma in the disability community: A call to action', *Rehabilitation Psychology*, **65**(4), p. 313.

Marmot, M.G., Allen, J., Goldblatt, P., Boyce, T., McNeish, D., Grady, M. and Geddes, I. (2010) *Fair society, healthy lives: Strategic review of health inequalities in England post-2010*, Available online: www.instituteofhealthequity.org/projects/fair-society-healthy-lives-the-marmot-review, Last Accessed 19/04/23.

Marmot, M., Allen, J., Boyce, T., Goldblatt, P. and Morrison, J. (2020a) *Health equity in England: The Marmot Review 10 years on*, London, Institute of Health Equity.

Marmot, M., Allen, J., Goldblatt, P., Herd, E. and Morrison, J. (2020b) Build back fairer: The COVID-19 Marmot Review. The pandemic, socioeconomic and health inequalities in England, London, Institute of Health Equity.

McGowan, V.J., Lowther, H.J. and Meads, C. (2021) 'Life under COVID-19 for LGBT+ people in the UK: Systematic review of UK research on the impact of COVID-19 on sexual and gender minority populations', *BMJ open*, **11**(7), p. e050092.

Mishra, V., Seyedzenouzi, G., Almohtadi, A., Chowdhury, T., Khashkhusha, A., Axiaq, A., Wong, W.Y.E. and Harky, A. (2021) 'Health inequalities during COVID-19 and their effects on morbidity and mortality', *Journal of Healthcare Leadership*, **13**, p. 19.

Phelan, J.C. and Link, B.G. (2015) 'Is racism a fundamental cause of inequalities in health?', *Annual Review of Sociology*, **41**, pp. 311–330.

Pickett, K.E. and Wilkinson, R.G. (2015) 'Income inequality and health: A causal review', *Social Science & Medicine*, **128**, pp. 316–326.

Power, A. and Bartlett, R. (2019) 'Ageing with a learning disability: Care and support in the context of austerity', *Social Science & Medicine*, **231**, pp. 55–61.

Public Health England (2021) *Public Health Profile for England 2021*, Available online: www.gov.uk/government/publications/health-profile-for-england-2021, Last Accessed: 02/02/22.

Radford, L., Corral, S., Bradley, C., Fisher, H., Bassett, C., Howat, N. and Collishaw, S. (2011) 'Child abuse and neglect in the UK today', London, National Society for the Prevention of Cruelty to Children (NSPCC).

Read, J.N.G. and Gorman, B.K. (2010) 'Gender and health inequality', *Annual Review of Sociology*, **36**, pp. 371–386.

Rummery, K. (2019) 'Disability and austerity: The perfect storm of attacks on social rights', in Heins, E., Rees, J. and Needham, C. (eds), *Social Policy Review 31: Analysis and Debate in Social Policy, 2019*, pp. 29.

Sakellariou, D. and Rotarou, E.S. (2017) 'Access to healthcare for men and women with disabilities in the UK: Secondary analysis of cross-sectional data', *BMJ open*, **7**(8), p. e016614.

Scambler, G. (2012) 'Health inequalities', *Sociology of Health & Illness*, **34**(1), pp. 130–146.

Sedlak, A.J., Mettenburg, J., Basena, M., Peta, I., McPherson, K. and Greene, A. (2010) 'Fourth national incidence study of child abuse and neglect (NIS-4)', *Washington, DC: US Department of Health and Human Services*, **9**, p. 2010.

Shakespeare, T., Watson, N., Brunner, R., Cullingworth, J., Hameed, S., Scherer, N., Pearson, C. and Reichenberger, V. (2022) 'Disabled people in Britain and the impact of the COVID-19 pandemic', *Social Policy & Administration*, **56**(1), pp. 103–117.

Strand, S. and Lindsay, G. (2009) 'Evidence of ethnic disproportionality in special education in an English population', *The Journal of Special Education*, **43**(3), pp. 174–190.

Toleikyte, L. and Salway, S. (2018) 'Local action on health inequalities: Understanding and reducing ethnic inequalities in health', London, Public Health England.

Tudor Hart, J. (1971) 'The inverse care law', The Lancet, 297(7696), pp. 405-412.

Webb, C., Bywaters, P., Scourfield, J., Davidson, G. and Bunting, L. (2020a) 'Cuts both ways: Ethnicity, poverty, and the social gradient in child welfare interventions', *Children and Youth Services Review*, **117**, p. 105299.

Webb, C., Bywaters, P., Scourfield, J., McCartan, C., Bunting, L., Davidson, G. and Morris, K. (2020b) 'Untangling child welfare inequalities and the "Inverse Intervention Law" in England', *Children and Youth Services Review*, **111**, p. 104849.

World Health Organisation (WHO) (2008) 'Closing the gap in a generation: Health equity through action on the social determinants of health', Geneva, WHO Commission on Social Determinants of Health.

Wilkinson, R. and Pickett, K. (2010) The spirit level: why equality is better for everyone.

Wilkinson, R.G. and Pickett, K.E. (2006) 'Income inequality and population health: A review and explanation of the evidence', *Social Science & Medicine*, **62**(7), pp. 1768–1784.

Williams, E., Buck, D. and Babalola, G. (2020) 'What are health inequalities?', London, The Kings Fund.

Zeeman, L., Sherriff, N., Browne, K., McGlynn, N., Mirandola, M., Gios, L., Davis, R., Sanchez-Lambert, J., Aujean, S., Pinto, N., Farinella, F., Donisi, V., Niedźwiedzka-Stadnik, M., Rosińska, M., Pierson, A., Amaddeo, F. and Network, H.L. (2018) 'A review of lesbian, gay, bisexual, trans and intersex (LGBTI) health and healthcare inequalities', *European Journal of Public Health*, **29**(5), pp. 974–980.

4

Social Policy and Inequality

Chapter overview

....

This chapter focuses on the actions taken by governments to address social problems and improve the health and wellbeing of citizens. It begins with the concept of
social welfare and the establishment of the welfare state in the decades following the
Second World War. Different types of welfare system are compared with reference
to political value positions such as liberalism and conservatism. Common critiques of
the welfare state are discussed alongside the increasing influence of neo-liberal policies in the 1980s and 1990s. The chapter proceeds to examine the unequal impact
of austerity measures following the financial crisis of 2007/08, and to consider the
effect of anti-discrimination and equalities legislation. It concludes with a discussion
of populism and divisive approaches to inequality, which have become a key feature
of the contemporary policy landscape.

Introduction

Inequality is a social and economic problem, which can be exacerbated or
mitigated by government policies as well as non-state actors including global institutions and corporations (see Chapter 5). There are many ways to define social policy
but here it is broadly taken to mean actions taken by the state to address these problems and influence the welfare of citizens. The areas targeted by social policy include
health services, education, social care, housing and homelessness, cash benefits and
pensions. Policies may be explicitly written down, as in proposals, draft legislation,
laws, statutory guidance, and so on, but are also implicit in decisions about investment, spending and taxation. The direction and impact of social policy depend on a
great many factors. Governments' ideological stance and political values are important, of course, because they tend to frame problems and solutions in a certain way.
This is particularly relevant to inequality, which not only can be defined and measured
in various ways but may be viewed as a necessary cost of other political objectives

such as economic growth. However, external events can lead to policies that deviate from the ideological position associated with a particular administration or regime. For example, a government elected on a manifesto to reduce taxes might end up having to raise money to pay for its response to a pandemic or the outbreak of war. Even when policies are aligned with intended reforms, their implementation has to address the complexity of change in social systems. Common problems include institutional inertia and resistance, the tension between central and local government agendas, variable enforcement and interpretation by 'street-level bureaucrats' (Lipsky, 1980), as well as unintended consequences that may counteract what the policy was designed to do (Hood, 2018). Such challenges are especially pertinent for welfare systems, which are not only highly complex but rely on large professional bureaucracies to deliver services to people, making change an unwieldy and unpredictable affair.

Welfare Systems

Baldock *et al.* (2011) observe that people tend to obtain social welfare from three main sources: their families, state-provided services, third sector and private provision. The 'mixed economy' of welfare will take different forms depending on a country's history, stage of development, and political values. For example, while families play the key role in looking after elderly relatives across the world, those in richer countries have more opportunity to draw on support and assistance from health and social care professionals. Whether such services should be provided by the state or through the market, and the extent to which they are universally available or 'means-tested' (i.e. only provided to those on low incomes) are some of the policy questions that shape the emergence of welfare systems in different countries and historical periods. These questions also have implications for inequality, as we shall see.

The Welfare State

Le Grand and Robinson (2018) identify three main features of the welfare state:

1 *Social security* – a system of income transfers from taxpayers to benefit recipients. This includes social insurance, to which individuals contribute while in employment so as to be entitled to cash payments when unemployed or sick, and to a pension when they reach retirement age.
2 *Benefits in kind* – taxpayer-funded services that are provided free at the point of access, such as universal healthcare and education, or in some cases means-tested for individual contributions, such as personal social services.
3 *Price subsidies* – designed to ensure the affordability of goods and services seen as socially essential, e.g. reduced fares for public transport or controlled rents for social housing.

In the UK, models of private social insurance started to give way to a more government-led approach to welfare provision at the beginning of the 20th century. The pioneering social studies of John Booth and Joseph Rowntree had raised awareness of the inadequate incomes and atrocious living conditions of the urban poor, while policymakers were also concerned about the poor physical health of enlisted soldiers (Cutler and Johnson, 2004). Extension of the right to vote to women and working-class men, combined with the electoral success of the newly formed Labour Party, provided a political incentive to widen access to unemployment and sickness benefits as well as old-age pensions. A rudimentary welfare state was therefore beginning to take shape before the Second World War but was hugely expanded in the post-war period, inspired by the 1942 Beveridge Report. Legislation passed by the Labour government of 1945–51 was intended to create a comprehensive, 'cradle to grave' welfare system. While the original model of provision has undergone numerous changes in subsequent decades, some of its basic principles, such as universal access to healthcare and education, are still evident in the UK today.

In other countries, welfare states evolved in different ways according to their respective historical, cultural and political contexts. Esping-Andersen (1990) analysed eighteen welfare regimes in the industrialised world, based on three defining characteristics:

- *Decommodification* – the extent to which people have to rely on the market to safeguard their welfare, particularly in relation to pensions or unemployment and sickness.
- *Social stratification* – the effect of the welfare state on the structure of social relations, particularly as regards class divisions, status differences and other forms of stratification.
- *Private-public mix* – the characteristic combination of family care with statutory, voluntary and private sector organisations, which together serve to provide welfare to citizens.

Esping-Andersen's analysis of these features led him to propose that there were three main types of welfare capitalism: Liberal, Conservative and Social Democratic. As outlined in Table 4.1, these labels reflect distinct ideological positions, or sets of political values, which include assumptions about inequality and what to do about it. For example, the generous, state-funded system of universal welfare typically associated with a Social Democratic country, such as Sweden, is aligned with a broader policy goal of reducing social divisions and promoting equality. In contrast, the more limited regime of means-tested benefits typically associated with a Liberal country, such as the United States, is aligned with the goal of incentivising individuals to make their own choices while minimising the role of the state. In recent decades, much of the debate about welfare and social policy has focused on the perceived influence of 'neo-liberal' attitudes to the state and public services, as will be discussed below.

Table 4.1 Basic ideological positions and their implications for welfare and inequality

Ideological position	Key priorities	Implications for welfare state	Assumptions about inequality
Conservatism	Maintain social order and stability Preserve class distinctions and traditional family values Minimal role for the state	Encourage traditional models of family-based care and assistance Welfare benefits should not undermine traditional caring roles, e.g. motherhood Residual state assistance provided when family's capacity is exhausted	Inequalities are inevitable and may reflect traditional values Promoting equality can be counter-productive, e.g. risk of social disorder
Liberal	Promote individual freedom of choice Emphasis on personal responsibility Encourage the role of markets and private provision	State benefits should be means-tested and targeted at low income and high need groups Incentives to work necessary to avoid welfare dependency Govts should encourage and if necessary subsidise private social insurance, to ensure choice within a market	Govts are not responsible for inequalities that result from people's life choices State intervention may be necessary to promote equality of opportunity
Social democratic	State should actively promote human rights and social justice Regulation of markets and private enterprise to avoid social divisions in access and opportunity Emphasis on state-funded welfare provision as a right of citizenship	Commitment to high level of provision and expenditure State has key role in providing welfare services and regulating private providers to ensure high standards Universal access to welfare services preferable to means-tested provision, e.g. to maintain solidarity and consensus	Greater social equality is a legitimate policy goal Some equalisation of outcomes is desirable even if complete equality is unrealistic Social justice should be pursued through normal democratic processes

Esping-Anderson's typology has been subject to numerous revisions and critiques since it was published (Bambra, 2007). For example, some researchers have found evidence for a 'Southern' model of the welfare state in the Mediterranean countries of Europe, such as Spain, Portugal, Greece and Italy (Ferrera, 1996), or for a 'Confucian' welfare state in East Asian countries, such as South Korea, Taiwan, Singapore and Japan (Aspalter, 2006). These typologies show that cultural values, including the mutual ties of social obligation in communities and the fundamental importance of families in providing a social safety net, underpin distinctive approaches to welfare provision in different parts of the world. There have also been efforts to incorporate gender inequalities into the analysis of welfare states, such as the extent to which they promote women's participation in the labour force (Korpi, 2000).

Debates about welfare connect with other policy approaches to poverty and inequality. For example, one argument in favour of the Social Democratic model (see Table 4.1) is that universal entitlements to benefits and public services maintain the political consensus needed for higher levels of taxation and public expenditure. However, this assumption can be criticised on the basis that universal provision does not do enough to redistribute wealth or resources and may even compound existing inequalities (as with the 'inverse care law' discussed in Chapter 3). From a liberal perspective, universal entitlement may be perceived as inefficient and as undermining individual responsibility. This critique points towards a targeted approach to welfare and a greater role for the private sector, which is more typical of liberal welfare systems. Korpi and Palme (1998) countered this argument by showing evidence for a trade-off between redistribution and targeting; their conclusion was that the more governments sought to target benefits at the poor, the less likely they were to reduce poverty and inequality (see Garcia-Fuente, 2021, for an updated analysis).

Neo-liberalism and the Critique of Welfare

Neo-liberalism is a broad term that invokes a set of assumptions about the role of the state and what kind of policies governments should pursue. It is widely regarded as the dominant paradigm for global governance, reflecting the central role of the United States in international institutions (see Chapter 5), and has also shaped economic and social policies in countries across the world (Campbell and Pedersen, 2001; Mudge, 2008). Neo-liberalism typically involves some combination of:

- *Institutional arrangements*, such as a residual welfare state, low taxation, minimal business regulation, flexible labour markets, weak unions, and removal of barriers to international capital; and
- *Normative principles*, the main one being that individualised, market-based competition is the best mode of social organisation, and always superior to government central planning.

Neo-liberalism originally emerged in opposition to social and economic policies implemented by many Western countries, including the UK, in the aftermath of the Second World War. During this period, the broad consensus was that governments should be prepared to intervene in the economy to achieve policy goals. Interventions might take the form of a state-funded welfare system, government spending on infrastructure projects to bolster demand and employment, and public ownership of utilities and other strategic assets. To neo-liberal thinkers such as Hayek (2001[1944]) such policies were misguided; societies dominated by state institutions would undermine people's freedoms, cause economic stagnation, lead to social unrest and encourage governments to become authoritarian. During the oil crisis and economic downturn of the 1970s, such notions gained currency as the post-war consensus on welfare capitalism broke down. The Reagan and Thatcher administrations of the 1980s exemplified the neo-liberal turn. They combined an individualist ethos with monetarist economic policies and an emphasis on traditional models of welfare:

> There's no such thing as society, only individuals and families. There are
> individual men and women and there are families. And no government
> can do anything except through people, and people must look after
> themselves first. It is our duty to look after ourselves and then, also, to
> look after our neighbours. (Thatcher, 1987)

Thatcher's quote, usually truncated to its famous opening phrase, shows how hostility towards the welfare state is embedded in neo-liberal thinking. Indeed, Hayek himself unsuccessfully sought to dissuade William Beveridge from making the recommendations in his 1942 report (Mudge, 2008). In essence, neo-liberals assert that welfare systems are expensive and create dependency, and that entitlements to benefits and support erode incentives to work while subordinating people to oppressive and inefficient government bureaucracies. When institutions are run by the state, people tend to be stuck with the service they are offered and so end up ceding power to professionals and bureaucratic decision-makers. Individual freedom of choice can therefore only be guaranteed within a competitive market[1]. Of course, as noted in Chapter 1, the neo-liberal claim that markets promote individual freedom can be contested on various grounds – not least because the operation of supposedly 'free' markets is enforced through an array of laws and regulations that happen to serve the interests of powerful elites.

A key driver of neo-liberal reforms to welfare systems has been the idea of choice – the citizen as consumer. This includes some policies that started off as progressive reforms to state-run institutions. An example in the UK is the policy of 'personalisation' in adult social care, which has been part of a broader shift to de-institutionalise the care and support provided to vulnerable adults in the community (Duffy *et al.*, 2010). However, the corollary of competition and choice is the drive to marketise

---

1   Neo-liberals also believe that no-one should be forced to pay for health or social insurance – hence the ongoing arguments in the United States about the 2010 Affordable Healthcare Act ('Obamacare').

and privatise parts of the public sector that have traditionally been considered off-limits to private providers. This includes areas where social workers operate, such as residential care and child protection (Jones, 2018). Even if full marketisation has not been possible, governments have tried to create quasi-markets through purchaser-provider splits and requirements for competitive tendering, commissioning and procurement (Le Grand and Bartlett, 1993), while also adopting management techniques from the private sector to improve performance and accountability. Indeed, from the 1980s onwards managerialism has become almost synonymous with modernisation of the welfare state (Clarke *et al.*, 2000). The consequences of such developments for social work are further discussed in Chapter 6.

Alternative Approaches to Welfare

While critique of the welfare state tends to be associated with conservative and right-wing politics, proposals for modernisation and reform have also come from progressive and left-wing circles. In contrast to the neo-liberal insistence on individuals choosing freely within a competitive market, such approaches tend to highlight the need for welfare systems to tackle contemporary social problems, adapt to technological change, and build connections between people and communities. From this perspective, the welfare state in its original form was a response to social problems and conditions in the mid-20th century, mainly in North America and Western Europe. For example, the 1942 Beveridge report set out a vision for reconstructing post-war British society, which even before the war had been blighted by global recession and mass unemployment during the 1930s. The world has changed enormously since then, putting pressure on institutions that often bear close resemblance to those established eighty years ago. For example, Cottam (2018) argues that a contemporary Beveridge report – one that was equally forward-thinking and revolutionary in its proposals – would focus on very different issues, such as the breakdown in social and ecological systems and the transformational effects of globalisation and digital technology. Tackling such problems requires a focus on capability, relationships and community, with 'horizontal and networked' institutions replacing the hierarchical, bureaucratic agencies through which help is currently 'delivered' to people.

The 'Social Investment State'

Influenced by the neo-liberal critique of welfare, many countries with a developed welfare state shifted during the 1990s to a 'social investment' policy strategy (Van Kersbergen and Hemerijck, 2012). The aim was to combine a neo-liberal focus on competitiveness and growth with social democratic concerns such as equality and inclusion. This policy agenda was pursued particularly by governments on the centre-left, in an effort to reframe welfare as a way of equipping citizens with the skills to compete for work in the era of globalisation (see Chapter 5). In the UK, the New Labour government that came to power in 1997 argued that social investment was needed to strengthen the structural competitiveness of the national economy. Rights and entitlements were explicitly connected to responsibilities, including the requirement for unemployed people to look actively for work. A commitment to 'make work pay' underpinned spending on education, training and subsidised employment, as well as tax credits for working families. Eligibility for disability benefits was progressively tightened through work capability assessments and medical testing (Beatty and Fothergill, 2015). Such policies continued the trend for the UK's welfare system to become more conditional and targeted. At the same time, receiving benefits became more stigmatised and people living in poverty increasingly exposed to divisive language from politicians and hostile stereotyping in the media (Dorling, 2015). These problems intensified after the global financial crisis of 2007–08, which set in motion a wave of austerity policies designed to reduce public spending.

Austerity and Inequality

The spread of neo-liberal policies during the 1980s is often cited as a contributory factor in the growth in income inequality observed in much of the industrialised world during that decade (Coburn, 2004; Cummins, 2018). Likewise, it could be argued that social investment strategies from the early 1990s, made possible by a sustained period of economic growth after the end of the Cold War, helped to stem the rise in income inequality, at least for people living in the affluent and victorious 'West' (Morel and Palier, 2011). However, social investment policies were largely predicated on neo-liberal doctrines, such as the primacy of competition and growth, as well as tacit acceptance of the wealth being amassed by people at the top of the income scale[2]. When a global banking crisis caused economic havoc in 2007–08, the stage was set for a huge retrenchment in spending on welfare. The cost of bailing out the banks, whose reckless lending and self-enrichment had nearly collapsed the world's financial system, was to be borne by the least affluent members of society.

The Meaning of Austerity

Austerity is often understood as a period of fiscal 'belt-tightening', inviting comparisons with households who have to restrict their spending during times of financial hardship. In policy terms, this is rather misleading, since the complex

---

2   Or even explicit acceptance. A former New Labour minister, Peter Mandelson, observed in a 1998 interview that his party was 'intensely relaxed about people getting filthy rich, as long as they pay their taxes'.

social and economic systems that make it possible for tens (or hundreds) of millions of people to live together bear little resemblance to what goes on in a household. Technically, austerity refers to the measures taken by a government to reduce the amount of public debt, usually in the form of tax rises and/or cuts to public expenditure. Which policies are chosen depends on a range of factors, including the ideological position of the government (see Table 4.1), the circumstances in which economic difficulties have arisen, and the political feasibility of the available options. From a UK perspective, it is worth noting that the Labour government of 1945–51 established the modern welfare state while simultaneously pursuing austerity policies in order to pay off huge overseas debts incurred during the Second World War. Specific policies included rationing, price controls, cuts in defence spending, and the continuation of high wartime levels of taxation. In contrast, the austerity policies implemented by the Coalition (Conservative/ Liberal Democrat) government of 2010–15 consisted largely of cuts to public expenditure, mainly levelled at social security and the funding of local government services. Similar policies were pursued in other countries across the world (Miller and Hokenstad, 2014; Ballas *et al.*, 2017; Garrett and Bertotti, 2017).

The meaning (and lived experience) of austerity depends on its objectives and the methods used to achieve them. For example, British wartime austerity was designed to ensure equitable distribution of food and staples and reinforce public support for the war effort; measures such as rationing and price controls generally led to more equal patterns of consumption than in the 1930s, and often improved the nutrition and diet available to the poorest families. Similarly, the decision to continue austerity measures after the Second World War was offset by the comprehensive welfare policies implemented by the Atlee government. This is not to suggest that wartime austerity was a panacea for equality; women were at a particular disadvantage, for example, being much more likely to sacrifice their allocation for the sake of children or husbands (Zweiniger-Bargielowska, 2000). Gender inequalities are also a marked feature of contemporary austerity, as discussed below. Nonetheless, the intention of austerity in the decade following the 2007–08 financial crisis differed in crucial ways from the social and economic policies of the 1940s and 1950s. Mainstream acceptance of neo-liberal ideas meant that 21st-century austerity did not aim to ensure equitable distribution of scarce resources during a time of national hardship[3] but rather to shore up the prevailing economic and financial order by reducing the obligations of the state to its citizens. Such priorities entailed a further shift towards a residual approach to welfare, including the removal of universal entitlements, stronger incentives for people to stay in (or move into) paid work, and steep cuts to taxpayer-funded services (Grimshaw and Rubery, 2012; Lambie-Mumford and Green, 2017).

---

3   Although the political rhetoric of austerity continues to draw on the idea of national sacrifice, former Chancellor of the Exchequer George Osborne introduced the first wave of austerity measures in 2009 with the slogan: 'We are all in this together'.

The Unequal Impact of Austerity

Due to the political choices discussed above, the burden of austerity policies has fallen disproportionately on groups that were already disadvantaged by existing social inequalities. As Rubery and Rafferty (2013) point out, women in the UK have long faced pay inequalities and poor employment conditions in the private sector, including poorly remunerated part-time work, limited access to occupational pensions, and inflexible working hours. Such disadvantages are even more pronounced for women from ethnically minoritised groups (Emejulu and Bassel, 2015). Women are more likely than men to work in the public sector, where pay and conditions tend to be more equitable and allow greater scope for family-friendly working arrangements (Colling and Dickens, 2001). It also means that women are more likely to claim benefits, particularly those related to low income, housing, and children. As a result, cuts to benefits and public sector investment have disproportionately affected women, who have not only borne the brunt of austerity in financial terms but have also been expected to maintain, and indeed increase, their unpaid work in informal caring roles (Rubery and Rafferty, 2013; Pearson, 2019). Women from racially minoritised groups have been further undermined by institutional racism and misrepresentation, e.g. being seen as either undeserving victims or as 'enterprising actors' within the entrepreneurial rationality of neo-liberalism (Emejulu and Bassel, 2015; Harries *et al.*, 2020).

Austerity cuts have led to a significant deterioration in the health and wellbeing of vulnerable and minoritised groups. Services for children and families have been a noticeable casualty, as subsidised childcare facilities along with flagship programmes such as Sure Start, launched during the heyday of social investment, have been scrapped or scaled back in favour of more targeted regimes of surveillance and intervention (Lambert and Crossley, 2017). Expenditure on adult social care services suffered huge cuts between 2010 and 2015, with significant consequences for elderly people and adults with disabilities. Between 2010 and 2014, the number of older people receiving council-funded social care decreased by over a quarter (Hood *et al.*, 2022). As pressure increased on the largely privatised residential care sector, hundreds of care home operators went bankrupt, causing harm and suffering to thousands of vulnerable residents and their families (Jones, 2018). Stewart (2019) points to evidence that increasingly punitive assessment of disability claimants has led to a crisis of mental health and preventable harm, while failing to achieve any significant increase in numbers of disabled people in paid employment. A UK survey carried out in 2014 reported that two-thirds of people claiming the main form of disability benefit[4] had suicidal thoughts and 'approaching half (43.2%) had made a suicide attempt at some point' (McManus, 2016: 296). Under what Dodd (2016) refers to as 'disablist austerity', cuts to social

---

4   People in the UK can apply for Employment and Support Allowance (ESA) if they have a disability or health condition that affects how much they can work.

care and social welfare have been accompanied by cultural demonisation and stigmatisation, making it harder for disabled people to assert their rights.

As always, there are intersections with other forms of discrimination and disadvantage. Austerity cuts have fallen disproportionately on deprived regions and cities (Centre for Cities, 2019) and people living in the poorest neighbourhoods have been the hardest hit (Mattheys *et al.*, 2018). Targeting cuts at areas with the highest levels of need has meant less money for preventative support for families, which has been associated in turn with a rise in statutory child welfare interventions (Hood *et al.*, 2019; Bennett *et al.*, 2021; Webb, 2021). Austerity has provided additional impetus to racialised discourses around immigration, national security, and integration, causing further detriment to minority groups whose access to welfare and public services have long been under attack from government policies and a hostile media (Collett, 2011; Hammerstad and Boas, 2015; Lowe *et al.*, 2017). Moreover, as Harries *et al.* (2020) point out, anti-racist and community organising has been undermined by the neo-liberal rationality of austerity, with its emphasis on competitiveness, enterprise and self-reliance as the model of citizenship. As organisations struggle to adjust to the constant pressures and insecurities produced by austerity, problems stemming from longstanding inequalities with their roots in the history of empire, slavery and colonialism (see Chapter 5) are effectively erased and reframed:

> Organizations have been pushed toward marketization and encouraged to become 'active citizens' without state support or recognition of the real value of anti-racist work. Market-based logics have thus provided the 'rhetorical cover' for major cuts in public spending but have also been employed as a convenient excuse to undermine anti-racist organizing and silence the voice that organizations give to the effects of stark inequalities and enduring racism. (Harries *et al.*, 2020: 35)

The Politics of Equality

The complexity of welfare systems reflects the need for social policies to balance different perspectives on equality, difference and identity. Baldock *et al.* (2011) suggest that modern welfare states are an unstable amalgam of such perspectives. The first is the traditional social welfare approach, which sees the role of the state as being to recognise and respond directly to what Titmuss (2004) called 'states of dependency', i.e. people's need for assistance, resources and support at different stages in their lives. Such services should be available to the whole population, so as to accommodate the differences between people and protect them from the inequalities of the market. The second is the (neo)liberal approach, which sees the state's role as ensuring basic legal protections and equality of opportunity within a meritocratic society, alongside marketised forms of welfare to promote individual choice and encourage economic dynamism. Finally, there is the politics of identity and recognition, which sees the role of the state as being to acknowledge new social movements whose political demands are based on the assertion of difference. Examples include the women's movement, anti-racist movement and disability rights movement, which point to the oppressive power dynamics often obscured by appeals to universal social rights. A politics of recognition seeks to go beyond issues of redistribution and equal opportunity to encompass the relationship between diversity and power, and highlight the importance of reciprocity and care for individual flourishing (Lovell, 2007).

Anti-discrimination Policies

Many countries have introduced anti-discrimination laws in order to promote equality and social justice (MIPEX, 2020). Such policies vary in their scope and application. For example, the UK's Equality Act 2010 makes it illegal to discriminate against someone because of a protected characteristic. Discrimination may be direct, as in treating a person less favourably than another, or indirect, as in imposing conditions that adversely affect members of a particular social group. There are currently nine protected characteristics:

- age
- disability
- gender reassignment
- marriage and civil partnership
- pregnancy and maternity
- race
- religion or belief
- sex
- sexual orientation.

Member states of the European Union have similar legislation, as do many other affluent democracies such as the United States, Canada and Australia. Elsewhere in the world, it is fairly common to find policies that outlaw discrimination on the basis of race and sex, particularly at work (Heymann *et al.*, 2021). Of course, the effectiveness of non-discrimination laws also depend on the degree to which they are enforced, highlighting the role of regulatory bodies and the political and legal authority vested in them. In the UK, for example, the Equality and Human Rights Commission (EHRC) is an independent statutory body that can use its enforcement powers to protect people against serious and systemic abuses of their rights as well as to clarify equality and human rights law (Spencer, 2008). Such frameworks provide a legal basis for redress, campaigning and activism, helping to improve pay and conditions for individuals, change attitudes and practices among employers and public institutions, and raise public awareness of equality issues.

While recognising the benefits of anti-discrimination laws, it is worth pointing out their limitations when it comes to broader issues of social justice. For example, feminist scholars have argued that sex discrimination laws are ill-equipped to challenge patriarchal power structures, many of which are based in private family life (Lacey, 1998). Structural disadvantages, such as the expectation that women perform the bulk of unpaid caring work while participating in a segregated labour market, tend to be reinforced during periods of political and economic instability and are difficult to challenge via anti-discrimination law. Similarly, policies that seek to address racial and ethnic inequalities co-exist with racialised policies aiming to restrict immigration (Capdevila and Callaghan, 2008), limit the rights of refugees and asylum seekers, and combat radicalisation (Thomas, 2016). Such contradictions make it hard for anti-discrimination policies to engage with the deep-rooted structures of racism in British society, including a long-overdue reckoning with the country's legacy of colonialism and slavery (see below). They also lend force to the argument that neo-liberal policies, including those with progressive agenda on equality, essentially promulgate a particular view of the individual: the White, able-bodied male negotiating his rights and interests within a capitalist marketplace. In rejecting this assumption, the political focus shifts to the rights and interests of different groups and their collective claim for recognition.

Populism and the Politics of Division

Brubaker (2017) defines populism as a repertoire of ideas and statements that have certain common elements, even though they may be deployed by people with very different goals and political affiliations. These common elements are:

- claiming to speak in the name of 'the people' against an 'elite' as well as against outside groups and forces;
- aggressive politicisation of topics that were not previously seen as political (e.g. statues, children's books);
- claiming to speak in the name of the majority against unfairly privileged minorities;
- valorising immediacy and directness against mediating institutions (e.g. mainstream media);
- economic, securitarian and cultural protectionism;
- a 'low-brow' style and deliberately flouting conventions of polite speech and behaviour.

Recent years have seen a resurgence of populism in many countries. Examples include the Brexit vote of 2016, the election of Donald Trump as US president in the same year, and the electoral gains made by European far right parties, such as the National Rally (previously National Front) in France, Vlaams Belang in Belgium, and Fidesz in Hungary. The growing potency and success of this strand of politics has a direct bearing on inequality. Most obviously, right-wing populism is characterised by xenophobia and racism, commonly articulated as hostility towards racially minoritised groups and particularly towards migrants and refugees. Moreover, populists exploit the impact of poverty and inequality *within* the majority group, seeking to win favour among people on low incomes by stoking resentment towards aspects of 'metropolitan elite' culture, or seeking to portray as 'elitist' any efforts to recognise and address the problems experienced by minority groups.For example, one of the features of populist discourse is the use of class and race to drive a wedge between the 'White working class' and people occupying a similar socio-economic position who do not identify as White. From a critical race perspective, it could be argued that the idea of a privileged racial identity (i.e. Whiteness), backed up by policies that undermine the welfare and dignity of people outside of that identity, actually serves as a (deeply unjust) stabilising force in societies marked by entrenched inequalities:

> Almost always, the injustices that dramatically diminish the rights of blacks are linked to the serious economic disadvantage suffered by many whites who lack money and power. Whites, rather than acknowledge the similarity of their disadvantage, particularly when compared with that of better-off whites, are easily detoured into protecting their sense of entitlement vis-à-vis blacks for all things of value. (Bell, 1992: 9)

Bell's view was that the rallying cry of racial superiority would always trump any other kind of shared political interests – in this case between Black and White communities in the United States – and so racism was likely to be a permanent feature of American society. Thirty years later, the force of his argument continues to resonate in light of the political response to the Black Lives Matter movement, which gained a global profile in the aftermath of the murder of George Floyd by a Minneapolis policeman in May 2020. In the UK, the movement forced a period of national reflection about structural racism, including the historic role of slavery and colonialism in the country's cultural institutions. This in turn provoked a backlash from right-wing media and politicians, who sought to frame themselves as the defenders of pride in British culture and history and in opposition to institutional 'wokeness' and censorious political correctness. Nonetheless, the government set up a Commission on Race and Ethnic Disparities, which reported in 2021. As Pilkington (2021) points out, the Commission's work was informed by scepticism among some of its members (including the Chair) about the role of institutional racism in causing racial disparities; the focus instead was on geographical and cultural factors, as well as the difficulties experienced by White working-class families. The report was controversial and widely criticised for its conceptual and methodological flaws. Such debates point to a cynical and divisive aspect of government social policy, which in recent years has sought to deploy so-called 'culture wars' to shore up political support in the face of widening disparities in power and money.

Conclusion

It is difficult to reconcile optimistic and pessimistic interpretations of social policy in relation to inequalities. On the one hand, the achievements of the post-war welfare state and the introduction of equalities legislation should not be overlooked or dismissed. They show that when governments are given an electoral mandate to mitigate the baleful effect of social divisions, they have introduced policies designed to improve people's lives in deprived and marginalised sections of society. On the other hand, the limitations of those policies are demonstrated by the persistence of poverty, deprivation and other forms of social inequality. Moreover, a combination of social change and neo-liberal economics are undermining welfare institutions built in the 20th century at a point when they need massive investment to address 21st-century problems. At the same time, a resurgence of right-wing populism means that identitarian tactics are being used to counter anti-racism, and other social movements with a progressive agenda such as trans and queer activism, with a view to preserving the status quo for established elites. It is a volatile political context that poses a number of challenges for social work, a profession that is embedded in the welfare state and whose code of practice is ostensibly rooted in a commitment to social justice. How social workers make sense of their statutory role in light of the direction and intention of social policy is one of the questions that will be examined in the second part of this book. Yet, as the Black Lives Matter movement goes to show, such questions are not confined to what goes on in individual countries but also reflect global concerns in an increasingly interconnected world. The next chapter will therefore look more closely at global inequalities and at the historical legacy of empire.

References

Aspalter, C. (2006) 'The east Asian welfare model', *International Journal of Social Welfare*, **15**(4), pp. 290–301.

Baldock, J., Vickerstaff, S. and Mitton, L. (eds) (2011) *Social policy*, Oxford, Oxford University Press.

Ballas, D., Dorling, D. and Hennig, B. (2017) 'Analysing the regional geography of poverty, austerity and inequality in Europe: A human cartographic perspective', *Regional Studies*, **51**(1), pp. 174–185.

Bambra, C. (2007) 'Going beyond the three worlds of welfare capitalism: Regime theory and public health research', *Journal of Epidemiology and Community Health*, **61**(12), pp. 1098–1102.

Beatty, C. and Fothergill, S. (2015) 'Disability benefits in an age of austerity', *Social Policy & Administration*, **49**(2), pp. 161–181.

Bell, D. (1992) *Faces at the bottom of the well: The permanence of racism*, New York, Basic Books.

Bennett, D.L., Webb, C.J.R., Mason, K.E., Schlüter, D.K., Fahy, K., Alexiou, A., Wickham, S., Barr, B. and Taylor-Robinson, D. (2021) 'Funding for preventative Children's Services and rates of children becoming looked after: A natural experiment using longitudinal area-level data in England', *Children and Youth Services Review*, **131**, p. 106289.

Brubaker, R. (2017) 'Why populism?', *Theory and Society*, **46**(5), pp. 357–385.

Campbell, J.L. and Pedersen, O.K. (2001) *The rise of neoliberalism and institutional analysis*, Princeton, NJ, Princeton University Press.

Capdevila, R. and Callaghan, J.E. (2008) '"It's not racist. It's common sense". A critical analysis of political discourse around asylum and immigration in the UK', *Journal of Community & Applied Social Psychology*, **18**(1), pp. 1–16.

Centre for Cities (2019) *Cities Outlook 2019*, Available online: www.centreforcities. org/reader/cities-outlook-2019/a-decade-of-austerity/, Last Accessed: 09 January 2020.

Clarke, J., Gewirtz, S. and McLaughlin, E. (eds) (2000) *New managerialism, new welfare?*, London, Sage.

Coburn, D. (2004) 'Beyond the income inequality hypothesis: Class, neo-liberalism, and health inequalities', *Social Science & Medicine*, **58**(1), pp. 41–56.

Collett, E. (2011) 'Immigrant integration in Europe in a time of austerity', Washington, DC, Migration policy institute.

Colling, T. and Dickens, L. (2001) 'Gender equality and trade unions: A new basis for mobilisation?', in Noon, M. and Ogbonna, E. (eds), *Equality, diversity and disadvantage in employment*, London, Palgrave Macmillan UK, pp. 136–155.

Cottam, H. (2018) *Radical Help: How we can remake the relationships between us and revolutionise the welfare state*, London, Virago.

Cummins, I. (2018) *Poverty, inequality and social work: The impact of neo-liberalism and austerity politics on welfare provision*, Bristol, Policy Press.

Cutler, D.M. and Johnson, R. (2004) 'The birth and growth of the social insurance state: Explaining old age and medical insurance across countries', *Public Choice*, **120**(1), pp. 87–121.

Dodd, S. (2016) 'Orientating disability studies to disablist austerity: Applying Fraser's insights', *Disability & Society*, **31**(2), pp. 149–165.

Dorling, D. (2015) *Injustice (revised edition): Why social inequality still persists*, Bristol, Policy Press.

Duffy, S., Waters, J. and Glasby, J. (2010) 'Personalisation and adult social care: Future options for the reform of public services', *Policy & Politics*, **38**(4), pp. 493–508.

Emejulu, A. and Bassel, L. (2015) 'Minority women, austerity and activism', *Race & Class*, **57**(2), pp. 86–95.

Esping-Andersen, G. (1990) *The three worlds of welfare capitalism*, Princeton, NJ, Princeton University Press.

Ferrera, M. (1996) 'The "Southern model" of welfare in social Europe', *Journal of European Social Policy*, **6**(1), pp. 17–37.

Garcia-Fuente, X. (2021) 'The paradox of redistribution in time: Social spending in 53 countries, 1967–2018: LIS Working Paper Series, No. 815', Luxembourg, Luxembourg Income Study (LIS).

Garrett, P.M. and Bertotti, T.F. (2017) 'Social work and the politics of "austerity": Ireland and Italy", *European Journal of Social Work*, **20**(1), pp. 29–41.

Grimshaw, D. and Rubery, J. (2012) 'The end of the UK's liberal collectivist social model? The implications of the coalition government's policy during the austerity crisis', *Cambridge Journal of Economics*, **36**(1), pp. 105–126.

Hammerstad, A. and Boas, I. (2015) 'National security risks? Uncertainty, austerity and other logics of risk in the UK government's National Security Strategy', *Cooperation and Conflict*, **50**(4), pp. 475–491.

Harries, B., Byrne, B., Garratt, L. and Smith, A. (2020) '"Divide and conquer". Anti-racist and community organizing under austerity', *Ethnic and Racial Studies*, **43**(16), pp. 20–38.

Hayek, F. (2001/1944) *The road to serfdom (Routledge Classics)*, Abingdon, Routledge.

Heymann, J., Bose, B., Waisath, W., Raub, A. and McCormack, M. (2021) 'Legislative approaches to nondiscrimination at work: A comparative analysis across 13 groups in 193 countries', *Equality, Diversity and Inclusion: An International Journal*, **40**(3), pp. 225–241.

Hood, R. (2018) *Complexity in social work*, London, Sage.

Hood, R., Goldacre, A., Abbott, S. and Jones, R. (2022) 'Patterns of demand and provision in English adult social care services', *The British Journal of Social Work*, Advance Access, https://doi.org/10.1093/bjsw/bcac011

Hood, R., Goldacre, A., Gorin, S. and Bywaters, P. (2019) 'Screen, ration and churn: Demand management and the crisis in children's social care', *The British Journal of Social Work*, **50**(3), pp. 868–889.

Jones, R. (2018) *In whose interest?: The privatisation of child protection and social work*, Bristol, Policy Press.

Korpi, W. (2000) 'Faces of inequality: Gender, class, and patterns of inequalities in different types of welfare states', *Social Politics: International studies in gender, state & society*, **7**(2), pp. 127–191.

Korpi, W. and Palme, J. (1998) 'The paradox of redistribution and strategies of equality: Welfare state institutions, inequality, and poverty in the Western countries', *American Sociological Review*, pp. 661–687.

Lacey, N. (1998) *Unspeakable subjects: Feminist essays in legal and social theory*, Oxford, Hart Publishing.

Lambert, M. and Crossley, S. (2017) '"Getting with the (troubled families) programme": A review', *Social Policy and Society*, **16**(1), pp. 87–97.

Lambie-Mumford, H. and Green, M.A. (2017) 'Austerity, welfare reform and the rising use of food banks by children in England and Wales', *Area*, **49**(3), pp. 273–279.

Le Grand, J. and Bartlett, W. (1993) *Quasi-markets and social policy*, Macmillan International Higher Education.

Le Grand, J. and Robinson, R. (2018) *Privatisation and the welfare state*, Abingdon, Routledge.

Lipsky, M. (1980) *Street level bureaucracy: Dilemmas of the individual in public services*, New York, Russell Sage Foundation.

Lovell, T. (2007) (Mis) recognition, social inequality and social justice: Nancy Fraser and Pierre Bourdieu, London, Routledge.

Lowe, S., Richmond, T. and Shields, J. (2017) 'Settling on austerity: ISAs, immigrant communities and neoliberal restructuring', *Alternate Routes: A Journal of Critical Social Research*, **28**.

Mattheys, K., Warren, J. and Bambra, C. (2018) '"Treading in sand": A qualitative study of the impact of austerity on inequalities in mental health', *Social Policy & Administration*, **52**(7), pp. 1275–1289.

McManus, S., Bebbington, P., Jenkins, R., Brugha, T. (2016) 'Mental health and wellbeing in England: Adult Psychiatric Morbidity Survey', Leeds, NHS Digital.

Miller, D.B. and Hokenstad, T. (2014) 'Rolling downhill: Effects of austerity on local government social services in the United States', *Journal of Sociology and Social Welfare*, **41**, p. 93.

MIPEX (2020) *Anti-discrimination*, Available online: www.mipex.eu/anti-discrimination.

Morel, N. and Palier, B. (2011) *Towards a social investment welfare state?: Ideas, policies and challenges*, Bristol, Policy Press.

Mudge, S.L. (2008) 'What is neo-liberalism?', *Socio-economic Review*, **6**(4), pp. 703–731.

Pearson, R. (2019) 'A feminist analysis of neoliberalism and austerity policies in the UK', *Soundings*, **71**(71), pp. 28–39.

Pilkington, A. (2021) 'Changing the narrative on race and racism: The Sewell Report and culture wars in the UK', *Advances in Applied Sociology*, **11**(8), pp. 1–20.

Rubery, J. and Rafferty, A. (2013) 'Gender, recession and austerity in the UK', in Karamessini, M. and Rubery, J. (eds), *Women and austerity: The economic crisis and the future of gender equality*. Abingdon, Routledge, pp. 123–144.

Spencer, S. (2008) 'Equality and Human Rights Commission: A decade in the making', *The Political Quarterly*, **79**(1), pp. 6–16.

Stewart, M. (2019) 'Preventable harm: Creating a mental health crisis', *Journal of Public Mental Health*.

Thatcher, M. (1987) *Interview for Woman's Own*, Available online: www.margaretthatcher.org/document/106689, Last Accessed: 27 March 2022.

Thomas, P. (2016) 'Youth, terrorism and education: Britain's Prevent programme', *International Journal of Lifelong Education*, **35**(2), pp. 171–187.

Titmuss, R. (2004) 'The social division of welfare: some reflections on the search for equity', in Deakin, N., Finer, C.J. and Matthews, B. (eds), *Welfare and the state: Critical concepts in political science (Volume II)*, Abindgon, Routledge, pp. 220–236.

Van Kersbergen, K. and Hemerijck, A. (2012) 'Two decades of change in Europe: The emergence of the social investment state', *Journal of Social Policy*, **41**(3), pp. 475–492.

Webb, C. (2021) 'In defence of ordinary help: Estimating the effect of early help/family support spending on children in need rates in England using ALT-SR', *Journal of Social Policy*, pp. 1–28.

Zweiniger-Bargielowska, I. (2000) *Austerity in Britain: Rationing, controls, and consumption, 1939–1955*, Oxford, Oxford University Press.

5
Global Inequalities

Chapter overview

This chapter considers various aspects of global inequality, starting with the huge gaps in income and wealth that exist between countries and individuals in the world. It proceeds to examine the ambiguous role of globalisation in the production and perpetuation of inequalities, looking at the significance of global institutions such as the World Bank, the activities of transnational organisations, and the impact of environmental racism. The chapter then takes a closer look at the relationship between inequality and imperialism, including the enduring legacy of European colonial empires. One such legacy is the structuring of the global economy as a power hierarchy, with rich and powerful core nations seeking to dominate and exploit the weaker and poorer societies on the periphery. Another is the enduring impact of settler colonialism on Indigenous peoples, something with profound implications for social work and its role within the welfare state. The chapter concludes with a discussion of migration and its connection to inequalities both between and within countries.

Introduction

The previous chapters have mostly been concerned with inequalities within countries rather than between them. However, international comparisons have also been used to examine the mechanisms driving inequality and to highlight its effect on people's lives. For example, differences in the distribution of income within and between rich countries are a key part of the literature on health inequalities (see Chapter 3). In this chapter, the focus is explicitly on global inequality, which not only means differences between aggregate populations, as in nations and countries, but also differences between the individuals of the world. A global perspective is essential for understanding social problems that cannot be analysed adequately at the local or national level. This includes obvious issues such as migration, wars and financial crises, which may directly affect individuals and families receiving support and intervention from social workers. However, it also means considering the social and economic impact of processes, activities and networks that are transforming societies across the world – through what is often termed 'globalisation'. It is also important to understand how globalisation connects with the history of Western imperialism, colonialism and exploitation, in which many contemporary inequalities are rooted. Before examining these issues in more depth, it is worth revisiting the evidence on inequalities from a global perspective.

Inequalities Across the World

Huge gaps in income and wealth exist across the world's population. International comparisons seeking to quantify these gaps face additional problems of measurement. For example, a given income – or its equivalent in an internationally traded currency such as US dollars – can buy different things in different countries. Economists use concepts such as 'purchasing power parity' (PPP) to adjust for the lower price levels in poorer countries, although exchange rates based on PPP can also be subject to error. Different measures of global inequality show different trends; for example, inequality *between* countries fell during the first two decades of the 21st century but was counteracted by an increase in inequality *within* countries over the same period (World Bank, 2016). Global averages can also be disproportionately affected by what happens in the most populous nations, such as China and India, making it important to consider regional trends and comparisons (Held and Kaya, 2007). It is also important to study inequalities in wealth, which tend to be much more pronounced than inequalities in income, as well as patterns of extreme wealth and extreme poverty. In a recent report on inequalities across the world, Chancel *et al.* (2022) report that:

- The richest 10% of the world's population accounts for 52% of global income and 76% of global wealth, whereas the poorest half of the world's population earns 8.5% of income and owns just 2% of global wealth.
- The most unequal region in the world is the Middle East and North Africa, while the most equal region is Europe.
- In 2020, about a third of global inequality was attributable to between-country inequality, and the rest was due to inequality within countries.
- Global inequality has always been very large – historically it rose steadily between 1820 and 1910 and shows little long-run trend between 1910 and 2020.
- Wealth inequalities have increased at the top of the distribution, with the share of global wealth owned by billionaires having risen from 1% in 1995 to 3% in 2020.
- There are considerable gender inequalities at the global level, with women's share of total incomes from work estimated to be below 35%.

The reality of such inequities is highlighted by the multiple forms of deprivation experienced by poor and marginalised sections of the world's population. To go beyond income-based measures (see Chapter 2), the United Nations Development Programme (UNDP) has constructed a global multidimensional poverty index, consisting of a weighted series of indicators around health (nutrition and child mortality), education (attendance and years of schooling) and standard of living (e.g. sanitation, drinking water, cooking fuel). Based on this index, the UNDP (2021) reports that:

- Around 1.3 billion people (over one-fifth of the world's population) live in acute, multidimensional poverty.
- Nearly 85% of this number live in Sub-Saharan Africa or South Asia, with roughly 84% living in rural areas.
- 788 million people live in a household with at least one undernourished person, and 568 million live more than 30 minutes' walk from a source of clean drinking water.
- Two-thirds of multidimensionally poor people live in households in which no girl or woman has completed at least six years of schooling, and the incidence of multidimensional poverty is positively associated with rates of intimate partner violence against women and girls.
- Minority ethnic groups in Sub-Saharan Africa, East Asia, and the Pacific show higher levels of multidimensional poverty, while Indigenous peoples are the poorest in most Latin American countries.
- Nearly 128 million people belong to ethnic groups in which 70% or more of the population is multidimensionally poor.
- In India, five out of six multidimensionally poor people are from a small number of socially excluded caste or class groups.

Covid-19 and Global Inequality

As discussed in Chapter 3, the Covid-19 crisis has both exposed and exacerbated health inequalities within countries. The poor and vulnerable have suffered a higher risk of infection, severe illness and death while also being disproportionately impacted by the wider consequences of the pandemic, e.g. on employment, education and violence (Arenas-Arroyo *et al.*, 2021; Cowie and Myers, 2021; Seifert, 2021; Wyper *et al.*, 2021). These disparities have been further magnified by differences between countries, both in terms of the resilience of health systems but also access to vaccines, personal protective equipment and therapeutic interventions. The World Bank estimated that just over 7% of people in low-income countries had received at least one vaccine dose by the end of 2021, compared to over 75% in high-income countries (Gopalakrishnan *et al.*, 2021). Across the world, the poorest 20% of people experienced the steepest fall in incomes during the pandemic and the divergence in impact increased over time, leading to around 100 million more people living in extreme poverty by the end of 2021 (Yonzan *et al.*, 2021). The pandemic also led to rising debt levels in low-income countries, many of which were at high risk of debt distress even before Covid-19 arrived (Gopalakrishnan *et al.*, 2021). Another World Bank report detailed the global disruption to education and its detrimental impact on children's learning, again disproportionately affecting the most marginalised children and young people (World Bank, 2021).

Globalisation and Inequality

The stark evidence of global inequalities invites us to look more closely at the policies and institutions that influence the development of countries and societies across the world. Historically, such processes have been associated with the waxing and waning of great civilisations and empires. Modern examples include the colonial empires of Britain and western Europe, the Soviet Union, the post-war alignment of NATO countries led by the United States of America, as well as the European Union and the growing economic and military clout of China. Empire-building through territorial expansion still does happen, of course, as demonstrated by Russia's recent invasion of Ukraine. Elsewhere, global institutions and governance structures provide the main underpinning for what Bieling (2012) calls 'world order politics'. Key global actors include the United Nations, NATO, the World Bank, World Trade Organisation, International Monetary Fund, and World Health Organisation, as well as an array of non-governmental organisations (NGOs). These institutions have contributed in various ways to increased interdependence of the world, particularly by creating and regulating international commitments to open trade and investment. While closer financial and economic ties lie at the heart of what is commonly known as 'globalisation', the term also encompasses important social and cultural elements, such as consumerism, technology and mass media. The idea that the world is becoming more interconnected suggests that many social problems will be partly caused by global processes and so require global solutions – the power of national governments to address them becomes more limited. Moreover, there are concerns that globalisation itself may contribute to global inequalities.

Does Globalisation Cause Inequality?

The links between globalisation and inequality are complex and disputed. As illustrated in Table 5.1, much depends on how these multi-faceted concepts are defined and measured. Some studies have focused on the connection between income inequality within countries and their integration in international trade and finance markets, both of which have been rising since the 1980s (Heimberger, 2020; Chancel *et al.*, 2022). Economists generally expect globalisation to reduce income differentials within developing countries, since opening up to trade should increase demand for unskilled labour and therefore push up real wages at the bottom of the scale. In contrast, trade openness will lead to greater inequality in more developed countries because their comparative advantage is in skilled labour at the top of the scale. However, empirical evidence does not entirely support this theory; a meta-analysis by Heimberger (2020) showed that economic globalisation has usually been found to increase income inequality, including in developing economies, and that financial globalisation has a stronger effect on inequality than trade globalisation. Similarly, Bergh and Nilsson (2010) found that liberalisation and globalisation were generally associated with increased inequality, particularly in more developed countries.

A more indirect approach is to examine the link between economic growth and inequality, on the premise that globalisation stimulates growth by opening up trade and allocating resources more efficiently. It is often assumed that income inequality will first increase and then decrease as countries develop their economies and become more open – a hypothesis known as the 'Kuznets curve' after its proponent (Kuznets, 1955). While some studies have reported that inequality does eventually decline with economic growth (Dollar, 2007; Jalil, 2012), others have found no systematic relationship (Deininger and Squire, 1996). It has been suggested that growth will only reduce inequality when a country's social and economic policies make sure the whole population benefits from it and not just privileged elites (Jovanovic, 2018; Ravallion and Chen, 2021). Moreover, the world's most developed countries have almost all experienced a rise in inequality over the past forty years. According to Milanovic (2016), the latter should be viewed as part of regular 'Kuznets waves', i.e. long-term cycles of waxing and waning inequality that are driven by externalities such as wars, epidemics, technological innovation, and social change. On this reading, globalisation can be expected to contribute to further increases in inequality until at some point in the future a combination of factors will push societies into reducing their steep gaps in income and wealth.

Table 5.1 Arguments for and against globalisation

Pro-globalisation arguments	Anti-globalisation arguments
• Globalisation increases growth and wealth and ultimately reduces inequality between countries.	• Developed countries that have globalised their economies have experienced widening inequalities.
• Countries like China that have opened up to trade and investment have benefited from high rates of growth and corresponding reductions in poverty.	• Not all developing countries have experienced the same trajectory as China. In some regions, such as Africa and the Middle East, inequality has increased and poverty remains high.
• Levels of extreme poverty have fallen and standards of living have improved across the world according to many indicators of health and wellbeing.	• Over a fifth of the world's population still lives in multidimensional poverty and resources and power remain unequal on a global scale.
• Globalisation creates new information flows and opportunities to raise awareness of inequalities, which helps empower people and develop social movements to create change.	• International institutions and governance structures perpetuate the advantages of rich countries and of privileged elites within poor countries, often reinforced by mass media.

(Continued)

Table 5.1 Arguments for and against globalisation (*Continued*)

Pro-globalisation arguments	Anti-globalisation arguments
• Globalisation has broken down borders, encouraging the movement of people and recognising the rights of refugees and asylum seekers.	• Fears of uncontrolled movement of people have led to a 'fortress mentality' among rich countries, more border controls, and fuelled nationalist and populist political parties.
• Global institutions have created a means for countries to address issues such as climate change that require concerted international action.	• Globalisation has exacerbated the forces underlying climate change, such as economic growth, urbanisation and consumerism.

Exercise 5.1: Is globalisation a good thing?

Read through the arguments that are made in Table 5.1, both in favour and against globalisation. Which do you find most convincing? What is your overall view on this complex debate?

Aspects of Global Inequality

While the merits of globalisation can be debated in various ways, some aspects of global inequality seem to reflect power imbalances in the current world order. For example, the emergence of transnational corporations means that some sectors of the global economy are now dominated by a few, powerful companies whose activities cannot easily be regulated by national governments. This can increase the risk of unethical and exploitative practices, as documented in the tobacco industry (Saloojee and Dagli, 2000), food industry (Boyd, 2012) and pharmaceutical industry (Gabriel and Goldberg, 2014). In the latter case, the dominance of 'Big Pharma' has been directly linked to global health inequalities, partly because of the ability of these companies to control prices for medicines (including vaccines) in poor countries where affordability is a problem, but also because they concentrate their research and development on diseases and health conditions that are prevalent in rich countries.

More broadly, transnational companies have been criticised for operating in countries with low regulatory standards, increasing the risk that their employees' health and safety will be compromised (Stiglitz, 2007). In high-income countries, the tendency for companies to shift their manufacturing base to low-income countries has been accompanied by the proliferation of low-paid and precarious employment in the 'gig economy', typified by zero-hours contracts and the minimisation of employment rights (Thelen, 2018). Such tendencies contribute to stagnating wages in rich countries but also the exploitation of cheap labour in poor countries. It has also been pointed out that international laws and agreements, e.g. around intellectual property, often seem to serve the interests of the richest countries at the expense of the poorest (Halabi, 2018). Global institutions such as the World Bank and International Monetary Fund have imposed structural reforms on developing countries as a condition of financial assistance, often worsening poverty and inequality in those countries without delivering the promised economic benefits (Forster *et al.*, 2019).

Consumerism is another aspect of globalisation in which inequalities are readily apparent. This is partly because disparities in income and wealth are reflected in rates of consumption. For example, the World Food Programme (2021) reported that 155 million people in 55 countries were experiencing a food crisis in 2021, the same year another UN report estimated that 17% of food worldwide was wasted. Consumerism also has a direct impact on societies. For example, health inequalities in some countries have been exacerbated by medical tourism, which contributes to a two-tier healthcare system in host countries and undermines public access to care and treatment (Snyder *et al.*, 2013). Some low-income countries have become increasingly dependent on tourism despite its social, economic and environmental consequences (Cooper, 2020). Consumerism is also linked to the global increase in rubbish, including toxic waste, to which poor and socially marginalised groups are unfairly exposed. Adam *et al.* (2001) discuss the concept of 'environmental racism', pointing out the parallels between the targeting of Black communities in the United States for waste dumping and environmental pollution and the practices of Western nations in Africa and India, e.g. oil companies in the Niger delta. Similarly, Nixon (2011) refers to the 'slow violence' of environmental degradation and resource exploitation perpetrated by rich countries in the developing world. Such evidence indicates that the environmental consequences of global economic growth, including pollution, climate change and rising water levels, are disproportionately borne by people who have benefited least from the proceeds of that growth.

Inequality and Empire

From a historical perspective, some aspects of global inequality can be linked to the legacy of European overseas empires, particularly those of the British, French, Spanish, Portuguese and Dutch. These empires were extractive in the sense of exploiting the raw materials and labour force of other countries in order to fuel their own economic growth and territorial expansion. Slavery and indentured labour, including the transatlantic shipment of Africans, formed a crucial part of the initial phase of conquest and colonisation, in some cases persisting well into the 'high imperial' period of the mid-19th to early 20th century (Morgan, 2007). Successive waves of migration led to the White settlement of overseas colonies and the dispossession, oppression and mass murder of Indigenous people. Social and economic integration of colonial territories helped to spread new technologies and institutions as well as Western ideas and values, often denigrating and silencing non-Western cultures and histories in the process (Said, 1994). After the Second World War, the emergence of new global institutions such as the United Nations coincided with independence struggles and the collapse of European colonial empires (Thomas and Thompson, 2014). However, the geopolitical order continued to be shaped by the ambitions and interests of global superpowers. The Cold War between the Soviet Union and the United States was a conflict largely played out in less powerful countries across the world, often with devastating results (O'Sullivan, 2014). The last two decades have seen China act ever more assertively in its national interests, presenting a new challenge to the US-led world order (Budd, 2021). As Russia's invasion of Ukraine sadly goes to show, imperial ambitions and the struggle for regional and global hegemony are as relevant today as they have been in most other periods of human history.

Debates about globalisation and empire show some interesting parallels with debates about inequality. Just as meritocratic arguments can be used to justify inequality between individuals (see Chapter 1), they can also be used to justify inequality between countries. In their crudest form, such arguments draw on racist stereotypes to compare entire populations and cultures, e.g. by suggesting that people in one country are less intelligent, hardworking or productive than those in another. Such characterisations became widespread during the era of European colonisation, whose ideology of conquest and control was often couched in moral terms as a type of 'civilising mission' (Grimshaw and Nelson, 2001). Civilisation could mean a variety of things, such as the conversion of Indigenous people to Christianity, the building of infrastructure such as railways and telegraph wires, and the integration of colonies into western-style capitalist markets. Notions of racial superiority were therefore embedded into notions of political and economic superiority. In the post-colonial era, such comparisons came to be framed in the technocratic language of economic development, in which countries are defined by their economic output. Put simply, the argument goes that developing countries have smaller economies than developed countries, so their populations tend to have worse health and wellbeing. To reduce global inequalities, those countries must therefore 'catch up', which typically means industrialisation, urbanisation and integration into world markets, as well as social and political reforms resembling those undertaken by their richer peers. In line with the 'Kuznets curve' theory of inequality (see above), any social upheaval caused by this transformation is justified by the longer-term goal of prosperity and growth.

Nowadays, global institutions such as the World Bank eschew the terms 'developing' and 'developed' in favour of country classifications based on per capita national income (Hamedeh *et al.*, 2021). An alternative classification uses the so-called 'Brandt line', proposed in the 1980s as a way of visualising the political and economic disparities between industrialised countries in the 'Global North' and the underdeveloped countries in the 'Global South' (Brandt, 1980)[1]. Since then, differential growth rates have changed economic relations to some extent, with countries like China and India helping to increase the South's share of global output over the past four decades (Lees, 2021). However, studies of politically relevant measures such as inequality and satisfaction have generally shown 'more evidence of continuity than change in the position of the Global South within the international system' (Lees, 2021: 104). The continued dominance of countries in the Global North suggests that structural inequalities have inhibited the convergence of wealth and income predicted by economists. A point of reference here is the world systems theory of Wallerstein (1974), who argued that the global economy was structured as a power hierarchy, with rich and powerful 'core nations' seeking to dominate and exploit the weaker and poorer societies on the periphery. According to this theory, globalisation tends to favour unequal exchange, leading to the systematic transfer of labour, raw materials and other resources from the periphery to the more advanced technological core. Global institutions and governance are therefore skewed towards the interests of the rich countries, allowing only a minor redistribution of power and wealth. Brandt's argument was that such stark divisions would ultimately lead to instability, conflict and war, creating an incentive for the North to engage with the South and agree to more equal arrangements.

The Impact of Colonialism

The world-system approach to global inequalities points to the enduring social, cultural, and economic impact of colonialism, which has continued to affect countries long after they achieved national independence. Drawing on the lived experience of Indigenous peoples in Canada, Czyzewski (2011) argues that colonialism is an ongoing historical process and should be treated as a social determinant of health similarly to other factors such as poverty and social exclusion:

> Colonialism is the guiding force that manipulated the historic, political, social, and economic contexts shaping Indigenous/state/non-Indigenous relations and account for the public erasure of political and economic marginalization, and racism today. These combined components shape the health of Indigenous peoples. At the intermediate level, this occurs

---

1   Nowadays the Global North would arguably include the United States, Canada, United Kingdom, countries in the European Union, as well as Singapore, Japan, South Korea, and some countries in the southern hemisphere, such as Australia, and New Zealand. The Global South, on the other hand, would include countries in Africa and Latin America, as well as the Middle East, Brazil, India, and parts of Asia.

via the funding and organization of the health care, education and labour systems; as well as the extent to which Indigenous peoples can operate their environmental stewardship and maintain cultural continuity. (Czyzewski, 2011: 4)

The Canadian context is an example of 'settler colonialism', described by Veracini (2013: 313) as 'circumstances where colonisers "come to stay" and to establish new political orders for themselves, rather than to exploit native labour'. Such actions were predicated on the control, domination and genocide of Indigenous peoples, typically obscured via a mythology of hardy pioneers exploring and settling 'Virgin Lands' (Wolfe, 2006). Even as settler colonial societies grew into independent nation states and were integrated into the global economy, Indigenous peoples continued to be subjected to brutal policies of exclusion, suppression and assimilation. In the process, the provision and administration of services for Indigenous communities, such as health, education and 'welfare', increasingly came under the purview of emerging professions such as social work (see Case Study 5.1). Indeed, social workers have contributed to settler colonial projects in various countries; examples include the 'Sixties Scoop' in Canada (Sinclair, 2007) and the 'stolen generations' in Australia (Krieken, 1999), terms that recall institutionally racist policies through which Indigenous children were forcibly removed from their families and placed in institutions in order to assimilate them within White settler society. Although such policies are no longer in place, the disproportionate removal of Indigenous children from their families continues to be a feature of the child welfare system in both countries (Blackstock *et al.*, 2020; Harnett and Featherstone, 2020).

Case Study 5.1: Settler colonialism and social work in Canada (Fortier and Hon-Sing Wong, 2019)

Fortier and Hon-Sing Wong (2019) show how the social work profession in Canada was consolidated as part of the settler colonial project. Following revisions to the Indian Act in 1951, social workers assumed key responsibilities for a range of educational and welfare services for Indigenous communities. This has given the profession a central role in three critical aspects of settler colonialism. The first is the dispossession and extraction of Indigenous peoples from their territories and communities. For example, the disproportionate removal of Indigenous children from their families and communities by social workers has been linked to the de-legitimisation of Indigenous practices of parenting and social support, as well as the social consequences of territorial dispossession and colonial violence. Second, social work has often confined itself to dispensing public services and assistance in ways that reproduce the settler state.

Continued

This includes efforts to mobilise the discourse of inclusion, recognition and reconciliation without following the lead of Indigenous communities as they seek to build their own structures of governance. Third, social work has become a technology of containment and pacification. Fortier and Hon-Sing Wong (2019) give the example of social service non-profit agencies set up in the Alberta tar sands, which facilitate the dispossession of Indigenous peoples and collaborate with law enforcement agencies to quell resistance among Indigenous communities. Underlying the theories and practices of social work are Euro-centric social structures and belief systems, many of which are not compatible with Indigenous cultural practices. In light of these difficulties, they discuss the possibilities for de-colonising social work, arguing that it would require such a radical transformation that social work would be left unrecognisable. Above all, such a process must be led by Indigenous peoples, whose resurgence can only be hindered by paternalistic and unsolicited 'help' from professionals.

Migration

According to statistics collected by the United Nations (McAuliffe and Triandafyllidou, 2022), there were 281 million international migrants globally in 2020, comprising 3.6% of the world's population. They included 169 million labour migrants and 89 million displaced persons. Migrants made international remittances of over $700 billion in 2020, of which $450 billion was received by low- and middle-income countries. As Black *et al.* (2005) point out, such figures are a powerful symbol of global inequalities, whether measured as income, job opportunities, lifestyles, or social and political stability. For many people, particularly those living in the Global South, international migration as well as internal migration (e.g. between rural and urban areas) represents an important strategy for improving their lives. Yet although migration is certainly rooted in inequalities, it does not necessarily reduce them (Palmary, 2020). Black *et al.* (2005) discuss a number of case studies, showing how the effect of migration varies significantly depending on access, i.e. who gets to migrate where, and opportunities that are available from different streams of migration. Social networks also act as a powerful mediator of access and opportunity. In rural Mexico, for example, middle- and upper-middle-class families find it easier to migrate to the United States than lower-class families and so remittances from abroad initially serve to increase inequalities. However, as international migration becomes more prevalent, network effects encourage poorer families to follow suit, which then serves to equalise the difference in remittances. Policies that restrict immigration tend to favour migrants who are already socially advantaged, forcing others into the informal 'grey economy' where they are vulnerable to exploitation. Such policies can reinforce existing inequalities around class or gender, as Siddiqui (2003) found to be the case for unskilled female migrants from Bangladesh. However, migration can also facilitate changes in social norms, including gender constraints on employment in traditional rural societies (Piper, 2013).

In receiving countries, migrants seek opportunities to improve their lives but also encounter various forms of discrimination, oppression and exploitation, including prejudicial treatment by statutory institutions (Carlisle, 2006; Fernandez-Reino, 2020). In the UK, the government has increasingly sought to restrict access to basic services, including healthcare (Taylor, 2009), for certain migrant groups, as part of general policy to create a 'hostile environment' for immigration (Wardle and Obermuller, 2019). Hostility towards migrants, particularly those from the Global South, has been a consistent feature of populist and nationalist political rhetoric in many countries in the Global North. Furthermore, as with many socially excluded groups, the harsh realities faced by migrants have been exposed by the health disparities of the Covid-19 pandemic. A particularly vulnerable group is constituted by children who seek asylum in another country without their parent or guardian. Global instability and conflict have led to increasing numbers of such children arriving in the UK and in other European countries, where they are sometimes referred to as 'unaccompanied asylum seeking children' (UASC). They face many challenges, including mental health problems, post-traumatic stress, language and cultural barriers, educational under-achievement, as well as numerous legal and institutional obstacles to their asylum status and leave to remain (Kohli, 2006). Social workers play a key role in supporting UASC both in the care system and as care leavers (Devenney, 2020).

Conclusion

This chapter has explored the global ramifications of inequality, pointing to the links between globalisation, geopolitics and the experience of socially disadvantaged groups across the world. Like some of the policy debates considered in the last chapter, adopting an historical perspective can shed light on contemporary social problems. For example, the extent to which racist attitudes were embedded in the imperial and colonial projects of European nations continues to have huge repercussions for racially marginalised communities. This includes Indigenous peoples such as the First Nations of Australia and Canada but also successive generations of immigrants to western Europe from those countries' former colonies. Such realities have profound implications for social work, which emerged as a profession during the age of empire and has subsequently become part of the apparatus of state within many former colonies as well as former colonial powers. Indeed, it could be argued that there are parallels between social work's role within 'settler colonialism' and its role within neo-liberal capitalism, when it comes to the surveillance and control of marginalised groups. Such arguments will be further explored in Chapter 7. At the same time, social work's value base and code of ethics gives practitioners at least some basis for challenging and transforming inequitable social arrangements. For example, social workers can play a vital role in supporting and advocating for refugees and asylum-seekers, including separated children. Navigating these tensions and conflicts is part of the challenge of social work, shaping the extent to which the profession is able to address inequality, as opposed to helping people to accommodate themselves to it.

References

Adam, H.M., Bullard, R.D. and Bell, E. (eds) (2001) *Faces of environmental racism: Confronting issues of global justice*, Oxford, Rowman & Littlefield.

Arenas-Arroyo, E., Fernandez-Kranz, D. and Nollenberger, N. (2021) 'Intimate partner violence under forced cohabitation and economic stress: Evidence from the COVID-19 pandemic', *Journal of Public Economics*, **194**, p. 104350.

Bergh, A. and Nilsson, T. (2010) 'Do liberalization and globalization increase income inequality?', *European Journal of Political Economy*, **26**(4), pp. 488–505.

Bieling, H.-J. (2012) 'European globalisation and world order politics', in Nousios, P., Overbeek, H. and Tsolakis, A. (eds), *Globalisation and European Integration*, Abingdon, Routledge, pp. 199–220.

Black, R., Natali, C. and Skinner, J. (2005) 'Migration and inequality', Washington, DC, World Bank.

Blackstock, C., Bamblett, M. and Black, C. (2020) 'Indigenous ontology, international law and the application of the Convention to the over-representation of Indigenous children in out of home care in Canada and Australia', *Child Abuse & Neglect*, **110**, p. 104587.

Boyd, C. (2012) 'The Nestlé infant formula controversy and a strange web of subsequent business scandals', *Journal of Business Ethics*, **106**(3), pp. 283–293.

Brandt, W. (1980) North South: A programme for survival; report of the Independent Commission on International Development Issues, London, Pan Books.

Budd, A. (2021) 'China and imperialism in the 21st century', *International Socialism Journal* (170), pp. 123–150.

Carlisle, F. (2006) 'Marginalisation and ideas of community among Latin American migrants to the UK', *Gender & Development*, **14**(2), pp. 235–245.

Chancel, L., Piketty, T., Saez, E. and Zucman, G. (2022) *World Inequality Report 2022*, Available online: wir2022.wid.world, Last Accessed: 14 February 2022.

Cooper, C. (2020) *Essentials of tourism*, London, Sage.

Cowie, H. and Myers, C.-A. (2021) 'The impact of the COVID-19 pandemic on the mental health and well-being of children and young people', *Children & Society*, **35**(1), pp. 62–74.

Czyzewski, K. (2011) 'Colonialism as a broader social determinant of health', *International Indigenous Policy Journal*, 2(1).

Deininger, K. and Squire, L. (1996) 'A new data set measuring income inequality', *The World Bank Economic Review*, **10**(3), pp. 565–591.

Devenney, K. (2020) 'Social work with unaccompanied asylum-seeking young people: Reframing social care professionals as 'co-navigators'', *The British Journal of Social Work*, **50**(3), pp. 926–943.

Dollar, D. (2007) 'Globalization, poverty and inequality since 1980', in Held, D. and Kaya, A. (eds), *Global inequality: Patterns and explanations*, Cambridge, Polity Press, pp. 73–103.

Fernandez-Reino, M. (2020) 'Migrants and discrimination in the UK', Oxford, The Migrant Observatory, University of Oxford.

Forster, T., Kentikelenis, A.E., Reinsberg, B., Stubbs, T.H. and King, L.P. (2019) 'How structural adjustment programs affect inequality: A disaggregated analysis of IMF conditionality, 1980–2014', *Social Science Research*, **80**, pp. 83–113.

Fortier, C. and Hon-Sing Wong, E. (2019) 'The settler colonialism of social work and the social work of settler colonialism', Settler Colonial Studies, **9**(4), pp. 437–456.

Gabriel, J.M. and Goldberg, D.S. (2014) 'Big Pharma and the problem of disease inflation', *International Journal of Health Services*, **44**(2), pp. 307–322.

Gopalakrishnan, V., Wadhwa, D., Haddad, S. and Blake, P. (2021) *2021 Year in Review in 11 Charts: The Inequality Pandemic*, Available online: www.worldbank.org/en/news/feature/2021/12/20/year-2021-in-review-the-inequality-pandemic, Last Accessed: 14 February 2022.

Grimshaw, P. and Nelson, E. (2001) 'Empire, "the Civilising Mission" and Indigenous Christian women in Colonial Victoria', *Australian Feminist Studies*, **16**(36), pp. 295–309.

Halabi, S.F. (2018) Intellectual property and the new international economic order: Oligopoly, regulation, and wealth redistribution in the global knowledge economy, Cambridge, Cambridge University Press.

Hamedeh, N., Van Rompaey, C. and Metreau, E. (2021) *New World Bank country classifications by income level: 2021-2022*, Available online: https://blogs.worldbank.org/opendata/new-world-bank-country-classifications-income-level-2021-2022, Last Accessed: 22 February 2022.

Harnett, P.H. and Featherstone, G. (2020) 'The role of decision making in the over-representation of Aboriginal and Torres Strait Islander children in the Australian child protection system', *Children and Youth Services Review*, **113**, p. 105019.

Heimberger, P. (2020) 'Does economic globalisation affect income inequality? A meta-analysis', *The World Economy*, **43**(11), pp. 2960–2982.

Held, D. and Kaya, A. (2007) *Global inequality: Patterns and explanations*, Cambridge, Polity Press.

Jalil, A. (2012) 'Modeling income inequality and openness in the framework of Kuznets curve: New evidence from China', *Economic Modelling*, **29**(2), pp. 309–315.

Jovanovic, B. (2018) 'When is there a Kuznets curve? Some evidence from the ex-socialist countries', *Economic Systems*, **42**(2), pp. 248–268.

Kohli, R.K. (2006) 'The sound of silence: Listening to what unaccompanied asylum-seeking children say and do not say', *British Journal of Social Work*, **36**(5), pp. 707–721.

Krieken, R.V. (1999) '"The Stolen Generations" and cultural genocide: The forced removal of Australian Indigenous children from their families and its implications for the sociology of childhood', *Childhood*, **6**(3), pp. 297–311.

Kuznets, S. (1955) 'Economic growth and income inequality', *American Economic Review*, **45**(1), pp. 1–28.

Lees, N. (2021) 'The Brandt Line after forty years: The more North–South relations change, the more they stay the same?', *Review of International Studies*, **47**(1), pp. 85–106.

McAuliffe, M. and Triandafyllidou, A. (eds) (2022) *World Migration Report 2022*, Geneva, International Organization for Migration (IOM).

Milanovic, B. (2016) Global inequality: A new approach for the age of globalization, Cambridge, MA, Harvard University Press.

Morgan, K. (2007) Slavery and the British empire: From Africa to America, Oxford, Oxford University Press.

Nixon, R. (2011) *Slow violence and the environmentalism of the poor*, Cambridge, MA, Harvard University Press.

O'Sullivan, P. (2014) *Geopolitics*, Abingdon, Routledge.

Palmary, I. (2020) 'Migration and inequality: an interdisciplinary overview', in Bastia, T. and Skeldon, R. (eds), *Routledge handbook of migration and development*, Abingdon, Routledge, pp. 95–102.

Piper, N. (2013) New perspectives on gender and migration: Livelihood, rights and entitlements, Abingdon, Routledge.

Ravallion, M. and Chen, S. (2021) 'Is that really a Kuznets curve? Turning points for income inequality in China', Cambridge, MA, National Bureau of Economic Research.

Said, E.W. (1994) *Culture and imperialism*, London, Vintage.

Saloojee, Y. and Dagli, E. (2000) 'Tobacco industry tactics for resisting public policy on health', *Bulletin of the World Health Organization*, **78**, pp. 902–910.

Seifert, A. (2021) 'Older adults during the COVID-19 pandemic–Forgotten and stigmatized?', *International Social Work*, **64**(2), pp. 275–278.

Siddiqui, T. (2003) 'Migration as a livelihood strategy of the poor: The Bangladesh case', Dhaka, Refugee and Migratory Movements Research Unit, Dhaka University.

Sinclair, R. (2007) 'Identity lost and found: Lessons from the sixties scoop', *First Peoples Child & Family Review: A Journal on Innovation and Best Practices in Aboriginal Child Welfare Administration, Research, Policy & Practice*, **3**(1), pp. 65–82.

Snyder, J., Crooks, V., Johnston, R. and Kingsbury, P. (2013) 'Beyond sun, sand, and stitches: Assigning responsibility for the harms of medical tourism', *Bioethics*, **27**(5), pp. 233–242.

Stiglitz, J.E. (2007) *Making globalization work*, London, Penguin.

Taylor, K. (2009) 'Asylum seekers, refugees, and the politics of access to health care: A UK perspective', *British Journal of General Practice*, **59**(567), pp. 765–772.

Thelen, K. (2018) 'Regulating Uber: The politics of the platform economy in Europe and the United States', *Perspectives on Politics*, **16**(4), pp. 938–953.

Thomas, M. and Thompson, A. (2014) 'Empire and globalisation: From "high imperialism" to decolonisation', *The International History Review*, **36**(1), pp. 142–170.

United Nations Development Programme (2021) *Global Multidimensional Poverty Index 2021: Unmasking disparities by ethnicity, caste and gender*, Available online: https://hdr.undp.org/sites/default/files/2021_mpi_report_en.pdf, Last Accessed: 14 February 2021.

Veracini, L. (2013) '"Settler colonialism": Career of a concept', *The Journal of Imperial and Commonwealth History*, **41**(2), pp. 313–333.

Wallerstein, I. (1974) *The modern world-system I: Capitalist agriculture and the origins of the European world-economy in the sixteenth century*, Oakland, CA, University of California Press.

Wardle, H. and Obermuller, L. (2019) '"Windrush generation" and "hostile environment": Symbols and lived experiences in Caribbean migration to the UK', *Migration and Society*, **2**(1), pp. 81–89.

Wolfe, P. (2006) 'Settler colonialism and the elimination of the native', *Journal of Genocide Research*, **8**(4), pp. 387–409.

World Bank (2016) 'Poverty and shared prosperity 2016: Taking on inequality', Washington, DC, World Bank.

World Bank (2021) 'The state of the global education crisis', Washington D.C., Paris, New York, The World Bank, UNESCO, and UNICEF.

World Food Programme (2021) *2021 Global report on food crises*, Available online: www.wfp.org/publications/global-report-food-crises-2021, Last Accessed: 15 February 2022.

Wyper, G.M., Fletcher, E., Grant, I., Harding, O., de Haro Moro, M.T., Stockton, D.L. and McCartney, G. (2021) 'COVID-19 and prepandemic all-cause inequalities in disability-adjusted life-years due to multiple deprivation: A Scottish Burden of Disease study', *The Lancet*, **398**, p. S94.

Yonzan, N., Kaner, C. and Mahler, D.G. (2021) *Is COVID-19 increasing global inequality?*, Available online: https://blogs.worldbank.org/opendata/covid-19-increasing-global-inequality, Last Accessed: 14 February 2022.

6

The Role of Social Work

Chapter overview

....

Chapter 6 explores the role of social work in tackling inequality in its various forms. Its starting point is the professionalisation of social work, which has implications for power relations, the institutional context of practice, and constraints imposed on the pursuit of social justice goals. The chapter then turns to some of the core activities of social work within the welfare state, looking particularly at assessment, casework, and social regulation in areas such as child protection and mental health. The contrast between clinical and structural practice models brings out some of the tensions and ambiguities within social work, and the extent to which it may unwittingly reproduce or even exacerbate inequalities in wider society. The chapter concludes with a discussion of advocacy, empowerment, and anti-discriminatory practice, which pave the way for the more radical and transformational approaches considered in Chapter 7.

Introduction

The last five chapters have examined aspects of social inequality that are particularly relevant to social workers. Over the next three chapters, attention turns to the profession's role in addressing inequality. Three broad perspectives are taken on this complex issue. The first is to see social work as embedded in the welfare state, as discussed in Chapter 4. This emphasises the statutory role of social workers, although welfare systems also encompass services delivered by voluntary and private sector organisations. The second perspective sees social work as a professional discipline that does – or could if need be – operate independently of the welfare state. This allows scope for approaches and practices that might challenge or resist certain government policies and priorities if they conflict with core professional values. The third perspective is to see social work as being about achieving communitarian objectives, whether these are to do with geographical places (as in neighbourhoods, cities, regions) or with shared identities and interests (as in groups, collectives, organisations). This view of social work highlights strategic and political activities, such as seeking consensus, constructing alliances, settling conflicts, and negotiating solutions, as well as experimenting with new ways of doing things. From each of these perspectives, social work has a different role to play in addressing inequality – what also differs is *who* decides what that role should be, i.e. the government, the profession, or the community. Our starting point is therefore social work's professional status: does it help or hinder efforts to tackle inequality?

Inequality and the Professions

Professions tend to share some common features: a body of specialist knowledge and expertise, university-accredited qualification, state-sanctioned regulator, and ethical code of practice (Macdonald, 1995). Applying such criteria enables societies to train people to do important work, deliver vital services, uphold standards of quality, and protect citizens from potential abuses of power. At the same time, professionalisation can be seen as a strategic project undertaken by certain occupations to establish market control over a particular sphere of work (Larson, 1977). This suggests a more sceptical attitude towards professionals as being motivated less by altruism and ethical values than by their own economic and social advantage (Johnson, 1972). Professionalisation also requires occupational groups to negotiate with governments, which have the power to grant them a monopoly over certain activities but also to regulate and sanction them. This relationship is particularly crucial for social workers, most of whom are employed by the state (Etzioni, 1969) and whose role requires them to implement government policies and follow statutory guidelines.

Professionalisation has various implications for social inequality. Achieving 'social closure', i.e. control over certain types of work, may entail or lead to exclusionary practices and therefore contribute to existing forms of discrimination (Witz, 1992). At the same time, entry to a profession is one of the main vehicles of social mobility (see Chapter 1) so it is worth noting that social work has a mainly female workforce and a relatively high proportion of ethnically minoritised groups compared to other professions (Department for Education, 2022; Skills for Care, 2022). For welfare professions, which include nurses and midwives as well as social workers, professionalisation may assist efforts to resist subordination to traditionally male-dominated fields such as medicine and law (Abbott and Wallace, 1990). Nonetheless, opportunities for professional advancement do not themselves resolve wider structural inequalities, such as the over-representation of minoritised groups among the recipients of social care services and statutory interventions (Ahmed *et al.*, 2022). Welfare professions have also been criticised for overstating their claims to specialist knowledge, eroding people's right to make decisions for themselves, and subjecting people to state surveillance and control (Wilding, 1982; Illich *et al.*, 2005).

Some of the thorniest debates around professionalisation concern questions of power and authority, which are also at the heart of inequality (see Chapter 1). Smith (2008) conceptualises power as 'the capacity, held individually or collectively, to influence either groups or individuals (including oneself) in a given social context'. Social workers may wield power over others because of their specialist knowledge and expertise, because of their agency role and mandate under the law, because they act as gatekeepers for resources and services that people want, or even because of the strength of their personality (French and Raven, 1968; Hasenfeld, 1987). All these forms of power may contribute to an unequal relationship with citizens. However, professional power also interacts with broader social inequalities, which may be relevant for Black social workers and practitioners from minoritised groups, for example, when it comes to working with affluent families (Bernard, 2019). In some countries, these power dynamics are aggravated by social work's contribution to settler colonial projects and the imposition of Eurocentric cultural norms on Indigenous peoples (see Chapter 5). In others, the embedding of social work within large government bureaucracies adds to the distance – both physical and metaphorical – between social workers and service users. In the UK, for instance, social workers may spend a lot of time in offices, secluded behind security doors, while their encounters with citizens are geared around assessments and reports (Jones *et al.*, 2013). Social work's success in becoming a regulated profession in the UK has coincided with the imposition of managerial controls on their work, leading to concerns that some aspects of practice have actually become de-professionalised, e.g. through a focus on specialist training in standardised tasks and procedures. On the other hand, social workers do still have scope to exercise their professional discretion (Evans, 2016) and may therefore find ways to leverage their professional status in pursuit of social justice goals (Fenton, 2019). A common theme in such debates is the profession's role within the welfare state.

Exercise 6.1: Should social work be a profession?

Consider the following statements about the profession of social work. Which do you agree or disagree with? How do you decide between conflicting views and which is more convincing overall?

- Social work should be a profession because it is an important job that needs people with the right knowledge and skills.
- Social work should not be a profession because it leads to social workers spending most of their time in the office typing reports rather than actually helping people.

Continued

- Social work should be a profession because it means social workers have to adhere to an ethical code of practice and the public is protected from unsuitable or incompetent practitioners.
- Social work should not be a profession because it means social workers have to do what the government wants, even if the government's policies are wrong.
- Social work should be a profession because it gives social workers more power to help people and give them access to services and support.
- Social work should not be a profession because it gives social workers too much power and makes it harder for them to relate to the people they work with.

Social Work and the Welfare State

In Chapter 4, it was observed that modern welfare systems tend to steer between different approaches to equality and difference: a social welfare perspective, which is about meeting people's needs for support and assistance; a liberal perspective, which is about making sure people can participate in society and fulfil their responsibilities as citizens, and a recognition perspective which is about working alongside marginalised groups to dismantle oppressive social structures. Through their professional activities of assessment and casework, social workers help to navigate the tensions and ambiguities between these approaches. In addition, social work has carved out a distinctive role at the 'sharp end' of the welfare state, where complex decisions are made about people's rights, responsibilities and best interests; in some cases, the law empowers statutory agencies to intervene in private life in order to safeguard people's health and wellbeing. This combination of functions gives social work a prominent role in the welfare state, which can be viewed through an inequalities lens.

Assessment and Decision-making

Historical overviews place the beginnings of social work in the philanthropic organisation of voluntary assistance within poor urban communities, which emerged as an aspect of rapid industrialisation and social change in 19th-century Britain and the United States (Stuart, 2019). Activities such as home visiting, interviewing applicants for relief, providing advice, and determining appropriate assistance were originally carried out by volunteers, then by paid employees, and ultimately by trained practitioners. Recognisably similar tasks are still carried out by social workers, albeit in a more professional and bureaucratised form. Ostensibly, this kind of work aligns with a social welfare approach to inequality, providing a framework through which collective resources can be allocated to citizens based on need. It may help to reduce inequality, e.g. through redistributive effects and improved access to opportunities. However, there is also potential for inequalities to become embedded in – and perpetuated by – institutional processes. This is partly because utilitarian considerations, i.e. how to deliver the most benefit to the greatest number of people, may implicitly be tied to the issue of desert, i.e. who deserves to be helped. Nowadays, such judgements tend to be framed in technocratic terms, such as eligibility or thresholds, but are nonetheless susceptible to bias, which makes it harder for some people to obtain help than others. For example, people from racially minoritised groups have been shown to experience inequitable treatment by welfare services, some of which is down to assessment practices and biases in decision-making (Bridges, 2016; Dettlaff and Boyd, 2020; Keddell, 2022).

The power dynamics of assessment reflect the issues discussed above in relation to professionalisation. In most social work settings, assessment is largely shaped by organisations' interpretation of statutory guidance, which in practice often takes the form of set lists of questions and pre-specified categories of response. The person being assessed has little control over the questions that are asked, the way information is perceived, and the judgements that are made. The overall – if unintended – effect is to prioritise professional knowledge and expertise over lived experience and 'what matters' to the person. Meanwhile, decisions about resources, eligibility or thresholds for intervention are often made at a remove from the person being assessed, e.g. by managers, commissioners or panels, based on reports completed by social workers and other professionals, and in meetings that the person may or may not attend. Indeed, it is important to distinguish between assessment and decision-making when analysing inequities in welfare provision. For example, Dettlaff *et al.* (2011) explored the impact of race on decisions made by child welfare services in Texas about alleged maltreatment, finding that children from all racial/ethnic groups were more likely to have concerns substantiated relative to White children, but this inequity only became apparent after the worker's risk perceptions were taken into account (see also Rivaux, 2008). In other words, racial bias was found to operate at the threshold for action rather than (or more measurably than) on the risk assessment itself. In their analysis of serious case reviews[1] involving Black children, Bernard and Harris (2019) also identified a lack of professional curiosity when it came to the salience of race in the children's lives, including 'the powerful influence of race on Black children's interaction with the child protection system', which meant that lessons in relation to children's cultural, racial, and religious experiences were not adequately addressed in such reviews (see also Bhatti-Sinclair and Price-Robertson, 2016).

---

1   In England, a serious case review (now called a safeguarding practice review) is a detailed local investigation that is held into any case of serious or fatal injury to a child occurring as a result of maltreatment, including when a child dies in custody.

Casework

Casework generally refers to activities undertaken by a social worker in relation to a defined set of needs and problems, often (but not necessarily) connected to a specific individual or family. Mary Richmond's (1922) foundational text on social casework was explicitly concerned with the relationship between individuals and their social environment; as Fjeldheim *et al.* (2015) point out, Richmond envisaged that 'direct' work with individuals should be combined with 'indirect' work focusing on the social environment. In subsequent decades, psycho-social models of casework were developed, based initially on psychodynamic approaches but gradually incorporating other techniques over time, partly as a result of the critique presented by 'radical' social work perspectives (see Chapter 7). In the 1980s and 1990s, the nature of casework was changed by the advent of case management, which reconfigured the social worker's role as an administrator or broker of services and coordinator of multi-agency care plans. Managerialism also increased recording and reporting requirements, leaving practitioners increasingly office-bound and with less time to spend with people in the community. Such developments in turn led to calls to reconfigure social work practice around 'relationships' (Ruch *et al.*, 2010) and to reduce the administrative burden on social workers in order to facilitate direct work. From an inequalities perspective, the challenge is to ensure that such calls to refocus on good practice in social work are allied to the kind of 'indirect' work advocated by Richmond, looking beyond the individual to the wider environment where structural barriers are to be found.

Risk and Regulation

According to Sparrow (2008), social regulation is about controlling and responding to risks to public safety and wellbeing. Examples include the reduction of environmental hazards such as noise and pollution, ensuring food safety, or clamping down on dangerous building practices. Social workers also undertake social regulation as part of their role in the welfare state, notably in areas such as child protection, adult safeguarding, mental health interventions, forensic social work, as well as specialist practice in relation to domestic violence, substance misuse and youth offending. It could be argued that there is an implicit regulatory aspect to any assessment of actual or potential risks to people's safety and wellbeing. However, it is more explicit in the practice of surveillance and investigation, enforcement and sanctions (for breaches of compliance), and non-voluntary or coercive intervention. Exercise 6.2 provides some examples of regulatory activity, alongside other examples of social work that (arguably) are not to do with regulation – see if you can distinguish them!

Exercise 6.2: Regulatory activities in social work

Which of these social work activities could be characterised as social regulation?

- Carry out an assessment under the Mental Health Act to determine whether a person needs to be admitted to hospital for treatment of a mental disorder.
- Help a foster child put together their life story book ahead of their move to an adoptive family.
- Investigate alleged financial abuse and exploitation of an elderly woman by her son's family.
- Help to organise a foodbank and clothing exchange in a local neighbourhood badly hit by a rise in the cost-of-living.
- Carry out a needs assessment for an adult with learning disabilities so that they may receive a direct payment for personalised support.
- Complete a court report on the welfare and living arrangements of a child whose parents have accused each other of emotional abuse and parental alienation.
- Refer someone to a local charity that supplies low-income families with household appliances such as fridges and washing machines.
- Apply to court for an emergency protection order to accommodate a child in out-of-home care.

Regulatory frameworks are designed to respond in a proportionate way, deploying an escalating series of sanctions to discourage behaviour and actions that pose a risk to the public. This is sometimes referred to as the regulatory pyramid (Braithwaite, 2002) because it is assumed that the majority of individuals and organisations will only require 'light touch' regulation, with more serious interventions reserved for the minority suspected of non-compliance. Health, education and social care services also have a pyramidal structure, in that they are organised as different tiers of provision that correspond to people's level of need. At the base of the pyramid, universal services in Tier 1, such as schools, GP surgeries and community centres, cater for the whole population. Specialist services in Tier 2, such as therapeutic interventions, provide targeted support to people whose needs cannot be met by universal services. At the 'top' of the pyramid, Tier 3 services, such as in-patient hospital wards or safeguarding and court teams, deal with acute or complex cases, which often means coordinating interventions from multiple professionals and agencies (Hood, 2015). Social workers may be engaged throughout the pyramid, but are typically found in Tier 2 and Tier 3 services, with aspects of social regulation becoming more prominent in the latter. In Exercise 6.2, for example, activities such as Mental Health Act assessments or the investigation of safeguarding concerns, which are legally mandated and may be carried out without people's consent, can be distinguished from services that are requested or voluntarily engaged in. Of course, the distinction is not always straightforward; the potential for services to escalate their response (i.e. refer 'up' the pyramid to higher tiers of provision) means people may feel they have little choice but to cooperate with social workers even when they have little desire to do so. Equally, it is incumbent on professionals to work in partnership with people, and in a respectful and non-oppressive manner, whichever tier they happen to be operating in. As Case study 6.1 shows, the balance between care and control can prove crucial for people who have suffered trauma and encounter social workers at a point of crisis in their lives.

Case Study 6.1: Osman

Osman is a 25-year-old cisgender heterosexual man of Black African heritage, who lives in South London. He has resided in the UK since 2007, after fleeing armed conflict in his home country of Sudan. Osman suffered traumatic experiences as a child, both in the war and subsequent journey to the UK, during which he was trafficked and exploited in Libya. On arrival in the UK, border officials did not believe him to be under 18 and a subsequent age assessment led him to be subject to adult detention procedures. Although Osman was eventually granted Leave To Remain as a refugee, he has found it hard to cope with linguistic, cultural and economic barriers to inclusion in UK society. He has also struggled with his mental health and two years ago had an episode of psychosis that led to compulsory admission to a psychiatric hospital for treatment under the Mental Health Act. He was diagnosed with schizophrenia, for which he now takes medication under the care of the community mental health team. His experiences have made him fearful of health and social care professionals; he worries that his illness has been reported to the Home Office and that he will be deported. A few months ago, Osman accompanied a friend to a local community centre for refugees and asylum seekers, where he found the staff and volunteers to be friendly and sympathetic. He has since become involved in activities to support separated children and wishes this type of help had been offered to him when he arrived in the country.

Questions to consider

1   What kind of services has Osman come into contact with since his arrival in the UK?
2   When would Osman have had contact with social workers? What role did they have in his life and how might he have experienced this contact?
3   Why do you think Osman has learned to be fearful of professionals, including social workers?

Continued

4   Osman may have met some social workers at the community centre he has
    been visiting – how is their role different from social workers contributing to
    age assessments or Mental Health Act assessments?
5   Do you think Osman's experience is typical of refugees entering the UK? What
    could be done to improve this situation?

The shift to higher tiers or thresholds of provision is often accompanied by a steep-
ening of the social gradient of intervention. In other words, inequalities are exacerbated in more regulatory forms of social work and social care. In a national study of
child welfare services in England, Goldacre and Hood (2022) found that for every
ten percentage point increase in the proportion of families on low incomes in a
small neighbourhood, the rate of referrals in that neighbourhood could be expected
to go up 62%; this figure then increased at every subsequent threshold until it
reached 80% for children placed on child protection plans. The threshold to child
protection marks a shift in the power of the state to monitor and intervene in private
family life – it is also the point at which statutory agencies 'decide more than ever
to concentrate their attention on poorer families' (Goldacre and Hood, 2022: 14).

As noted in Chapter 3, research shows that people from racially minoritised
groups face difficulties in accessing care and support at the same time as they are
disproportionately subjected to coercive and stigmatising interventions; examples include compulsory admission to psychiatric hospital (Barnett *et al.*, 2019),
labelling with behavioural disorders (Strand and Lindsay, 2009), and punitive
and degrading treatment by the police (Gamble, 2022). Similar experiences are
prevalent among refugees and asylum seekers (Cemlyn and Nye, 2012; Given-
Wilson *et al.*, 2016; Hlass, 2019), as suggested by Case study 6.1. Contributing to
such problems is substantial evidence from both the US and the UK that Black
children are subject to 'adultification' by professionals (Dancy, 2014; Goff *et al.*,
2014; Davis and Marsh, 2020), meaning they are seen as less vulnerable and
more adult-like, with the result that services 'overlook their needs and disregard
their legal rights to be protected, supported and safeguarded' (Davis and Marsh,
2020: 255). For example, a 2022 child safeguarding practice review into the abusive strip-search by police of a 15-year-old girl at her school in London supported the view that this was a racist incident linked to adultification bias, citing
evidence from custody suites that such practices were disproportionately used by
police for Black and minority ethnic detainees (Gamble and McCallum, 2022).

Practice Models

Social work has an eclectic theory base, drawing on disciplines as varied as
law, psychology, sociology, bio-medical science and the philosophy of ethics.

Having to weave together such disparate strands means there are countless ways to do social work. In this respect, practice models play a vital mediating role They enable social workers to implement theories in a coherent and consistent way, ensure their work is informed by research evidence as well as ethical principles, and help them deliver the most appropriate service for the person in their environment. It is therefore worth considering how questions of social justice are treated within different practice models, and how this affects social work's contribution to addressing inequality.

Clinical Models

Clinical practice models are familiar to most social workers, even if they do not see themselves as clinicians[2]. The term highlights the way practitioners in most helping professions, whether social workers or nurses or therapists, tend to structure their work in a similar way to medical professionals carrying out diagnosis and treatment In other words, there is an assessment stage, in which the professional uses their expertise to understand the problem at hand, followed by an intervention stage, in which an appropriate course of action is agreed and implemented. Of course, this process can be undertaken in a way that respects people's autonomy and expertise when it comes to their own lives. It is possible for assessments to locate problems in the social environment as well as highlighting aspects of individual behaviour and functioning. Interventions may be based around activities such as relationship-building, partnership working and goalsetting as opposed to implementing expert recommendations. Nonetheless, many practice models used in social work have a recognisably clinical structure. Well-known examples include:

1 *Psychodynamic approaches* – help people understand how early childhood experiences can help to shape their personality and behaviour in later life, paying particular attention to unconscious drivers and motivations. For example, a social worker might use video-interaction guidance to help a parent bond and interact sensitively with their young child, with a view to promoting the security of attachment (Maxwell and Rees, 2019).
2 *Cognitive behavioural approaches* – focus on people's conscious thoughts, beliefs and perceptions as a way of addressing problematic behaviour and attitudes. For example, social workers might undertake a three-phase trauma-focused cognitive behavioural treatment plan with a child who was traumatised by the events surrounding her parents' arrest and incarceration (Morgan-Mullane, 2018).

---

2   The term 'clinical social worker' is not commonly used in the UK but is prevalent in some countries, such as the United States.

3   *Task-centred approaches* – help people to identify the key problems they
    want to address before proceeding to define goals and agree tasks that
    enable progress towards achieving those goals (Marsh and Doel, 2005).
    For example, a social worker might support someone wishing to move
    back into paid employment after a period of illness, drawing up a plan with
    incremental steps that are reviewed at specified intervals.

4   *Solution-focused approaches* – help people to change their lives by focusing
    on their strengths and drawing on their ideas about what would constitute a
    'problem-free' future. For example, a social worker might work with a child
    and their family on a safety plan to ensure that the risk of physical abuse in the
    home is appropriately monitored and managed (Turnell and Edwards, 1999).

5   *Crisis intervention approaches* – focus on short-term help for people whose
    health and wellbeing is at risk because they are faced with a situation they
    cannot solve with their usual resources or coping mechanisms (Roberts,
    2005). For example, a social worker might need to respond quickly
    to arrange care and treatment for someone whose mental health has
    deteriorated following a family bereavement.

6   *Systemic approaches* – focus on the relationships and interconnections
    between people, paying particular attention to cyclical patterns and wider
    influences on people's actions and behaviours. For example, a social worker
    might use systems ideas to work with a family where there are concerns that
    the youngest child is being blamed for 'bad behaviour' as a way of resolving
    parental conflicts and tensions (Yahav and Sharlin, 2002).

The list is not meant to be exhaustive and readers will doubtless be able to think of
many other ways of doing social work that follow an assessment-intervention tem-
plate, such as narrative approaches (Abels, 2001), relationship-based approaches
(Ruch *et al.*, 2010), restorative approaches (Molloy *et al.*, 2021), trauma-informed
approaches (Mersky *et al.*, 2019), and so on. From an inequalities perspective,
it is necessary to interrogate such models in terms of how they address the
professional–client power dynamic, or how the clinical process accounts for the
contribution of structural factors to the problems that people face. For example,
in the study of a trauma-focused CBT intervention cited above, the author notes
that 'alongside parental incarceration, the mediating effects of racism, poverty, low
educational attainment, and a variety of other social barriers make it essential for
the social worker to acknowledge that a client's socioeconomic and demographic
circumstances can interact with or contribute to their trauma' (Morgan-Mullane,
2018: 209). As part of the process of creating a therapeutic alliance, or its equivalent, clinical approaches operate on the premise that people are the experts in their
own lives. Nonetheless, the focus of the work will generally be on achieving change
on an individual level rather than addressing structural barriers in wider society.
This limits the practitioners' ability to think about what has been called 'socially
engineered trauma' (Avruch and Shaia, 2022); for example, resulting from racism,

colonialism and the historical context of social and political experiences around race and racialisation. Many social workers are aware of the dangers of 'context-blindness' (Shaia *et al.*, 2019), and such awareness has contributed to the development of structural approaches to go alongside the main clinical models of practice.

Pause and reflect

....

What clinical practice models are you familiar with? Do you have a preferred way of working? Does your organisation have a practice model? Consider the strengths and limitations of these approaches.

Structural Models

Structural models of practice form part of social work training and are explicitly or implicitly recognised by regulatory bodies. They aim to ensure that social workers are sensitive to individual and cultural differences, able to reflect on their own biases and assumptions, prepared to challenge discriminatory attitudes and behaviour, and take steps to address structural barriers and disadvantages. The professional standards for social workers in England, for example, include an injunction to 'recognise differences across diverse communities and challenge the impact of disadvantage and discrimination on people and their families and communities' (Social Work England, 2020). Most, if not all, social workers would probably agree that practising in a non-discriminatory way is a cornerstone of their profession. The same professional standards refer to 'balancing rights and risks and enabling access to advice, advocacy, support and services' (Social Work England, 2020. Such statements confer legitimacy on the advocacy role of social work, even if there is a tension with the regulatory aspects of the work, as we shall see. Nor does the profession's recognition of structural models of practice necessarily mean a wholehearted embrace of the critical theories that underpin them. Nonetheless, they form a valuable counterbalance to clinical models, reminding practitioners of the need to understand and address wider issues of equality, power and social justice as a means of facilitating individual change.

Anti-discriminatory Practice

Thompson (2012: 48) describes anti-discriminatory practice in the following terms:

> An approach to practice which seeks to reduce, undermine or eliminate
> discrimination and oppression, specifically in terms of challenging
> sexism, racism, ageism and disabilism and other forms of discrimination
> or oppression encountered in practice.

Thompson's definition makes it clear that anti-discriminatory practice (ADP) should not be interpreted in a legalistic way, i.e. it is not only about complying with anti-discrimination laws or statutory guidance but is also about challenging the social structures that give rise to inequality and injustice. Since there is potential for social work practice itself to be discriminatory, ADP is fundamentally about the profession's contribution to broader social justice goals. There can be no 'middle road' – social work is either part of the solution or part of the problem. Such a stance makes ADP broadly synonymous with 'anti-oppressive' approaches, although other writers such as Dominelli (2002) and Dalrymple and Burke (2007) have sought to distinguish between the two. Thompson (2012) suggests that both concepts are emancipatory in their aims, advancing a model of social work practice that is not content to help people adjust to an unjust and oppressive society but links the individual to cultural and structural analyses of discrimination. Having understood how they interact to create inequitable outcomes, the challenge for social workers is to intervene holistically on all three levels while operating within the constraints of their legal, institutional and professional role.

Both ADP and anti-oppressive practice (AOP) draw on the radical and critical perspectives on social work discussed in the next chapter. In some ways, these models can be understood as a bridging concept, designed for social workers who are mainly trained in clinical approaches to gain an understanding of multiple forms of structural disadvantage. They encourage social workers to reflect on their own positionality, be open to discussion and debate, and join (or establish) coalitions and support groups. Of course, like any model, they have their limitations. For example, because ADP/AOP deal with practice, they have more to say more about how social work is done than about what it *is*. The core principles of 'no middle ground' and 'good practice is anti-discriminatory practice' suggest that social workers can (and should) make an active choice to be a progressive force for social change. On the other hand, part of the point of structural analysis is that social workers are not necessarily able to *practise* their way out of an oppressive role within institutional frameworks that are fundamentally unjust. What are social workers to do if their role requires them to function as bureaucratic administrators, or agents of a repressive state? Another way of putting this dilemma is to ask whether empowerment is always possible within social work, or only under certain conditions.

Empowerment

Empowerment is an influential concept in social work. The term may be used in a broad sense to describe activities that seek to give citizens a greater voice in services and decisions that affect them, the power to exercise their legal rights, or choice and control over resources and budgets (Solomon, 1976; Lee, 2001; Dalrymple and Burke, 2007; Thompson, 2016). More narrowly, it describes a way of doing social work, a practice model that places professional skills and resources at the disposal of citizens to support a process of change. Empowerment is not something social workers can do to or for people, since the starting point and endpoint are people's lived experience, capabilities and goals. There are some similarities to models of self-actualisation (Maslow, 1970), counselling (Rogers, 1973) and skilled help (Egan, 2013). Like practitioners in those fields, social workers who wish to work in an empowering way must cultivate the virtues of honesty and authenticity, develop skills in active and empathetic listening, build relationships with people, and remain open to questioning and challenge (Mackay, 2007). The main difference is that social workers who seek to practise empowerment may find it necessary to join and undertake political action in order to remove the 'power blocks' that stand in people's way (Solomon, 1976). This includes addressing aspects of social work that make people feel powerless and oppressed, such as complicated, bureaucratic procedures, use of professional jargon in correspondence and meetings, and Eurocentric assumptions about families and relationships. It also emphasises what Rose (1990) calls the 'collectivity principle' in work that aims to be socially transformative; in practice, this might consist of building coalitions and networks, undertaking group work and community work (Northen and Kurland, 2001), as well as advocacy.

Advocacy

Advocacy is often associated with empowerment in the social work literature (e.g. Rose, 1990; McKay, 2007) and is likewise seen as a way of promoting social justice and protecting human rights. Wilks (2012) cites the following definition:

> Advocacy involves a person(s), either a vulnerable individual or group or their agreed representative, effectively pressing their case with influential others, about situations which either affect them directly or, and more usually, trying to prevent proposed changes with, will leave them worse off. Both the intent and outcome of such advocacy should be to increase the individual's sense of power; help them to feel more confident, to become more assertive and gain increased choices. (Brandon, 1995, cited in Wilks, 2012: 2)

In these terms, advocacy is an activity that can be undertaken by anyone, including professionals but also volunteers and private citizens. Advocacy can also be a distinct role that requires specialist training and is differentiated from care or support, as with independent mental capacity advocates (Lee, 2007) or independent domestic violence advocates (Robinson and Payton, 2016). Advocates may also be 'non-instructed' if they are speaking on behalf of people who have significant barriers to communication or temporarily lack capacity to express a view about a proposed intervention or decision. In social work, there is a tradition of advocacy being used as a practice tool, including legal representation, citizens advice, community evelopment and activism, campaigning and self-help. Peer advocacy and self-advocacy have had a strong impact on the service user movement, contributing to important policy shifts in social care, such as de-institutionalisation and person-isation (Black and Rose, 2002). Echoing Mary Richmond's comments on social case work (see above), Brandon and Brandon (2001) distinguish between direct and indirect advocacy: the former being about representing citizens directly and the latter about supporting groups of citizens to represent their collective interests. These activities may operate on the micro level, such as helping someone to make a benefits application, or on the macro level, such as supporting a neighbourhood group to pressure the local authority into undertaking repairs on council property.

Advocacy may come into tension with other aspects of the social work role. For example, Wilks (2012) describes a scenario about a 66-year-old woman who is experiencing a crisis in their mental health. In this case, the social worker is also an Approved Mental Health Professional (AMHP), who is trained to apply elements of mental health law alongside medical practitioners. This is a sensitive and coercive area of practice, as under some circumstances people may be admitted to hospital for psychiatric assessment against their will. However, the social worker is able to present a social perspective on mental health care, communicate with the family using an interpreter, represent their views within a multi-disciplinary context, and use their procedural knowledge and understanding to negotiate a creative solution that can meet with everyone's agreement. Wilks contends that advocacy has an important role to play in such contexts, where the imbalance in power mean that people's voices are more likely go unheard.

Exercise 6.3: What does anti-discriminatory practice mean in practice?

....

Think about your own approach to social work, either on placement as a student or in your role as a qualified practitioner. How have you tried to implement the principles of ADP? Are there things you wish you could have done but were unable to, for whatever reason? What skills and resources would help you to practise in a more anti-discriminatory way? Some suggestions below for things to consider:

1   *Personal and professional development* – this includes training and education but also your own efforts to increase your awareness of power, intersectionality and privilege.

2   *Case preparation* – this relates to the work that you do before you meet with an individual or family, which again might include specific reading, reflection or discussion with colleagues, as well as a search for relevant research and evidence.

Continued

3   *Assessment* – for example, reviewing theoretical assumptions and assessment tools for cultural appropriateness, reflecting on unconscious bias, eliciting 'counter-stories' to the dominant narrative about someone's situation, or working with an independent advocate to engage someone in the assessment process.

4   *Decision-making* – this might include reflecting on unconscious bias, resisting 'group-think' during multi-agency meetings, or insisting on participatory forms of decision-making such as family group conferences.

5   *Supervision*, e.g. reflecting on a critical incident during a structured peer discussion, bringing an issue of concern to the team meeting, or challenging organisational priorities in relation to costs and budgets.

6   *Support* – this might include advocating for the individual or family, referring them to an independent advocate, supporting them to challenge unjust decisions (e.g. by housing or benefits agencies).

7   *Intervention* – e.g. making sure that care plans are produced jointly with service users and carers, address what matters to them, draw on a wider support network, and include sufficient funding to meet their needs.

Organisational Models

Models of social work practice are often considered in isolation from their organisational context. Yet, as Etzioni (1969) pointed out, social workers – like nurses and teachers – are largely dependent on their institutional setting and have less power and autonomy than some other professionals such as doctors and lawyers. Many social workers are employed by regional or local governments, where their roles are shaped by organisational functions, protocols and procedures, managerial controls, audit and quality assurance, inspections, and so on. Regional and local governments are important stakeholders in the profession and often influence the direction of practice. For example, many children's social care services in England have implemented 'Signs of Safety', a solution-focused approach to child protection work that originated in Australia and has been transferred to other countries (Baginsky *et al.*, 2017; Sheehan *et al.*, 2018). Another approach is to blend different models and tools into a 'practice framework', which can be tailored to the local context and organisational priorities. For example, one local authority in England has developed an Adult Social Care Practice Framework, as part of which social workers are trained in techniques such as motivational interviewing, family group conferencing and 'making safeguarding personal' (Coventry City Council, 2022).

From an inequalities perspective, organisational models are interesting because they incorporate professional practice within a framework for the design and delivery of services. After all, if the social work role is geared towards social justice ends within a framework that has organisational buy-in, there is a better chance that policies and resources will follow suit. For example, in 2015–16 the city of Leeds developed a 'Family Valued' framework for children's social care, funded by a government innovation programme (Mason *et al.*, 2017). The framework drew on principles of restorative practice to underpin a shift towards family group conferencing and locality-based delivery of Early Help and family support. In subsequent years, during a period of acute budgetary pressures on local authorities, maintaining investment in Early Help was justified by the continued reduction in the number and proportion of children accommodated in public care (Tariq, 2020), leading to similar models being adopted by other local authorities. Indeed, the cost-effectiveness of spending on prevention in children's social care has lately been corroborated by research (Webb *et al.*, 2022) and is becoming more widely accepted in policy reports (MacAlister, 2021). Organisational practice models can therefore play an important role in translating social goals into localised service delivery, and ensuring a better fit between professional and institutional priorities.

Conclusion

This chapter has explored social work's contribution to addressing inequalities, which mainly stems from professional values and expertise being deployed within a state-funded welfare system. As ever, there is the double-edged sword of power relations – the leverage that social workers have to make an impact on people's lives, often for the better, may also contribute to the surveillance and control of already oppressed and marginalised groups. Social workers are involved in highly contentious intrusions of the state into private and family life, including compulsory detention in psychiatric hospital and the removal of children into public care. Structural practice models are necessary to complement and critique the clinical approaches that underpin much psycho-social casework, case management and risk assessment. In recent decades, the dominance of neo-liberal approaches to welfare makes this an increasingly tricky balancing act, while in many countries the profession continues to struggle with the legacy of colonialism and paternalism. The next chapter will therefore turn to critical and radical approaches to social work, which seek to confront these challenges head-on.

References

Abbott, P. and Wallace, C. (eds) (1990) *The sociology of the caring professions*, Basingstoke, The Falmer Press.

Abels, S.L. (2001) *Understanding narrative therapy: A guidebook for the social worker*, London, Springer.

Ahmed, N., James, D., Tayabali, A. and Watson, M. (2022) 'Ethnicity and children's social care', London, Department for Education.

Avruch, D.O. and Shaia, W.E. (2022) 'Macro MI: Using motivational interviewing to address socially-engineered trauma', *Journal of Progressive Human Services*, **33**(2), pp. 176–204.

Baginsky, M., Moriarty, J., Manthorpe, J., Beecham, J. and Hickman, B. (2017) 'Evaluation of signs of safety in 10 pilots', London, Department for Education.

Barnett, P., Mackay, E., Matthews, H., Gate, R., Greenwood, H., Ariyo, K., Bhui, K., Halvorsrud, K., Pilling, S. and Smith, S. (2019) 'Ethnic variations in compulsory detention under the Mental Health Act: A systematic review and meta-analysis of international data', *The Lancet Psychiatry*, **6**(4), pp. 305–317.

Bernard, C. (2019) 'Recognizing and addressing child neglect in affluent families', *Child & Family Social Work*, **24**(2), pp. 340–347.

Bernard, C. and Harris, P. (2019) 'Serious case reviews: The lived experience of Black children', *Child & Family Social Work*, **24**(2), pp. 256–263.

Bhatti-Sinclair, K. and Price-Robertson, R. (2016) 'Evaluation: Serious case reviews and anti-racist practice', in Williams, C. and Graham, M. (eds), *Social work in a diverse society: Transformative practice with black and minority ethnic individuals and communities*, Bristol, Policy Press, pp. 217–228.

Black, B. and Rose, S. (2002) *Advocacy and empowerment: Mental health care in the community*, Abingdon, Routledge.

Braithwaite, J. (2002) *Restorative justice & responsive regulation*, Oxford, Oxford University.

Brandon, D. and Brandon, T. (2001) *Advocacy in social work*, London, BASW.

Bridges, K.M. (2016) 'The deserving poor, the undeserving poor, and class-based affirmative action', *Emory Law Journal*, **66**, p. 1049.

Cemlyn, S.J. and Nye, M. (2012) 'Asylum seeker young people: Social work value conflicts in negotiating age assessment in the UK', *International Social Work*, **55**(5), pp. 675–688.

Coventry City Council (2022) *Adult Social Care Practice Framework: Adults and their carers at the heart of practice*, Available online: www.coventry.gov.uk/adult-social-care-strategies-policies-plans/adult-social-care-practice-framework, Last Accessed: 12/12/2022.

Dalrymple, J. and Burke, B. (2007) *Anti-oppressive practice*, Buckingham, Open University Press.

Dancy, T.E. (2014) 'The adultification of Black boys: What educational settings can learn from Trayvon Martin', in Fasching-Varner, K.J., Reynolds, R.E., Albert, K.A. and Martin, L.L. (eds), *Trayvon Martin, race, and American justice*, Boston, Brill, pp. 49–55.

Davis, J. and Marsh, N. (2020) 'Boys to men: The cost of "adultification" in safeguarding responses to Black boys', *Critical and Radical Social Work*, **8**(2), pp. 255–259.

Department for Education (2022) *Children's social work workforce*, Available online: https://explore-education-statistics.service.gov.uk/find-statistics/children-s-social-work-workforce, Last Accessed: 26 May 2022.

Dettlaff, A.J. and Boyd, R. (2020) 'Racial disproportionality and disparities in the child welfare system: Why do they exist, and what can be done to address them?', *The ANNALS of the American academy of political and social science*, **692**(1), pp. 253–274.

Dettlaff, A.J., Rivaux, S.L., Baumann, D.J., Fluke, J.D., Rycraft, J.R. and James, J. (2011) 'Disentangling substantiation: The influence of race, income, and risk on the substantiation decision in child welfare', *Children and Youth Services Review*, **33**(9), pp. 1630–1637.

Dominelli, L. (2002) *Anti oppressive social work theory and practice*, Basingstoke, Palgrave Macmillan.

Egan, G. (2013) The skilled helper: A problem-management and opportunity-development approach to helping, Brooks/Cole, Belmont: CA.

Etzioni, A. (1969) *The semi-professions and their organisation*, New York, Free Press, Macmillan.

Evans, T. (2016) Professional discretion in welfare services: Beyond street-level bureaucracy, Abingdon, Routledge.

Fenton, J. (2019) Social work for lazy radicals: Relationship building, critical thinking and courage in practice, London, Red Globe Press.

Fjeldheim, S., Levin, I. and Engebretsen, E. (2015) 'The theoretical foundation of social case work', *Nordic Social Work Research*, **5**(sup1), pp. 42–55.

French, J. and Raven, B. (1968) 'The bases of social power', in Cartwright, D. and Zander, A. (eds), *Group dynamics: Research and theory*, New York, Harper and Row, pp. 259–269.

Gamble, J. (2022) 'Local Child Safeguarding Practice Review: Child Q', London, CHSCP.

Gamble, J. and McCallum, R. (2022) 'Local Child Safeguarding Practice Review: Child Q', London, The City & Hackney Safeguarding Children Partnership (CHSCP).

Given-Wilson, Z., Herlihy, J. and Hodes, M. (2016) 'Telling the story: A psychological review on assessing adolescents' asylum claims', *Canadian Psychology-Psychologie Canadienne*, **57**(4), pp. 265–273.

Goff, P.A., Jackson, M.C., Di Leone, B.A.L., Culotta, C.M. and DiTomasso, N.A. (2014) 'The essence of innocence: Consequences of dehumanizing Black children', *Journal of Personality and Social Psychology*, **106**(4), p. 526.

Goldacre, A. and Hood, R. (2022) 'Factors affecting the social gradient in children's social care', *The British Journal of Social Work*, Available online, https://doi.org/10.1093/bjsw/bcab255

Hasenfeld, Y. (1987) 'Power in social work practice', *Social Service Review*, **61**(3), pp. 469–483.

Hlass, L. (2019) 'The adultification of immigrant children', *Geography Immigration LJ*, **34**, p. 199.

Hood, R. (2015) 'A socio-technical critique of tiered services: Implications for interprofessional care', *Journal of Interprofessional Care*, **29**(1), pp. 8–12.

Illich, I., Zola, I.K., McKnight, J., Caplan, J. and Shaiken, H. (2005) *Disabling professions*, London, Marion Boyars.

Johnson, T.J. (1972) *Professions and power*, London, Macmillan.

Jones, R., Bhanbhro, S.M., Grant, R. and Hood, R. (2013) 'The definition and deployment of differential core professional competencies and characteristics in multiprofessional health and social care teams', *Health & Social Care in the Community*, **21**(1), pp. 47–58.

Keddell, E. (2022) 'Mechanisms of inequity: The impact of instrumental biases in the child protection system', *Societies*, **12**(3), p. 83.

Larson, M.S. (1977) *The rise of professionalism: A sociological analysis*, London, University of California Press.

Lee, J. (2001) *The empowerment approach to social work practice*, New York, Columbia University Press.

Lee, S. (2007) 'Making decisions. The Independent Mental Capacity Advocate (IMCA) service', London, Office of the Public Guardian.

MacAlister, J. (2021) 'Independent Review of Children's Social Care: Final Report', London, Independent Review of Children's Social Care.

Macdonald, K.M. (1995) *The sociology of the professions*, London, Sage.

Mackay, R. (2007) 'Empowerment and advocacy', in Lishman, J. (ed.), *Handbook for practice learning in social work and social care*, pp. 269–284.

Marsh, P. and Doel, M. (2005) *The task-centred book*, London, Routledge.

Maslow, A. (1970) *Motivation and personality* (2nd Edition), New York, Harper & Row.

Mason, P., Ferguson, H., Morris, K., Munton, T. and Sen, R. (2017) *Leeds Family Valued Evaluation Report*, London, Department for Education.

Maxwell, N. and Rees, A. (2019) 'Video interaction guidance: A return to traditional values and relationship-based practice?', *The British Journal of Social Work*, 49(6), pp. 1415–1433.

Mersky, J.P., Topitzes, J. and Britz, L. (2019) 'Promoting evidence-based, trauma-informed social work practice', *Journal of Social Work Education*, 55(4), pp. 645–657.

Molloy, J.K., Keyes, T.S., Wahlert, H. and Riquino, M.R. (2021) 'An exploratory integrative review of restorative justice and social work: Untapped potential for pursuing social justice', *Journal of Social Work Education*, pp. 1–16.

Morgan-Mullane, A. (2018) 'Trauma focused cognitive behavioral therapy with children of incarcerated parents', *Clinical Social Work Journal*, 46(3), pp. 200–209.

Northen, H. and Kurland, R. (2001) *Social work with groups*, New York, Columbia University Press.

Richmond, M. (1922) *What is social case work? An introductory description*, New York, Russell Sage Foundation.

Rivaux, S.L., James, J., Wittenstrom, K., Baumann, D., Sheets, J., Henry, J. and Jeffries, V. (2008) 'The intersection of race, poverty, and risk', *Child Welfare*, 87(2), pp. 151–168.

Roberts, A.R. (2005) Crisis intervention handbook: Assessment, treatment, and research, Oxford, Oxford University Press.

Robinson, A. and Payton, J. (2016) 'Independent advocacy and multi-agency responses to domestic violence', in Hilder, S. and Bettinson, V. (eds), *Domestic violence: Interdisciplinary perspectives on protection, prevention and intervention*, London, Palgrave Macmillan UK, pp. 249–271.

Rogers, C. (1973) 'The interpersonal relationship: The core of guidance', in Maslowski, R. and Morgan, L. (eds), *Interpersonal growth and self actualization in groups*, New York, Arno Press, pp. 176–189.

Rose, S.M. (1990) 'Advocacy/empowerment: An approach to clinical practice for social work', *Journal of Sociology and Social Welfare*, 17, p. 41.

Ruch, G., Turney, D. and Ward, A. (eds) (2010) *Relationship-based social work: Getting to the heart of practice*, London, Jessica Kingsley.

aia, W.E., Avruch, D.O., Green, K. and Godsey, G.M. (2019) 'Socially-engineered trauma and a new social work pedagogy: Socioeducation as a critical foundation of social work practice', *Smith College Studies in Social Work*, **89**(3–4), pp. 238–263.

eehan, L., O'Donnell, C., Brand, S., Forrester, D., Addis, S., El-Banna, A., Kemp, A. and Nurmatov, U. (2018) 'Signs of safety: findings from a mixed methods systematic review focused on reducing the need for children to be in care', Cardiff, Cardiff University.

ills for Care (2022) *Headline social worker information: Social workers employed by local authorities in the adult social care sector*, Available online: www. skillsforcare.org.uk/adult-social-care-workforce-data/Workforce-intelligence/ publications/Topics/Social-work/headline-social-work-information.aspx, Last Accessed: 26 May 2022.

nith, R. (2008) *Social work and power*, Basingstoke, Palgrave Macmillan.

cial Work England (2020) *Professional Standards*, Available online: https://www. socialworkengland.org.uk/media/1640/1227_socialworkengland_standards_prof_ standards_final-aw.pdf, Last Accessed: 26/02/2023.

lomon, B. (1976) *Black empowerment: Social work in oppressed communities*, New York, Columbia University Press.

arrow, M. (2008) *The character of harms: Operational challenges in control*, Cambridge, Cambridge University Press.

rand, S. and Lindsay, G. (2009) 'Evidence of ethnic disproportionality in special education in an English population', *The Journal of Special Education*, **43**(3), pp. 174–190.

uart, P.H. (2019) *Social work profession: History*, NASW Press and Oxford University Press.

riq, S. (2020) 'Report of the Director of Children and Families', Leeds, Leeds City Council.

hompson, N. (2012) 'Anti-discriminatory practice: Equality, diversity and social justice', Basingstoke, Palgrave Macmillan.

rnell, A. and Edwards, S. (1999) 'Signs of safety: A solution oriented approach to child protection casework, London, WW Norton.

ebb, C., Bennett, D., Bywaters, P. and Hood, R. (2022) 'Impact of investing in prevention on demand for statutory children's social care', London, NCB.

ilding, P. (1982) *Professional power and social welfare*, Abingdon, Routledge.

ilks, T. (2012) *Advocacy and social work practice*, Maidenhead, Open University Press.

itz, A. (1992) *Professions and patriarchy*, London, Routledge.

ahav, R. and Sharlin, S.A. (2002) 'Blame and family conflict: Symptomatic children as scapegoats', *Child & Family Social Work*, 7(2), pp. 91–98.

7
Radical and Critical Social Work

Chapter overview

....

This chapter examines the role of critical and radical social work in addressing inequality. These approaches use a structural analysis of social problems to understand how services can be aligned with emancipatory social justice aims. The profession's radical core is traced from progressive elements of the 19th-century Settlement movement to social work's response to the social upheavals of the post-war period. The chapter then follows distinctive strands of radicalism, starting with Marxist and socialist perspectives and proceeding to examine a range of critical approaches to practice: feminist social work, anti-racist social work, Indigenous social work, the social model of disability, and LGBTQ+ affirmative social work. Intersectionality is highlighted as a key conceptual framework for placing the concerns of multiply marginalised groups and identities at the centre of an inequalities agenda. Possibilities for reform and transformation of services in the neo-liberal context of contemporary welfare systems are examined with reference to themes such as interest convergence, postcolonialism and allyship.

Introduction

The last chapter examined social work's role in addressing social inequalitie within contemporary welfare systems. Questions were raised about the abilit of social workers to implement structural models of practice, including ant discriminatory and anti-oppressive approaches, in an institutional context dom nated by individualistic approaches to social problems (see Chapter 5). Radica and critical approaches, which are the subject of this chapter, address thes questions by stepping outside of the status quo and reimagining social wor through the vision of a transformed society. For example, the social model c disability argues for the removal of disabling barriers that undermine people' apabilities (see Chapter 1); this certainly includes practical help with everyday living but goes beyond this to envisage a social environment in which people with impairments can thrive and lead fulfilled lives. Such approaches apply a distinct analysis to the systemic basis of oppression, seeking ways to uproot[1] the causes of injustice in order to create a fairer society. Radical theories and methods are often linked to emancipatory social movements, which are global in their scope and influence; they include the disability movement, the women's liberation movement, the civil rights movement, and lesbian and gay movements. Activists inspired by these movements have often been in the vanguard of new forms of social welfare and helped to shape the direction of social work; for example, the women's liberation movement was instrumental in establishing women's refuges and drawing attention to the social problem of male violence against women (Rose, 1985).

The radical tradition in social work has developed and is understood in different ways across the world. For example, the terms 'critical' or 'structural' social work may be more familiar to practitioners in the United States, Canada and Australia, where there has also been a focus on anti-oppressive practice. In some countries, the cultural and historical legacies of conquest, colonialism and slavery have played a central role in shaping radical approaches, whereas in others addressing social divisions based around class, caste or gender have been more prominent. The environmental movement has been gaining more recognition within social work, particularly in countries affected by climate change (Dominelli, 2018). The diversity of radical and critical social work means that concerns and priorities may not always align. For example, issues of identity may be more important in some strands of radical social work, whereas socio-economic issues may predominate in others. Some people find that their voices and experiences are overlooked and marginalised within movements that have traditionally been associated with a particular group or perspective. Intersectional frameworks, which have been developed by Black feminist and critical race scholars, can help to analyse and work through some of these tensions and debates.

Pause and reflect

....

What does radicalism mean to you? Are you a member of a trade union, activist group or social movement? Have you ever taken part in social actions such as campaigns, lobbying, protests, marches, strikes, 'sit-ins', or media activism? If so, what was the purpose of the action and was there a connection to inequality? If not, what is your opinion of this type of activity and the people involved?

---

[1] The word 'radical' stems from the old Latin word 'radix', meaning root.

Social Work's Radical Core

This section will argue – perhaps in contrast to the impression given in the previous chapter – that social work does have a core of radicalism. While radical social work tends to be associated with a strand of critique that emerged in the 1970s, its roots go back to the profession's origins in the newly industrialising cities of Europe and America in the 19th century. A key question – never to be satisfactorily resolved – was whether the social problems that emerged with modernity should be addressed by reforming individuals to fit in with society, or by reforming society. Despite being drawn constantly towards the former, social work has refused to abandon entirely the idea of social change as the foundation for individual betterment. It has been suggested that the Settlement movement of the 1880s (see Chapter 6) represented a more progressive version of social work in contrast to the paternalist and judgemental approach of the COS (Mullaly 1997; Powell, 2001). A key difference was that Settlement houses were located within poor urban communities, which meant that middle-class volunteers lived and worked alongside people from more disadvantaged backgrounds. As well as providing services such as education and healthcare, the movement also advocated for social reforms to alleviate poverty and improve working conditions. In the United States, it was actively involved in organising strikes and campaigning on social issues such as child labour (Reisch and Andrews, 2014). Nonetheless, as Ferguson and Woodward (2009) point out, there were limits to the radicalism of the Settlement movement, particularly in Britain, where it increasingly steered away from political action. The shift towards professionalisation reinforced this tendency and social work in the early and mid-20th century became largely synonymous with psycho-social casework and the core activities of assessment and intervention.

The profession went through a major change in the 1970s, when a concerted challenge arose to clinical and psychodynamic models of practice. There were various reasons for this: the persistence of chronic poverty and deprivation in the midst of economic growth and expansion of the welfare state, the limitations of casework in addressing structural problems, the spread of trade unionism in social work departments, the influence of 1960s counterculture and the waves of popular protest that spread throughout the world towards the end of that decade. Not least, there was the inspiration provided by social movements such as feminism, anti-colonialism, and the civil rights movement. New ideas and forms of practice influenced by these movements, as well as radical educationalists such as Paolo Freire, or the 'anti-psychiatrist' R.D. Laing, were developed by social workers and loosely grouped under the rubric of radical social work (Bailey and Brake, 1975). Their aim was not to supplant more established forms of practice but rather to align them with collective and political approaches that were prepared to challenge the status quo. Ferguson and

Woodward (2009) argue that the new radicalism influenced social work theory and practice in three main ways:

• Group work and community work became a stronger component of training and education, as did teaching on sociological themes and knowledge of benefits payments and other aspects of the welfare system.
• Collective approaches, including group work, became more embedded in professional practice, with some local authorities opting to invest in community workers and enabling statutory social workers to undertake and support projects in the community alongside more conventional casework activity.
• There was a transformation in the profession's value base, as the core principles of anti-oppressive and anti-discriminatory practice became widely accepted and to some extent reflected in regulatory standards and expectations.

Since the 1980s, the encroachment of neo-liberal approaches to social work (see Chapter 5) have arguably eroded some of these achievements. In the UK, the exposure of social work students to group and community work has arguably declined in line with an increasing emphasis on statutory placements, although they remain an important part of social work training in other jurisdictions. Meanwhile, the evolution of social work's value base has probably had more effect on how social workers think about their work than on what kind of work they do. There are questions about how to move beyond the terminology of equality, diversity and inclusion when it comes to developing a social justice agenda in social work training and education (Lerner and Fulambarker, 2018). Intersectionality has emerged as the principal framework for examining power and inequality (Bernard, 2021), spurring a re-evaluation of theory and practice within the different strands of radical and critical social work. In what follows, we briefly examine some of these strands, each associated with specific social movements and a distinctive structural (and in some cases post-structural) analysis of the world.

Exercise 7.1: Politics in social work

Many social workers consider themselves to be on the left of the political spectrum, although this is by no means always the case. Some social workers may view strong political or ideological convictions, including religious beliefs, as irrelevant or even problematic, for example because they are potential sources of bias or prejudicial attitudes. However, political convictions often underpin critical and radical approaches to social work. It is therefore worth considering your own political views

Continued

and the extent to which you see them as relevant to your work. The following exercise is designed to help you explore these questions.

1   Examine your own political leanings by going to the political compass website (www.politicalcompass.org) and taking their informal 'test' – a series of propositions designed to identify roughly where you stand politically along two scales: an economic scale (left vs right), and a social scale (authoritarian vs libertarian).
2   Reflect on the results – do they represent what you consider to be your political stance? What is inaccurate or missing? What terms would you use to describe your political views?
3   Consider whether and how your political stance (in your own terms) affects the following:

   a.   Your reasons for becoming a social worker.
   b.   How you understand the problems, needs and strengths of the individuals and families you work with.
   c.   The kind of support and interventions you want to put in place to help people and reduce risks to their safety and wellbeing.
   d.   Your feelings (positive or negative) about the organisation you work for and the job you do.

Marxist and Socialist Social Work

The radical turn of the 1970s, particularly in the UK, was heavily influenced by Marxist and socialist perspectives. Marxism is distinguished by its analysis of class conflict within capitalist societies, which stems from inequalities in ownership of the 'means of production', i.e. the resources and facilities needed to produce goods and services. Marxists seek to achieve a transition away from capitalism, in which an economically dominant class controls the resources necessary for human flourishing and exploits everyone else, towards socialism, in which resources are collectively owned and fairly allocated so that everyone has a chance to flourish. However, the relationship between Marxism and socialism is a complicated one. The latter may also be understood in a broader (i.e. non-Marxist) sense to denote a range of policies pursued by governments on the 'left' of the political spectrum, such as raising taxes to fund a generous welfare state, placing utilities and transport infrastructure in public ownership, and giving legal recognition to trade unions and grassroots political organisations. Moreover, there is a longstanding tradition of libertarian socialism, usually known as anarchism, which offers a critique of centralised political authority, including the powerful state apparatus associated with Marxist regimes, and argues instead for the radical democratisation of institutions at all levels of society. To add to the confusion, a broadly socialist policy platform may be termed 'liberal' in the United States, where libertarianism is unfortunately associated with ultra-conservative right-wing ideas! Overall, it is important to remember that socialist theory takes many forms, having influenced and been influenced by other social movements, including feminism, environmentalism and anti-racism.

As Vickers (2019) points out, there is a distinction between Marxist approaches to social work within capitalist societies and those within socialist societies. In the former, there is a tension between meeting people's immediate needs or support and working towards longer-term social change. Social workers within state welfare systems must find ways to reconcile these contradictory aspects of their professional role, for example by helping people to organise to pursue their collective interests at the same time as negotiating resources for individually tailored support. In this respect, Lavalette (2019) refers to 'popular social work', in the sense of an engagement with popular movements for social justice, being necessary to innovate and revitalise a profession that might otherwise become drawn into a pathologising and controlling function within the capitalist state. Other insights are provided by the role of social work, or its equivalent, in countries whose political and economic order is (or was) based on socialist principles, albeit often moderated by market reforms since the 1980s. Vickers (2019) draws on international literature to describe some of these programmes and initiatives. In communist China, for example, Workers' Cultural Palaces provided a wide range of activities, education and training to workers, while in Vietnam, the revolutionary government integrated the local 'Phöôøng' into its welfare system, a pre-colonial 'cooperative organisation where people helped each other to build houses, take care of the weak and the sick and bury the dead' (Oanh, 2002; cited in Vickers, 2019: 11). In Cuba, social work roles were created as part of community health initiatives but also contributed to efforts to increase democratic participation. For example, Strug (2006, cited in Vickers, 2019: 11) describes 'empirical social workers', activists who 'facilitated the entry of women into the labor market, promoted their economic, political and social involvement with the Revolution, and organised community members for participation in major educational and public health initiatives'.

In relation to inequality, Marxist analysis insists on the importance of class struggle within a material (economic and political) account of society under capitalism. From this standpoint, Coburn (2004) and Scambler (2012) take issue with some of the health inequalities literature discussed in Chapter 3, which they see as overlooking the political and structural causes of social gradients in health and wellbeing in favour of a psycho-social analysis of stress, stigma and shame[2].

Scambler (2009) advances an alternative sociological explanation for health inequalities, foregrounding the strategic decision-making of capitalist elites, which he terms the 'Greedy Bastards Hypothesis'.

While the latter has found ready acceptance within social work, being well aligned with the conventions of psycho-social casework, analysis from a Marxist perspective is inclined to be sceptical about discussions of inequality that appear disinterested in politics, including those stemming from epidemiological and system theories. Marxists also prefer material and economic explanations to questions of culture and identity, which is perhaps one reason why the social work literature on anti-discriminatory and anti-oppressive practice has been somewhat reluctant to engage with Marxist theory, preferring to treat class, not as the major structuring principle of capitalist society, but rather as one of many different aspects of identity, oppression and social stratification. Indeed, Thompson (2016) chooses to omit class entirely from his introduction to ADP, arguing that it has been given sufficient attention elsewhere. Since the 1970s, interest in Marxist theories of class conflict has perhaps waned in mainstream social work, although they arguably continue to influence contemporary debates about poverty, the cost of living and health and welfare inequalities.

Case Study 7.1: Priscilla, Steven, Jake and Hayley

Priscilla is a 29-year-old woman from a Black British African background, and the mother of two boys and a girl: Steven (8), Jake (5) and Hayley (3). Priscilla is separated from the children's father, Joseph (35), who is White British and lives in the same part of East London. Joseph was abusive and violent towards Priscilla and has a restraining order that requires him to stay away from her home and refrain from contacting her. The family were living in a privately rented flat but were evicted with two weeks' notice by the landlord, who is planning to refurbish the flat in order to charge higher rent. The council has a shortage of social housing and offered Priscilla emergency accommodation twenty miles away in another London borough. However, she did not want to move there as it was too far to commute to her job as a cleaner and to take her children to school. The council then found her to be intentionally homeless and called the police when she refused to leave the housing office. The police referred Priscilla to the children's social care team, where a social worker, Karin, carried out multi-agency safeguarding checks and met with the family. Following these actions, Priscilla was offered emergency accommodation locally. She has been told that the waiting list for social housing in the area is over twenty years, but her earnings are not enough to cover private rental costs. She has been offered a move to Birmingham, which is 130 miles away from London and where she has no connections. Priscilla has told Karin that she is feeling depressed and is struggling to care for her children in the cramped single room in which the family is currently living. Steven has told Karin that he cannot sleep properly and is refusing to go to school, saying he cannot concentrate in class and that he is worried about his mother. Jake says that at the weekend they saw his father in the street near where they live, although he did not speak to them.

Case Study 7.2: A Marxist and socialist perspective

A conventional case formulation, particularly within child welfare services, might focus on the risks to family members caused by de-facto homelessness and its knock-on effects on their physical and psychological welfare, including possible contact with an abusive ex-partner. Critical and radical approaches consider these risks in the context of multiple structural factors, which interact uniquely for every individual. A Marxist or socialist perspective would pay particular attention to Priscilla's class identity and its intersection with gender, race and ethnicity. Social factors such as low pay, gentrification and the marketisation of social housing would be considered relevant to the family's predicament, arguably an unjust consequence of economic forces that concentrate wealth and income among property-owning classes and prioritise the maximisation of profits above meeting people's basic needs for shelter and security. The local authority's enforcement of the eviction, refusal to provide the family with alternative accommodation, and efforts to move them somewhere they have no connections or support, also reflect the tendency for housing policy in places like London to favour the rich and cause hardship for those who are less well-off. For the social worker there is a requirement to engage in culturally competent practice to engage with Priscilla as a Black, working-class woman with African heritage, and with her children as dual-heritage children from a working-class background. This includes sensitivity to the way in which institutional misogyny, racism and unconscious bias may manifest themselves in the approach taken by services, e.g. to Priscilla's efforts to advocate for her family in the housing office, or to Steven's refusal to attend school. Alongside trauma-informed responses to addressing individual wellbeing and safety, the social worker might consider ways to put pressure on the council to rehouse the family locally, for example by contacting a local activist group that campaigns on behalf of those affected by eviction and lack of affordable housing[3]. More broadly, the family's situation could prompt the social worker to argue within her organisation for preventative work and community outreach to identify and support families struggling with rent, food and fuel poverty.

Points to consider:

1 In what other ways might this case study be examined from a Marxist or socialist perspective?
2 How likely do you think it is that the social worker would include this type of analysis in her assessment or report? What might encourage or hinder her from doing so?
3 Is an activist role – e.g. encouraging someone to challenge a housing department decision when you work for another part of the council – compatible with a professional role?

---

3   This part of the case study was suggested by the work of Focus E15, a campaign organisation based in Stratford, London (see Hardy and Gillespie, 2016).

Feminist Social Work

Social work has a long and complex association with feminism. Beyond the obvious fact that women have always been at the heart of social work, both as providers and recipients of services, the profession's development since the 19th century has been strongly influenced by feminist theory and practice. The role of changing feminism(s) is evident in particular areas of practice, such as child and family social work, but also in areas of shared concern: the importance of identity, the value of critical reflection, and recognition of the political dimension of interpersonal relationships and family dynamics. Debates and controversies among feminists have been mirrored in social work, such as how to engage male perpetrators of violence against women, or to address the complexity of gendered identity. From a critical perspective, Orme (2003) argued that feminist social work should embrace postmodern ideas about power and oppression which have undermined simplistic constructions of femininity and masculinity. In similar vein, Phillips and Cree (2014) point to the advent of a 'fourth wave' of feminism, rooted in online discourses (and conflicts) around inclusivity and positionality; they approach the dilemma of how to preserve the emancipatory project of feminism in the context of increasing gender diversity, including genderqueer and non-binary perspectives (see also Monro, 2019). Meanwhile, Black feminist approaches rooted in critical race theory have directed social workers to think about interlocking categories of identity, oppression and privilege, rather than viewing women's experiences via a single analytical lens.

From an inequalities perspective, critical feminism involves a move away from essentialist and universalising positions on gender while continuing to mobilise against patriarchal power structures that enable men to oppress women. This raises some challenging questions for social work in its organisational context. For example, how are services that ostensibly work with people from all genders, such as child protection or adult social care, to understand and address the fact that they deal predominantly with women, or (in some jurisdictions) disproportionately with women from racialised and minoritised groups? Alternatively, how are specialist services that are intentionally geared towards women, such as mother and baby units, or refuges for female survivors of domestic abuse, to understand and address the differences between women from different class and ethnic backgrounds, or between cisgender and transgender women? Such questions demand a flexible and innovative approach to provision, not a one-size-fits-all approach. Another issue is the importance of material considerations in relation to questions of culture, language and difference. Material explanations point to the need to raise consciousness, build coalitions, and organise collective responses to patriarchal structures. Cultural and linguistic explanations point to the need to challenge oppressive stereotypes and generate new frameworks of understanding to underpin social transformation. For example, Moya Bailey and

Trudy (2018) discuss their development of misogynoir as a theory and language to describe the anti-Black racist misogyny that Black women experience, particularly in popular culture and digital spaces. While material and socio-cultural approaches are complementary, they may be difficult to address within a single service or intervention.

The complex interplay between feminism and social work is illustrated by the field of domestic abuse and child protection, in which feminist theory and practice have played an important role. For example, the Duluth model is a well-known framework for understanding and addressing male abuse and violence towards women. It conceptualises intimate partner violence as a range of ways, including but not limited to physical aggression, in which men seek to establish power and control over women (Snead *et al.*, 2018). The model has been influential in risk assessment as well as in social work interventions with fathers who are abusive towards their partners and/or the mothers of their children (Scott *et al.*, 2021). At the same time, research drawing on a feminist perspective has highlighted the tendency of child protection systems to hold mothers responsible for their children's safety, showing that for women suffering abuse and violence in an intimate relationship, obtaining help and support often comes at the cost of surveillance, stigma and dislocation (Hester, 2011; Ferguson *et al.*, 2019; Wild, 2022). Studies have also found that survivors of domestic abuse are disproportionately likely to include women with disabilities, younger women, and women living in poverty (Nixon and Humphreys, 2010; Skafida *et al.*, 2022). There has been longstanding concern about the absence of fathers from child welfare practice in relation to domestic abuse (Featherstone and Peckover, 2007; Nygren *et al.*, 2019), while preventative and rehabilitative work to stop male violence against women has been problematic in various ways (Flood, 2015). Such findings highlight the need for intersectional approaches that recognise and address the multiple structural inequalities impacting on people's circumstances, as well as their readiness to engage with services.

Case Study 7.3: A feminist perspective

From a feminist perspective, the risks faced by Priscilla and her family are rooted in patriarchal social structures that are also characterised by deep divisions along the lines of class, race and ethnicity. Contributing factors include the social problem of male abuse and violence towards women, the feminisation of poverty, as well as gendered inequalities in employment, income and caring responsibilities. Also relevant is the problematic tendency of child welfare agencies to make mothers who suffer domestic abuse accountable for their children's safety, even though these mothers

Continued

are often multiply disadvantaged, while failing to challenge and engage with men who harm. Black female survivors of domestic abuse may find particular difficulties in accessing support, for example because of a lack of appropriate safe spaces, cultural stereotypes around strength and resilience, or experience of institutional racism within the police and criminal justice system. Culturally competent practice will therefore require careful reflection on all these aspects of identity and experience, in order to work in partnership with Priscilla and her children. Adopting a holistic and trauma-informed approach assessment and intervention may require the social worker to challenge not only overly punitive risk-based responses but also overly transactional responses focused purely on resolving the family's housing issue. More broadly, the family's situation could prompt the social worker to advocate within her organisation to review services for Black women and women from other minoritised groups who suffer domestic abuse, as well as intervention and support offered to fathers who harm their partners. With that in mind, there is also a need to consider differences within any ethnic or racialised group. Family structures and relationships are usually considered from a psycho-social lens, but they are also political in the sense of reflecting intergenerational impact of phenomena such as imperialism and colonialism.

Anti-racist Social Work

Bonnett (2005: 3) suggests that a minimal definition of anti-racism is that 'it refers to those forms of thought and/or practice that seek to confront eradicate and/or ameliorate racism'. Different forms of anti-racism may differ in terms of how they define racism and underlying concepts such as race, ethnicity, racialisation and minoritisation (see Chapter 2 for a brief discussion of these terms). The murder of George Floyd in 2020 and the resulting profile of the Black Lives Matter movement, along with inequalities exposed by the global Covid-19 pandemic, put a spotlight on problems surrounding race and racism in the profession of social work (Cane and Tedam, 2022). Given that such issues long predated the events of 2020, they also highlighted a general lack of anti-racism knowledge and skills within the profession. Various reasons for this deficit have been proposed. In educational settings, anti-racist practice seems to have been subsumed within the general category of anti-oppressive or anti-discriminatory practice, diluting the explicit focus on racism that arose from the civil rights movement and post-war struggles against racism and colonialism in the Global North. The UK social work standards, for example, refer to discrimination and social justice but make no mention of racism. Williams and Bernard (2018) also point to the influence of neo-liberalism, which has sought to promote a 'neo-assimilationalist language of diversity and difference' that results in the experiences of Black people being minimised and overlooked. Meritocratic arguments for a classless society see Chapter 1) have also been extended to suggest we live in a 'post-race' society, enabling political leaders to deny the continued existence and impact of institutional racism. Political and media hostility to critical race theory and intersectionality, a regular feature of the so-called 'culture wars', may also have constrained the use of these theoretical positions to underwrite social work programmes and training courses (McCoy, 2020; Gates *et al.*, 2021; Pilkington, 2021). It has also limited critical analysis of Whiteness, particularly in local contexts perceived as 'predominantly White', in which the salience of race and ethnicity is often overlooked (Williams and Parrott, 2014). These (and many other) barriers make it harder for students and practitioners from minoritised groups to find their place in the profession, while also increasing the likelihood of racial bias in social work assessment and intervention.

In relation to inequalities, the difficulties attending anti-racist practice in social work point to an uphill struggle; first to prevent social work from unwittingly contributing to racism in society, and second to develop forms of social work that could help make society less racist. It seems reasonable to assume that progress must be made on the first objective before embarking on the second. Yet the evidence of significant racial and ethnic inequalities in provision (see Chapter 3), the continuing legacy of imperialism and colonialism (Chapter 4), and inequities associated with social work's regulatory role in the welfare state (Chapter 5), suggests that progress is uneven. It is therefore unsurprising that anti-racist social work has often been concerned with the foundations of anti-racist practice, such as decolonising education and training, awareness of unconscious bias and assumptions, challenging normative Whiteness and privilege, developing cultural competence, and ensuring greater diversity and representativeness among the workforce (including in management positions and 'fast-track' qualifying routes) (Cane, 2021; Cane and Tedam, 2022). Until these foundations are firmly established, it will be harder for social work to pursue a truly transformative role.

Critical Race Theory (CRT) offers a set of core themes that are relevant to the development of anti-racist social work (Delgado and Stefancic, 2023). For example, the theory of interest convergence (see Chapter 2) holds that members of the 'majority' group will only take an interest in the welfare of racialised or minoritised groups when doing so is to their own political, economic, or psychological benefit. Similar observations have been made elsewhere in the political history of equality and human rights. For example, social historians have suggested that advances in female suffrage in the UK owed much to women's vital role in the country's war economy during the First World War (Hicks, 2013), and that the introduction of health insurance at the start of the 20th century had less to do with altruism than with concerns about the poor health of conscripts fighting in the Boer War (Cutler and Johnson, 2004). Interest convergence holds that political systems in countries such as the US and UK, which are dominated by powerful white elites, are unlikely to support an equalities agenda unless doing so serves the economic and financial interests of those elites (see Chapter 5). At the same time, another core theme of CRT is the critique of liberalism and its reliance on basic legal rights and equal treatment under the law; these principles, it is suggested, are sufficient only to prevent the most obvious and egregious forms of discrimination (see also Arvin *et al.*, 2013, for a critique from an Indigenous feminist perspective).

CRT has important implications for social work. It predicts that concrete advances in anti-racist practice are likely to meet with a backlash or gradual erosion of meaningful gains – perhaps under cover of meritocratic arguments or neo-liberal concerns with efficiency and effectiveness. Such tendencies might suggest that social work should orient itself more strongly towards equality of outcome rather than equality of opportunity (see Chapter 1). Another implication is that social workers might need to work directly with (and for) marginalised groups to create alternative welfare institutions – arguably the strategy pursued by some First Nations in settler colonial societies (see below). Delgado and Stefanic (2023) also examine the tension between materialist and idealist approaches to anti-racist practice, with the former focusing on the distribution of material benefits in society, and the latter highlighting the importance of culture, language and identity. The debate is relevant to social workers, who might actively engage in mobilising and organising collective action to improve people's political and socio-economic power, while also seeking to ensure that they are culturally competent, representative of the communities they serve, and sensitive to the nuances of intersecting identities when undertaking assessments and interventions. In this respect, CRT points to the risk that welfare institutions will co-opt elements of anti-racist practice that represent incremental progress but that do not present an existential threat to the institution itself. A dilemma for anti-racist practitioners is that fundamental change might require the kind of rupture and transformation that cannot easily be accommodated within a professional context.

Case Study 7.4: An anti-racist perspective

....

An anti-racist perspective would acknowledge the impact of historical, structural and institutional racism on the problems experienced by the family, as well as their experience of and treatment by professionals and institutions. Relevant to the former are racial and ethnic inequalities in employment, income, housing, physical and mental health. An intersectional approach would not consider these factors in isolation but see them as connected to multiple, overlapping and unequal power relations based on gender, age, ability, sexuality, class, and other markers of identity. These factors affect how social problems are understood and constructed by professional agencies, including discriminatory attitudes that make it less likely for Black service users

Continued

to be seen as vulnerable or traumatised and as needing support, and more likely for them to be perceived as angry and aggressive, or alternatively as robust, resilient or 'adultified'. At the same time, the experience of anti-Black racism is complex and should not be generalised across Black ethnic and cultural groups, nor assumed to transfer straightforwardly to other racialised or minoritised groups. In Priscilla's case, such biases might have played a part in how services responded to her distress in the housing office, or might have influenced how education welfare services choose to respond to Jake's school non-attendance. A cultural humility framework (Gottlieb, 2021) would ask us to de-centre our own knowledge as part of our commitment to an ongoing process of self-awareness and inquiry, a stance of being open and teachable, and being vigilant to power imbalances and the impact of social systems on people's lived experience. Social workers can support their assessment and decision-making by drawing on a debiasing framework such as the BRAC2eD model set out by Cane (2023) in relation to adoption work. A trauma-informed approach would also seek to position the family history and prior experience of abuse and violence in the context of intersectional inequalities, the legacy of racism and colonialism not only on families over generations but also on the institutional approach taken by services, so that power differentials are not unwittingly reproduced in professional interactions. The involvement of specialist agencies with a deep understanding of the intersectionality of racism and gender-based violence may be helpful and necessary in ensuring such support[4]. More broadly, the experience of Priscilla and her family should alert all the services involved – including housing, police and child welfare agencies – of the specialist resources, training and provision required to respond appropriately to such situations and prevent their recurrence. At the same time, there is a need to connect culturally specific services to the rest of the social care system, both to avoid creating further marginalisation and isolation on an institutional level but also to ensure that learning is shared and anti-racist practice is adopted within mainstream services. From a CRT perspective, there is a risk that social care services will struggle to uphold basic rights for families from racialised and minoritised groups when doing so would conflict with the capitalist interests of mainly White elites.

Indigenous Social Work

According to Gray and Coates (2010), there are two strands of literature concerning Indigenous social work, both connected to regions with a history of colonisation. One strand relates to countries in the Global South, including Africa, Asia and South America and the South Pacific (Mafile'o and Vakalahi, 2018) – whereas the other relates to settler colonial contexts in the Global North, such as the USA,

---

4   Two examples of organisations in London who offer this kind of support are Southall Black Sisters (https://southallblacksisters.org.uk/) and Sistah Space (https://www.sistahspace.org/).

Canada and Australia, where it is 'associated primarily with professional education and practice relating to Aboriginal or First Nations Peoples' (Gray and Coates, 2010: 615). Similar dynamics relating to the *bentude* (native and local) and *bentuhuade* (imported and adapted) have pertained in China, albeit refracted through a rather different political and ideological context (Yan and Tsang, 2008). Common features include an insistence on culturally specific knowledges and practices, resistance to the importing of Eurocentric models and approaches, and calls to redress the injustices of colonisation. Such changes require political mobilisation and support, as well as the development of indigenous research and scholarship. While being culturally specific, Indigenous social work can also lead to cross-cultural applications; for example, family group conferences, which originated in the Maori culture of Aotearoa New Zealand, have been adopted by child welfare systems in many countries across the world (Frost *et al.*, 2014; Thørnblad *et al.*, 2016; Burford, 2017).

In Canada, efforts to develop and implement Indigenous approaches to social work have involved:

- Acknowledgement of the history and continuing impact of colonisation, social work's contribution to both, and the need to engage wholeheartedly with truth and reconciliation processes (Baskin and Sinclair, 2015; Yee *et al.*, 2015; Choate *et al.*, 2022).
- Decolonisation of social work education and training (Choate *et al.*, 2022), much of which is based on Eurocentric values and understandings and is therefore inappropriate for working with Indigenous peoples. This includes frameworks such as attachment theory, which is commonly taught as being universally applicable and used to underpin social work interventions viewed as culturally insensitive and oppressive by Indigenous peoples, such as the removal of children into the care system and adoption outside of their culture.
- Incorporation of Indigenous world knowledge into teaching and learning, including the importance of family and community, the collective and temporal dimension to health and wellbeing, the interconnectedness between people and the world around them, and the positive role of spirituality and ancestral knowledge.
- Establishing separate services that are under Indigenous control, not only in First Nations communities but also in urban centres. Such services require sufficient resources and funding, culturally appropriate accountability standards, and strong relationships between Indigenous and mainstream social services so as not to further marginalise minoritised groups from the wider social care system.
- Addressing barriers to university and social work qualification for Indigenous practitioners, including lack of funding, distance to travel, family and caring responsibilities, as well as the Eurocentrism of programmes and courses.

Ensuring that services take up the knowledge and skills of Elders, traditional teachers and healers, who may not have the 'qualifications' valued by policymakers but are considered the most qualified to help people in their communities.

Of course, this is far from being a comprehensive list and, as Choate *et al.* (2022) note, such initiatives only place the profession at the 'start of the curve'. They nonetheless serve to illustrate the kind of holistic changes in policy, theory and practice that would reflect the aims of Indigenous social work in this particular context. They also raise the vexed question of allyship, which is germane to anti-racism and Indigenous social work but also applies to other radical perspectives that inspire people to join the fight against social injustice. Gates *et al.* (2021) note that while activist groups have generally promoted allyship as a way for (non-Black, Indigenous and other People of Colour) social workers to contribute to anti-racist initiatives, it has also been criticised for becoming performative, 'an identity disembodied from any real mutual understanding of support' (Indigenous Action, 2014, cited in Gates *et al.*, 2021: 2). The authors propose that 'critical allyship' is defined by action, a lifelong commitment to anti-racist knowledge and practice, and reflexive examination of power and privilege. In similar vein, Howard (2021) discusses the shift from being a 'non-racist', with its connotations of passivity and complacency, to being 'anti-racist', which involves a commitment to challenging and changing the status quo. Allyship is often viewed in personal terms, but as Baskin and Sinclair (2015) point out, institutions and organisations can also be significant allies; they give the example of universities actively seeking to recruit Indigenous scholars and regularly inviting Elders, Knowledge Keepers and service users to share their knowledge and experiences with students. In this sense, social work as a profession must itself move towards critical allyship, going beyond statements of support to 'allegiance with marginalised communities and decisive actions to redress colonial and structural inequalities' (Yassine and Tseris, 2022: 196).

The Social Model of Disability

Since its emergence in the 1970s, the social model of disability has greatly influenced social care policy and practice and has become embedded in social work training and education (Morgan, 2012). Indeed, one of its main proponents, Mike Oliver, taught social work students for many years at the University of Kent. Key tenets of the social model, such as the critique of individualist, deficit-led approaches to impairment and focus on structural barriers to dignified living and participation in society (see Chapter 2) give practitioners a framework for understanding disability and for working in partnership with disabled people to make services more responsive to their needs. At the same time, the idea of a contrast between medical and social models has contributed to social work's own professional project, for example in underpinning its distinctive role in multi-agency settings such as community mental health teams (Walker, 2005). It is also important to note the differences between a social work perspective and a social model perspective. For example, Woodcock and Tregaskis (2008) found that parents of children with disabilities wanted help to overcome systemic barriers to obtaining joined-up services for their children, while social work assessments tended to focus on aspects of parenting and to employ a 'one-size-fits-all' interpretation of impairment and need. Recent years have seen increasing interest in critical disability theory as a way of challenging ableist assumptions in social work education and practice, as well as examining intersectional differences (Flynn, 2020; Stafford, 2020).

Nonetheless, the social model remains significant for the radical strand in social work, especially in the UK where the profession contributed actively to its uptake and promotion. It both informs and critiques social work's contribution to an equalities agenda. A key question is the degree to which social workers can use their discretion to address systemic barriers, given the constraints of their institutional and organisational context, as well as wider socio-political factors. An obvious example is the impact of post-2010 austerity policies (see Chapter 5) which have cut or reduced many of the services previously available to help individuals and families, as well as raising thresholds for statutory support (Power and Bartlett, 2019; Ryan, 2020). Such policies have put social workers in a difficult position, given their role in carrying out eligibility and needs assessments that, despite their best efforts, mean that some people will not get the care and support they require. From an ethical perspective, such dilemmas might be viewed as a necessary tension between utilitarian and deontological principles for action, i.e. social workers rightly focus on the person-in-context but also have to ensure that scarce resources go to those who need them most (see Hood, 2018). The social model suggests that attention should also be paid to the socio-political dimensions of ethical practice, e.g. whose interests does austerity and rationing welfare really serve (Hood *et al.*, 2020)?

The social model can also be used to interrogate the concept of personalisation, or personalised care, which emerged on the policy and practice agenda in the late 2000s and since then has arguably become the dominant paradigm for social work with older adults and people with disabilities (Duffy *et al.*, 2010; Lymbery, 2012; Beresford, 2014a). Duffy (2010) describes the origins of personalisation in the disability movement and its demand that society address disabled people's right to independent living. Built on principles of mutual support and self-advocacy, the disability movement drove a shift towards de-institutionalisation, de-segregation, and the dismantling of paternalistic structures of care and control for disabled people. As community-based support become the norm, tools were developed to enable disabled people to take as

uch control of their lives as possible, such as personal budgets, direct pay-
ents and other types of self-directed support. Such tools were subsequently
corporated into mainstream adult social care services, as part of wide-ranging
forms designed to diversify the range of providers beyond the state, creating
oice for the 'citizen-consumer' (Scourfield, 2007).

The mainstreaming of personalisation led to concerns that what was originally
rights-based concept had been largely co-opted by neo-liberal approaches to
elfare, with counterproductive effects for the people supposedly benefiting from
em (Ferguson, 2012; Spicker, 2013; Beresford, 2014b). It has been pointed out
at the neo-liberal equation of personalisation with consumerism (i.e. individual
oice in a market of services) does little to address structural inequities and
ay even exacerbate them. For example, the 'inverse care law' (see Chapter 2)
ould predict that more affluent and educated people will generally be better
navigating the bureaucracy of direct payments and articulating their need for
rvices. There is some evidence to support this view; for example, Malbon *et al.*
019) studied one of the world's largest personalisation schemes (in Australia)
d found that 'the very design of these schemes can not only entrench existing
equalities in the social determinants of health but widen them'. Such findings
allenge social workers to look beneath the surface of such attractive-sounding
ncepts as personalisation and examine carefully the structures and systems
rough which they are delivered.

GBTQ+ Affirmative Social Work

espite a growing literature and evidence-base, LGBTQ+ affirmative social work
ractice, sometimes shortened to affirmative practice, still has a relatively low
rofile in the profession and has yet to be properly integrated into social work
ducation and training (Mallon, 2008; Dentato, 2017; Wagaman *et al.*, 2018;
rguello, 2019; Austin *et al.*, 2021). It is also very diverse, so worth noting that
ractitioners may use different terms to refer to their work in this area. Accord-
g to Arguello (2019), affirmative practice seeks to facilitate an 'opening up of
ossibilities' for allyship with marginalised groups, including LGBTQ+ communi-
es, in pursuit of social justice aims. Cultural competence is an important aspect
f this work but needs to be accompanied by actions and interventions that
firm and validate queer identities 'along the spectrum of sexualities and gen-
ers' (Arguello, 2019, p. 79). In line with theories of minority stress (Alessi, 2014;
n *et al.*, 2019), interventions with LGBTQ+ people and communities should
cognise and address the health and welfare inequalities that stem from oppres-
ve and phobic social structures. For example, Austin *et al.* (2021) report on an
GBTQ+ affirmative parenting intervention with foster parents in the United
ates, noting that evidence-informed interventions are needed to address the

identity-based victimisation that LGBTQ+ young people often face in the care system. Fabbre (2017) explores the concept of queer ageing and its implications for social work practice with LGBTQ+ older adults, which includes increasing the attention paid to structural issues in direct work. At the same time, as noted in Chapter 2, affirmative practice steers away from a deficit lens and towards the recognition of 'trans joy' and the emancipatory potential of genderqueer identities (Shuster and Westbrook, 2022; Holloway, 2023).

The flourishing of LGBTQ+ affirmative scholarship and practice has contributed greatly to social workers' efforts to understand the intersectional identities of the people they work with and tailor services accordingly. For example, the case studies assembled by Arguello (2019) encompass a range of issues such as trans-affirming care for teenagers, addiction services for elderly gay men, or mental health support for Black women experiencing racist micro-aggressions at work. While LGBTQ+ identities may be foregrounded in many of these vignettes, they also show how considering factors like religion, disability or immigration status have proved crucial for formulating cases in a culturally responsive way. Like all radical approaches for working with marginalised groups, affirmative practice is inherently intersectional in that it never restricts itself to viewing a person along just one structural axis. Indeed, it should be clear to anyone reading this chapter that an intersectional lens is the common thread that links all the critical perspectives that have been reviewed so far. For this reason, intersectionality itself is the final radical approach to be considered.

Intersectionality and Social Work

Intersectionality was introduced in Chapter 1 as a key theoretical framework for analysing complex power relations and multiply marginalised identities within societies characterised by inequality. It is rooted in the activism, scholarship and research of Black feminists and critical race theorists (e.g. Crenshaw, 1991, 2017; Nash, 2008; Mehotra, 2010; Collins and Bilge, 2020). In recent years, intersectionality has gained increasing prominence within social work, both in terms of generally encouraging an intersectional lens to be applied to questions of identity, oppression and discrimination, but also as a paradigm for critical and radical social work in its own right (Yamada et al., 2015; Nayak and Robbins, 2018; Almeida et al., 2019; Joy, 2019; Bernard, 2021; Matsuzaka et al., 2021). Bernard (2021) argues that intersectionality is useful to social workers as a way of bridging the gap between theory and practice, providing them with a conceptual framework to understand better 'how interlocking oppressions manifest in everyday experiences' (Bernard, 2021: 25). In individual casework, employing an intersectional lens can help practitioners to understand the multiple dimensions of someone's situation and work respectfully with them to create a plan of ction that takes account of their intersectional identity. Social workers can also use intersectionality to examine how social inequalities frame people's lives and contribute to the risks they face themselves, or pose to others; an intersectional framework can facilitate a reflective space in which to consider and critique the multiplying effects of racism, sexism, disabilism, classism, ageism and hetero-normativity on people's health and wellbeing. Indeed, Mattsson (2014) incorporates intersectionality into a critically reflective tool, using critical incidents from practice (Fook and Gardner, 2007) to develop 'awareness and knowledge of how power relations work and affect the social worker, and how the social worker herself functions as a bearer of these structures' (Mattson, 2014: 14).

As a radical form of practice, intersectionality can also underpin forms of social work developed by and with specific communities whose multiple marginalisation is not adequately recognised or addressed by conventional services. The implied connection between activism and practice is made explicit by the contributions to Nayak and Robbins (2018), who argue for an 'activism of intersectionality' aiming to disrupt mainstream social work structures and discourses and build collective spaces for transformation. For example, Kumar (2018) considers the role of Black-led women's organisations working to end violence against women and girls, while Held and McCarthy (2018) discuss the lived intersectional experiences of asylum-seeking women, drawing on the work of the Lesbian Immigration Support Group in Manchester. Such examples and explorations challenge social workers, particularly in statutory settings, to reimagine what services might look like if they were really co-produced with and geared towards the concerns of marginalised groups and communities. Writing on the Aotearoa New Zealand context, Joy (2019) considers the links between intersectionality and the perspective of *mana wāhine*, a 'space where Māori women can, on our own terms and in our own way, (re) define and (re)present the multifarious stories and experiences of what it means, and what it meant in the past, to be a Māori woman in Aotearoa New Zealand' (Simmons, 2011, cited in Joy, 2019: 45). Krumer-Nevo and Komem (2015) discuss a critical feminist programme for social work with girls, implemented in after-school centres for Jewish and Arab girls in Israel, which used intersectional theory to develop 'positional dialogues' around gender, ethnicity, class, sexuality and employment. Zufferey (2016), meanwhile, develops an intersectional approach to social work and homelessness, aiming to show how an understanding of intersecting inequalities can help to transform practice, expand the use of advocacy and draw attention to the diverse voices of people affected by homelessness.

Conclusion

This chapter has discussed (in a very introductory way) some of the radical and critical strands of social work, in which the social justice aims of the profession are brought to the fore. Of course, there is much more to say and other types of critical practice that could have been explored (see Shaikh *et al.*, 2022, and Webb 2019, for a more comprehensive overview). Every radical tradition has its own field of interest, relating to the arbitrary social divisions used to underpin oppressive power structures, unequal distribution of resources, and unfair disparities in health and wellbeing. Because these divisions are intimately connected to identity and self-perception, any structural analysis must also encompass the subjective experience of inequality and oppression, which differs for individuals in their specific contexts and at particular times. The need to apply an intersectional lens to the analysis of social inequalities has become more widely accepted, while the emergence of intersectionality has drawn attention to the multi-layered identities and experiences of Black women and global majority of women across the world. On the whole, there are grounds for both optimism and pessimism about the prospects for radical and critical social work. On the positive side, there is clearly scope and enthusiasm for embedding feminist, anti-racist, Indigenous and disability and LGBTQ+ affirmative practice into the core elements of psychosocial casework. On the other hand, the dominance of neo-liberal assumptions in contemporary welfare systems makes their fundamental reform unlikely, given that such transformation would serve the interests of marginalised groups rather than those of national and global elites. The prospects and possibilities for radical change may therefore lie more in engagement with grassroots activism and community-level initiatives than with appeals to ministers and civil servants in remote political centres. It is therefore community social work, arguably the oldest yet least fashionable of all types of social work, to which we turn in the next chapter.

References

Alessi, E.J. (2014) 'A framework for incorporating minority stress theory into treatment with sexual minority clients', *Journal of Gay & Lesbian Mental Health*, **18**(1), pp. 47–66.

Almeida, R.V., Werkmeister Rozas, L.M., Cross-Denny, B., Lee, K.K. and Yamada, A.-M. (2019) 'Coloniality and intersectionality in social work education and practice', *Journal of Progressive Human Services*, **30**(2), pp. 148–164.

Arguello, T. (2019) *Queer social work: Cases for LGBTQ+ affirmative practice*, New York, Columbia University Press.

Arvin, M., Tuck, E. and Morrill, A. (2013) 'Decolonizing feminism: Challenging connections between settler colonialism and heteropatriarchy', *Feminist Formations*, pp. 8–34.

Austin, A., Craig, S.L., Matarese, M., Greeno, E.J., Weeks, A. and Betsinger, S.A. (2021) 'Preliminary effectiveness of an LGBTQ+ affirmative parenting intervention with foster parents', *Children and Youth Services Review*, **127**, p. 106107.

Bailey, M. and Trudy (2018) 'On misogynoir: Citation, erasure, and plagiarism', *Feminist Media Studies*, **18**(4), pp. 762–768.

Bailey, R. and Brake, M. (eds) (1975) *Radical social work*, London, Edward Arnold.

Baskin, C. and Sinclair, D. (2015) 'Social work and Indigenous peoples in Canada', *Encyclopedia of social work*, Available online, https://doi.org/10.1093/acrefore/9780199975839.013.953

Beresford, P. (2014a) *Personalisation*, Bristol, Policy Press.

Beresford, P. (2014b) 'Personalisation: from solution to problem?', in Beresford, P. (ed.), *Personalisation*, Bristol, Policy Press, pp. 1–26.

Bernard, C. (2021) Intersectionality for social workers: A practical introduction to theory and practice, Abingdon, Routledge.

Bonnett, A. (2005) *Anti-racism*, Abingdon, Routledge.

Burford, G. (2017) Family group conferencing: New directions in community-centered child and family practice, Abingdon, Routledge.

Cane, T. (2021) 'Attempting to disrupt racial division in social work classrooms through small-group activities', *The Journal of Practice Teaching and Learning*, **18**(1–2).

Cane, T. (2023) 'BRAC2eD model: An approach to de-bias decision-making in adoption assessments with prospective adopters from minoritised ethnic groups', *Adoption & Fostering*, **47**(1), pp. 58–76.

Cane, T.C. and Tedam, P. (2022) '"We didn't learn enough about racism and anti-racist practice": Newly qualified social workers' challenge in wrestling racism', *Social Work Education*, pp. 1–23.

Choate, P.W., St-Denis, N. and MacLaurin, B. (2022) 'At the beginning of the curve: Social work education and Indigenous content', *Journal of Social Work Education*, **58**(1), pp. 96–110.

Coburn, D. (2004) 'Beyond the income inequality hypothesis: class, neo-liberalism, and health inequalities', *Social Science & Medicine*, **58**(1), pp. 41–56.

Collins, P.H. and Bilge, S. (2020) *Intersectionality (2nd Edition)*, Cambridge, Polity Press.

Crenshaw, K. (1991) 'Mapping the margins: Identity politics, intersectionality, and violence against women', *Stanford Law Review*, **43**(6), pp. 1241–1299.

Crenshaw, K.W. (2017) *On intersectionality: Essential writings*, New York, The New Press.

Cutler, D.M. and Johnson, R. (2004) 'The birth and growth of the social insurance state: Explaining old age and medical insurance across countries', *Public Choice*, **120**(1), pp. 87–121.

Delgado, R. and Stefancic, J. (2023) *Critical race theory: An introduction*, New York, New York University Press.

Dentato, M.P. (2017) Social work practice with the LGBTQ community: The intersection of history, health, mental health, and policy factors, Oxford, Oxford University Press.

Dominelli, L. (2018) *The Routledge handbook of green social work*, Abingdon, Routledge.

Duffy, S. (2010) 'The citizenship theory of social justice: Exploring the meaning of personalisation for social workers', *Journal of Social Work Practice*, **24**(3), pp. 253–267.

Duffy, S., Waters, J. and Glasby, J. (2010) 'Personalisation and adult social care: Future options for the reform of public services', *Policy & Politics*, **38**(4), pp. 493–508.

Fabbre, V. (2017) 'Queer aging: Implications for social work practice with lesbian, gay, bisexual, transgender, and queer older adults', *Social Work*, **62**(1), pp. 73–76.

Featherstone, B. and Peckover, S. (2007) 'Letting them get away with it: Fathers, domestic violence and child welfare', *Critical Social Policy*, **27**(2), pp. 181–202.

Ferguson, G., Featherstone, B. and Morris, K. (2019) 'Framed to fit? Challenging the domestic abuse "story" in child protection', *Critical and Radical Social Work*, Available online, https://doi.org/10.1332/204986019X15668424450790

Ferguson, I. (2012) 'Personalisation, social justice and social work: A reply to Simon Duffy', *Journal of Social Work Practice*, **26**(1), pp. 55–73.

Ferguson, I. and Woodward, R. (2009) *Radical social work in practice: Making a difference*, Bristol, Policy Press.

Flood, M. (2015) 'Work with men to end violence against women: A critical stocktake', *Culture, Health & Sexuality*, **17**(sup2), pp. 159–176.

Flynn, S. (2020) 'Theorizing disability in child protection: Applying critical disability studies to the elevated risk of abuse for disabled children', *Disability & Society*, **35**(6), pp. 949–971.

Fook, J. and Gardner, F. (2007) Practising critical reflection: A resource handbook: A handbook, McGraw-Hill Education (UK).

Frost, N., Abram, F. and Burgess, H. (2014) 'Family group conferences: Context, process and ways forward", *Child & Family Social Work*, **19**(4), pp. 480–490.

Gates, T.G., Bennett, B. and Baines, D. (2021) 'Strengthening critical allyship in social work education: Opportunities in the context of# BlackLivesMatter and COVID-19', *Social Work Education*, pp. 1–17.

Gottlieb, M. (2021) 'The case for a cultural humility framework in social work practice' *Journal of Ethnic & Cultural Diversity in Social Work*, **30**(6), pp. 463–481.

Gray, M. and Coates, J. (2010) '"Indigenization" and knowledge development: Extending the debate', *International Social Work*, **53**(5), pp. 613–627.

Hardy, K. and Gillespie, T. (2016) *Homelessness, health and housing: Participatory action research in East London*, Available online: http://www.e15report.org.uk/, Last Accessed 11 May 2023.

Held, N. and McCarthy, K. (2018) '"They like you to pretend to be something you are not": An exploration of working with the intersections of gender, sexuality, "race", religion and "refugeeness", through the experience of Lesbian Immigration Support Group (LISG) members and volunteers', *Intersectionality in Social Work*, Routledge, pp. 142–155.

Hester, M. (2011) 'The three planet model: Towards an understanding of contradictions in approaches to women and children's safety in contexts of domestic violence', *British Journal of Social Work*, **41**(5), pp. 837–853.

Hicks, D.L. (2013) 'War and the political zeitgeist: Evidence from the history of female suffrage', *European Journal of Political Economy*, **31**, pp. 60–81.

Holloway, B.T. (2023) 'Highlighting trans joy: A call to practitioners, researchers, and educators', *Health Promotion Practice*, Available online, https://doi.org/10.1177/15248399231152468

Hood, R. (2018) *Complexity in social work*, London, Sage.

Hood, R., O'Donovan, B., Gibson, J. and Brady, D. (2020) 'New development: Using the Vanguard Method to explore demand and performance in people-centred services', *Public Money & Management*, pp. 1–4.

Howard, L. (2021) 'Becoming an anti-racist ally', in Moore, T. and Simango, G. (eds), *The Anti-Racist Social Worker*, St Albans, Critical Publishing, pp. 43–54.

Joy, E. (2019) '"You cannot take it with you": Reflections on intersectionality and social work', *Aotearoa New Zealand Social Work*, **31**(1), pp. 42–48.

rumer-Nevo, M. and Komem, M. (2015) 'Intersectionality and critical social work with girls: Theory and practice', *British Journal of Social Work*, **45**(4), pp. 1190–1206.

umar, C. (2018) 'Fault lines: Black feminist intersectional practice working to end violence against women and girls (VAWG)', *Intersectionality in Social Work*, Abingdon, Routledge, pp. 170–184.

avalette, M. (2019) *What is the future of social work?*, Bristol, Policy Press.

rner, J.E. and Fulambarker, A. (2018) 'Beyond diversity and inclusion: Creating a social justice agenda in the classroom', *Journal of Teaching in Social Work*, **38**(1), pp. 43–53.

mbery, M. (2012) 'Social work and personalisation', *British Journal of Social Work*, **42**(4), pp. 783–792.

afile'o, T. and Vakalahi, H.F.O. (2018) 'Indigenous social work across borders: Expanding social work in the South Pacific', *International Social Work*, **61**(4), pp. 537–552.

albon, E., Carey, G. and Meltzer, A. (2019) 'Personalisation schemes in social care: Are they growing social and health inequalities?', *BMC Public Health*, **19**(1), p. 805.

allon, G.P. (2008) *Social work practice with lesbian, gay, bisexual, and transgender people*, New York, Routledge.

atsuzaka, S., Hudson, K.D. and Ross, A.M. (2021) 'Operationalizing intersectionality in social work research: Approaches and limitations', *Social Work Research*, **45**(3), pp. 155–168.

attsson, T. (2014) 'Intersectionality as a useful tool: Anti-oppressive social work and critical reflection', *Affilia*, **29**(1), pp. 8–17.

cCoy, H. (2020) 'Black lives matter, and yes, you are racist: The parallelism of the twentieth and twenty-first centuries', *Child and Adolescent Social Work Journal*, **37**(5), pp. 463–475.

ehrotra, G. (2010) 'Toward a continuum of intersectionality theorizing for feminist social work scholarship', *Affilia*, **25**(4), pp. 417–430.

onro, S. (2019) 'Non-binary and genderqueer: An overview of the field', *International Journal of Transgenderism*, **20**(2-3), pp. 126–131.

organ, H. (2012) 'The social model of disability as a threshold concept: Troublesome knowledge and liminal spaces in social work education', *Social Work Education*, **31**(2), pp. 215–226.

ullaly, R. (1997) *Structural social work: Ideology, theory, and practice*, Oxford, Oxford University Press.

ash, J.C. (2008) 'Re-thinking intersectionality', *Feminist Review*, **89**(1), pp. 1–15.

ayak, S. and Robbins, R. (2018) Intersectionality in social work: Activism and practice in context, Abingdon, Routledge.

ixon, J. and Humphreys, C. (2010) 'Marshalling the evidence: Using intersectionality in the domestic violence frame', *Social Politics*, **17**(2), pp. 137–158.

ygren, K., Walsh, J., Ellingsen, I.T. and Christie, A. (2019) 'What about the fathers? The presence and absence of the father in social work practice in England, Ireland, Norway, and Sweden – A comparative study', *Child & Family Social Work*, **24**(1), pp. 148–155.

rme, J. (2003) '"It's feminist because I say so!" Feminism, social work and critical practice in the UK', *Qualitative Social Work*, **2**(2), pp. 131–153.

Phillips, R. and Cree, V.E. (2014) 'What does the "fourth wave" mean for teaching feminism in twenty-first century social work?', *Social Work Education*, **33**(7), pp. 930–943.

Andrew, P. (2021) 'Perspective Chapter: Black Lives Matter and the Anti-Woke Campaign in the UK', in Erick, G. (ed), *Effective Elimination of Structural Racism*, Rijeka, IntechOpen, Chapter 7.

Powell, F.W. (2001) *The politics of social work*, London, Sage.

Power, A. and Bartlett, R. (2019) 'Ageing with a learning disability: Care and support in the context of austerity', *Social Science & Medicine*, **231**, pp. 55–61.

Reisch, M. and Andrews, J. (2014) The road not taken: A history of radical social work in the United States, New York, Routledge.

Rose, H. (1985) 'Women's refuges: Creating new forms of welfare?', in Ungerson, C. (ed), *Women and social policy: A reader*, London, Macmillan Education UK, pp. 243–259.

Ryan, F. (2020) *Crippled: Austerity and the demonization of disabled people*, London, Verso.

Scambler, G. (2009) 'Capitalists, workers and health: Illness as a 'side-effect' of profit-making', *Social Theory & Health*, 7, pp. 117–128.

Scambler, G. (2012) 'Health inequalities', *Sociology of Health & Illness*, **34**(1), pp. 130–14€

Scott, K., Dubov, V., Devine, C., Colquhoun, C., Hoffelner, C., Niki, I., Webb, S. and Goodman, D. (2021) 'Caring dads intervention for fathers who have perpetrated abuse within their families: Quasi-experimental evaluation of child protection outcomes over two years', *Child Abuse & Neglect*, **120**, p. 105204.

Scourfield, P. (2007) 'Social care and the modern citizen: Client, consumer, service use manager and entrepreneur', *British Journal of Social Work*, **37**(1), pp. 107–122.

Shaikh, S., LeFrancois, B. and Macias, T. (eds) (2022) *Critical social work praxis*, Halifax, NS, Fernwood Publishing.

Shuster, S.M. and Westbrook, L. (2022) 'Reducing the joy deficit in sociology: A Study of transgender joy', *Social Problems*, Available online, https://doi.org/10.1093/socpro/spac034

Skafida, V., Morrison, F. and Devaney, J. (2022) 'Prevalence and social inequality in experiences of domestic abuse among mothers of young children: A study using national survey data from Scotland', *Journal of Interpersonal Violence*, **37**(11–12 pp. NP9811-NP9838.

Snead, A.L., Bennett, V.E. and Babcock, J.C. (2018) 'Treatments that work for intimate partner violence: Beyond the Duluth Model', *New frontiers in offender treatment*, Springer, pp. 269–285.

Spicker, P. (2013) 'Personalisation falls short', *British Journal of Social Work*, **43**(7), pp. 1259–1275.

Stafford, L. (2020) 'Disrupting ableism in social work pedagogy with Maurice Merleau-Ponty and critical disability theory', in *The Routledge handbook of critical pedagogies for social work*, Abingdon, Routledge, pp. 359–372.

Tan, K.K., Treharne, G.J., Ellis, S.J., Schmidt, J.M. and Veale, J.F. (2019) 'Gender minority stress: A critical review', *Journal of Homosexuality*, pp. 1471–1489.

Thompson, N. (2016) 'Anti-discriminatory practice: Equality, diversity and social justice', Basingstoke, Palgrave Macmillan.

Thørnblad, R., Strandbu, A., Holtan, A. and Jenssen, T. (2016) 'Family group conferences: From Maori culture to decision-making model in work with late modern families in Norway', *European Journal of Social Work*, **19**(6), pp. 992–1003.

Vickers, T. (2019) 'Marxist social work: An international and historical perspective', *The Routledge handbook of critical social work*, Routledge, pp. 24–34.

Wagaman, M.A., Shelton, J. and Carter, R. (2018) 'Queering the social work classroom: Strategies for increasing the inclusion of LGBTQ persons and experiences', *Journal of Teaching in Social Work*, **38**(2), pp. 166–182.

Walker, S. (2005) 'Releasing potential – the future of social work and CAMHS', *Journal of Social Work Practice*, **19**(3), pp. 235–250.

Webb, S. (2019) The Routledge handbook of critical social work, Abingdon, Routledge.

Wild, J. (2022) 'Gendered discourses of responsibility and domestic abuse victim-blame in the English children's social care system', *Journal of Family Violence*, Available online, https://10.1007/s10896-022-00431-4

Williams, C. and Parrott, L. (2014) 'Anti-racism and predominantly "white areas": Local and national referents in the search for race equality in social work education', *British Journal of Social Work*, **44**(2), pp. 290–309.

Williams, C. and Bernard, C. (2018) 'Black History Month: A provocation and a timeline', *Critical and Radical Social Work*, **6**(3), pp. 387–406.

Woodcock, J. and Tregaskis, C. (2008) 'Understanding structural and communication barriers to ordinary family life for families with disabled children: A combined social work and social model of disability analysis', *British Journal of Social Work*, **38**(1), pp. 55–71.

Yamada, A.M., Rozas, L.M.W. and Cross-Denny, B. (2015) 'Intersectionality and social work', *Encyclopedia of Social Work*.

Yan, M.C. and Tsang, A.K.T. (2008) 'Re-envisioning indigenization: When bentuhuade and bentude social work intersect in China', in Gray, M. and Coates, J. (eds), *Indigenous social work around the world: Towards culturally relevant education and practice*, Abingdon, Routledge, pp. 191–202.

Yassine, L. and Tseris, E. (2022) 'From rhetoric to action: confronting whiteness in social work and transforming practices', *Critical and Radical Social Work*, **10**(2), pp. 192–208.

Yee, J.Y., Hackbusch, C. and Wong, H. (2015) 'An anti-oppression (AO) framework for child welfare in Ontario, Canada: Possibilities for systemic change', *The British Journal of Social Work*, **45**(2), pp. 474–492.

Zufferey, C. (2016) Homelessness and social work: An intersectional approach, Abingdon, Routledge.

8
Community Social Work

Chapter overview

··

This chapter focuses on community social work, which is broadly defined to encompass various types of community development, community organising and social action. Different understandings of community are considered and a brief history of community work provides some key reference points, including its origins in colonial projects and the Settlement movement, the connections to trade unionism and the activity of radical organisers such as Saul Alinsky, and the later development of state-sponsored community work as part of urban policy and planning. The chapter continues with a discussion of skills in community practice, the benefits and pitfalls of professionalisation and voluntarism, and the pluralist approach adopted by social workers in locality-based settings. There is a brief introduction to approaches developed in the United States, such as broad-based and asset-based community development. The chapter concludes with a discussion of radical community work, which in recent years has become increasingly concerned with intersecting inequalities.

Introduction

As a starting point for thinking about community work, Twelvetrees (2017: 5) suggests that we consider it as a form of empowerment: 'the process of assisting people to improve their community by undertaking autonomous collective action, that is, by working together'. As this definition implies, community work and social work are occupations with common roots, values and skill sets. However, they are also different in many ways – for example, social work has a social justice orientation but often also a distinct role at the interface between the state and the individual. It follows that community social work can be interpreted narrowly, as types of social work that resemble or incorporate elements of community practice, or more broadly, as the potential for social workers to undertake almost any kind of community work. This chapter will adopt the latter, i.e. broader interpretation of what community social work is – or could be. One reason for this is to further explore aspects of the critical and radical traditions that were introduced in the previous chapter and which are directly concerned with inequality. That is not to say community work is inherently radical, or necessarily pursues social justice objectives – as we shall see below, there are similar tensions within community work as there are in social work. Nonetheless, radical strands of community work overlap with similar currents of theory and practice in social work, so that it makes sense to consider them alongside each other. The broad spectrum of community work offers possibilities of transformation for future social work even if they are not necessarily evident in contemporary social work. At the same time, it is important to recognise that community work is a distinct and varied field, encompassing an extensive theory base and a global sphere of practical application. This distinctiveness derives from the ambiguous yet powerful concept that lies at its heart: the idea of community.

Understanding Community

Community can be understood in various ways. On a descriptive level, the term may be used in relation to a locality or geographical area, often also referred to as a neighbourhood, or in relation to a group of people who are linked by shared aspects of identity, such as the 'Black community' or 'LGBTQ+ community', or in relation to other groups that form around shared interests and experiences, e.g. carers, or recovering addicts. On an evaluative level, the term reflects the contested terrain on which questions of identity and belonging are worked out – our belief that a community exists in a particular place, or among certain people, might say more about our own preconceptions and assumptions than anything meaningful about how people perceive themselves and their relations to others. Yet despite its slippery meaning, community often means something positive and even idealised to many people – for some, perhaps, harking back to a nostalgic view of the past as a time of greater social cohesion and intimacy. Such connotations suggest that communities could even be a site of resistance and opposition to the individualism and transactional relationships encouraged by neo-liberal frameworks. On the other hand, the idea of community can be leveraged to give a positive 'spin' to institutions and services that operate in a mainly individualistic way, or even as a means of suppressing dissent and pre-empting social unrest.

Exercise 8.1

Explore and reflect on the different meanings of community by considering the following questions:

1   What does community mean to you personally? Do you consider yourself to be part of one or more communities?

Continued

2   Think about a community with which you are familiar (it is not necessary that you identify as a member). What defines its boundaries, i.e. who or what decides whether someone is part of that community? How open is the community, i.e. how easy is it for someone to join or leave?

3   You may come across the following terms in social work. What types of community are they referring to?

    a   Community care
    b   Community mental health team
    c   Community of practice
    d   Community-based assessment
    e   Youth and community centre

A Brief History of Community Work

As Popple (2015) points out, the tension between radical and paternalist strains of community work has deep historical roots. During the age of European imperialism, for example, Indigenous communities were a key site of anti-colonial resistance, and have since maintained a vigorous tradition of autonomous social action and cultural reclamation (Samson and Gigoux, 2016). At the same time, community work was an integral part of the colonial project itself, associated with the work of Christian missionaries, educational initiatives, and infrastructure projects aiming to integrate new territories into a global economic system dominated by the Global North (Kwo, 1984; Hintjens, 1998; Cohen *et al.*, 2021). Post-independence, governments in settler colonial societies have continued to sponsor community development among Indigenous peoples as part of a political agenda of assimilation and 'welfare colonialism' (Bernardi, 1997; Jarpa-Arriagada, 2020; Cohen *et al.*, 2021).

In the UK, community social work emerged as part of the Settlement movement, which was introduced in Chapter 7. The Settlement ethos encouraged social workers to spend time living and working in poor neighbourhoods, providing educational and welfare services with a focus on alleviating poverty, as well as advocating for social and political reform on behalf of people in the neighbourhood. Elements of this ethos can be discerned in later models of locality-based or 'patch-based' social work (Martinez-Brawley, 1988; Adams and Krauth, 2017), as well as the tradition of 'neighbourhood houses' staffed by social workers in the US (Trolander, 1982). However, the movement's 'benevolent paternalism' (Popple, 2015) also played a role in moderating social unrest in communities affected by deprivation and inequality; the emphasis on cooperation rather than conflict meant that Settlement workers were rarely in the vanguard of protest and social reform. At the same time, more radical forms of community action emerged from

ade unionism and the labour movement. An early example was the 1915 Glas-
ow tenants' strike, which sought to link labour disputes with concerns about
naffordable rents and poor housing conditions in working-class communities.
he suffragette movement provided another link between community organisa-
on and political radicalism, foregrounding the feminist challenge to patriarchal
onceptions of family and community (Dominelli, 2019). Anti-racist community
ork, inspired by the US civil rights movement and anticolonial independence
ovements, contributed to the aims of racially and ethnically minoritised groups
 defend their rights, fight discriminatory policies and practices, and improve
eir living and working conditions.

   In the United States, a distinctive approach to community organisation was
ioneered by the political activist, Saul Alinsky. His approach to bringing about
ocial change, resisting oppression and improving the lives of people in American
hettoes was deliberately confrontational and anti-establishment. For example,
e Back of the Yards Neighborhood Council (BYNC), which Alinsky co-founded
 a deprived area of Chicago in 1939, rallied a diverse local population to mount
irect action against meatpacking companies, slum landlords and the city gov-
nment, achieving tangible benefits for residents and workers alike. Alinsky's
pproach was characterised by a rugged insistence on self-determination – the
YNC's motto was (and still is) 'We the people will work out our own destiny' –
 well as the tactical use of conflict to unite people around collective aims
d challenge powerful institutions. His most famous book, *Rules for Radicals*
Alinsky, 1971), outlines a set of principles for grassroots community organising
at are still widely read and applied by activists today. Although seen by some
 overly confrontational, Alinsky's methods influenced subsequent generations
f US community organisers, such as Ed Chambers, Cesar Chavez and Dolores
uerta (Banks and Westoby, 2019).

   The post-war development of welfare systems in many countries was accom-
anied by a growth in government-funded community work. In the UK, such
itiatives were a feature of urban policy and often had a dual purpose; first to
ddress unemployment and crime in deprived neighbourhoods, and second to
romote the 'integration' of newly settled immigrant communities. These priori-
es were typified by the Urban Programme, announced in 1968 in the context
f escalating racist rhetoric by right-wing politicians as well as a series of gov-
rnment-commissioned reports advocating further intervention in working-class
eighbourhoods. In practice, the Urban Programme was considered ineffective at
aching ethnically minoritised groups, although for many years it did provide a
nding mechanism for local authorities and charities to establish and run com-
unity projects and clubs in deprived areas. As Marxist and socialist perspectives
ecame more influential in community work during the 1970s, such activities
ere sometimes criticised for adopting a 'community pathology' approach to
ocial problems, overlooking the structural inequalities experienced by racialised

and working-class communities. In contrast, the National Community Develop
ment Project (NCDP), launched one year after the Urban Programme, gave rise t
a radical critique of poverty and inequality across the twelve different neighbou
hoods covered by the project. Reports published by local CDPs drew attentio
to the impact of industrial decline, recession and under-investment, while als
advocating reforms to address the unequal distribution of power and resource
in society (Banks and Carpenter, 2017). Such trenchant analysis was probabl
not what the government had in mind; in 1976, the CDPs all had their fundin
withdrawn!

The rise of neo-liberal approaches to welfare in the 1980s saw further expar
sion of state-sponsored community work, often focused on employment. Cuts t
local authority budgets constrained the funding available for activist communit
groups, while the shift to short-term commissioning and procurement also ince
tivised community workers to gear their proposals to government priorities an
targets. In the 1990s and 2000s, the role of community work in social policy wa
given a boost by urban regeneration and neighbourhood programmes, such a
the New Deal for Communities (NDC) in the UK. As Lister (2001) points out, thes
programmes essentially continued the tradition of area-based targeting in urba
policy, characterised by a managerialist approach that sought to break dow
systemic problems into discrete outcomes such as school attendance or teer
age pregnancy. The result was to downplay the role of deep structural inequal
ties, 'with the danger that the problem is constructed as lying primarily withi
deprived neighbourhoods and the motivation of the individuals living in then
with potentially stigmatising consequences' (Lister, 2001: 434). Like most othe
community-based services, the resources available for neighbourhood regenera
tion were drastically curtailed with the 2008/09 financial crisis and subsequer
imposition of austerity policies (see Chapter 5). On the other hand, increasin
public awareness of social inequality over the past decade has also led to a ris
in activism, often linked to concerns about climate change, which has harnesse
the power of social media and digital technology (Glenn, 2015).

Community Social Work

If the history of community work suggests a tension between radical/activist an
consensual/state-funded forms of practice, it is the latter that has often forme
the basis for community social work, or what might also be described as commu
nity practice within social work (Banks et al., 2003). Examples include establish
ing or facilitating community groups, coordinating community care, contributin
to the work of voluntary organisations, running community-based projects, o
undertaking specialist work in areas such as hate crime. In the 1970s and 1980
it was quite common to find patch-based community social workers doing th

ind of work, operating out of small neighbourhood offices that provided a range f services, including housing and social care (Martinez-Brawley, 1988; Adams nd Krauth, 2017). Each local office would be provided with a small discretion- ry budget to address areas of particular concern to local residents, practitioners nd councillors. Social workers in these offices were embedded in communities, ı some ways reminiscent of the old Settlement Houses, which enabled them to uild relationships and gain an understanding of community life. This in turn ıade it easier for professionals to undertake their formal duties in areas such as hild safeguarding, as illustrated in Case Study 8.1.

Case Study 8.1: Community social work and child safeguarding (Davies, 2016)

Davies (2016) reflects on her time as a community social worker in a patch-based office in Islington, North London, during the 1980s. At one point, she came up with a plan to set up a children's clothing exchange as a way of developing community networks in a deprived housing estate. The idea met with strong criticism from some of her colleagues, who thought that local working-class families would find it demeaning for their children to wear second-hand clothes. However, their concerns proved to be unfounded and the clothing exchange was a great success, as many parents were strug- gling with the expense of new children's clothing and saw nothing wrong with recycling good quality clothes that had been outgrown. Over time, the exchange helped to break down barriers between families, reduced the need for parents to request money for clothes from social workers (which they did find demeaning), and increased levels of trust between professionals and residents. As a result, the community also started to play a more active role in keeping children safe from abuse and exploitation:

> The local community got to know us better as local social workers and began to alert us when they were worried about children being abused. They had their own understanding of what was and was not acceptable and appreciated a relationship where they could check out with us whether or not we thought a child was at risk and there needed to be an investigation. Because social workers were supporting the clothing project, the families were more willing to open up to us with concerns and this enabled some issues to be responded to effectively with the help of community networks.

Although this is an example from the 1980s, when patch-based offices were more prevalent, Davies points out that community networks have continued to underpin statutory protection processes; for example, by helping services to identify and respond to child sexual abuse, or to monitor and rehabilitate serious sex offenders through 'circles of trust and accountability' (see also Davies, 2004; Wilson et al., 2010; Nelson, 2016).

Of course, the notion of citizen-assisted state surveillance has a dark side too – most notoriously in the massive civilian informant networks run by the Stasi in East Germany, but also echoed in the contemporary 'civilianisation' of counter terrorism security in the UK and other countries (Sliwinski, 2013). Social workers operating at the sharp end of the state's intrusion into private family life must therefore negotiate the boundary between oppressive and empowering forms of community practice. Social workers are also required to recognise and intervene along with other professionals, when communities act oppressively towards their own members, as with cases of honour-based violence (Gill, 2012; Idriss, 2018). At the same time, in keeping with the radical tradition discussed in the previous chapter, social workers may look out for opportunities to support people in upholding their rights, campaigning for reform, and acting against oppressive systems. Many different activities can fall within the scope of community social work, requiring a broad range of skills and expertise.

Skills in Community Practice

Community social work largely belongs to what Popple (2015) calls the 'pluralist' tradition of community work, which focuses more on practical skills and less on ideological debates and structural analysis. Here, the main question is how to go about engaging people in a neighbourhood or network, with a view to working together to identify and address communal problems. An example of this type of approach is provided by Twelvetrees (2017), who discusses three types of community work:

- **Community development** – supporting members of a community to organise themselves collectively to address shared problems and needs.
- **Social action** – when a community group tries to persuade the government, or another organisation, to do (or stop doing) something, in accordance with the community's wishes.
- **Social planning** – efforts to influence service providers directly, e.g. by setting up and running a project rather than working through a community.

As might be expected, such work demands a considerable range of skills. For example, planning and preparing for a community project will involve activities such as setting objectives, managing budgets, fund-raising, getting buy-in from stakeholders, making and following up contacts, 'sowing seeds', undertaking surveys and focus groups, developing a community profile (or 'needs analysis') and considering what the outcomes of the work should be (Twelvetrees, 2017). A key concern is how to organise community groups, sustain their purpose and involvement, and deal with the complexity of relationships and partnerships. Some of the capabilities involved will be familiar to social workers undertaking social casework, such as the need to plan and record activity, reflect on practice and eview outcomes. A more distinctive skillset is that of the community facilitator, which involves (among other things):

bringing people together and helping them to identify specific needs and objectives;

helping people set up and maintain an organisation to achieve those objectives;

helping people to formulate a plan of action and then monitor, evaluate and review the results;

helping people to gain access to resources and acquire relevant skills;

helping people to make decisions as a group, including the allocation of tasks, roles and responsibilities;

helping the group to acknowledge and deal with conflict and disagreement;

helping the group to build relationships with other groups and agencies.

More radical approaches to community organisation (e.g. Ledwith, 2020) suggest additional methods designed to empower people who are marginalised and oppressed by mainstream society. This does not mean directing community groups to work towards pre-defined social goals but is more about raising consciousness and encouraging a sense of shared purpose and agency. Drawing on the critical pedagogy of Paulo Freire, Ledwith (2020) points to the transformative power of narrative and story-telling, arguing that stories 'offer the basis of analysis for critical consciousness and social change'. She highlights the work of the Adult Learning Project (ALP), an initiative set up in Glasgow at the end of the 1970s to implement the kind of 'praxis' advocated by Freire (Kirkwood and Kirkwood, 2011). Reeves (2020) describes the ALP process as employing participatory dialogue in four non-sequential stages:

Investigating social reality – e.g. by getting to know people in the local area to find out about their lives and what is important to them.

Coding and decoding that reality and *identifying social problems* – e.g. bringing people together around a photo of a well-known event, or some other cultural artefact, in order to explore its meaning and significance for each person.

Learning programmes – further study of themes and issues in the life of the community, which have been identified in the investigation stage but need to be explored in more depth, e.g. by joining a women's history project or learning more about parenting in other cultures.

Action outcomes – learning projects lead to community development projects that try to tackle the issues raised by group members, e.g. setting up a parents' centre, skills exchange or writers' workshop.

Is there anything to stop social workers from carrying out such activities? In the neo-liberal era, opportunities to do so have arguably become more restricted, particularly in statutory settings where locality-based social work has long been in decline (Adams and Krauth, 2017). Even in the voluntary sector, the reliance on state funding, the short-term nature of commissioning, the technocratic focus on measuring effectiveness and outcomes, along with a range of other pressures (Davies and Evans, 2012), have made it more difficult to sustain open-ended projects with long-term social aims. In some countries, social work education and training may include some preparatory grounding in community work theory and practice, laying a foundation for social workers to become effective community organisers. At the time of writing, groupwork skills or knowledge of group processes, although still taught on some social work courses, were not mentioned anywhere in the professional standards in England (Social Work England, 2020). Instead, community work has arguably become a secondary field of knowledge and practice, which social workers may pursue independently of their professional qualification – as is the case with other specialist areas such as play therapy or forensic assessment.

Professionalisation vs Voluntarism

Is community work a profession? The literature on community work, whether pluralist or radical, is somewhat ambiguous on this question. On the one hand it seems fair to say that effective community work requires at least some people with specialist skills and experience, particularly in organisational and facilitative roles. The pathway to acquiring expertise often means doing a relevant qualification, such as youth and community work, while agencies employing community workers will presumably favour accreditation as well as experience. On the other hand, community work is not a regulated profession, nor likely to become one. It encompasses a variety of roles and activities, many which are carried out by unpaid workers, including residents, citizens and volunteers, as well as people from cognate professions, such as teachers and social workers. The involvement of professionals in community groups can have its downsides, such as off-putting jargon and a fondness for bureaucracy. For example, Twelvetrees (2017) recalls a Director of Social Services who met with a local Age Concern group and suggested at one point that they should 'write to me on that' (telling him about it was presumably not enough!). It also ties into the relationship between professions and the state, which can limit the scope for campaigning and dissent. Saul Alinsky, the American community organiser, was notoriously hostile towards social workers in Settlement Houses, whom he regarded as being out of touch with neighbourhoods and incapable of radical action (Trolander, 1982). Alinsky's views on 21st-century community work might have been even more trenchant: a survey of practitioners in 2006 found evidence that 'a high proportion of paid workers spend a relatively small amount of time in direct contact with communities' (Hendersen and Glen, 2006; cited in Bunyan, 2010: 115).

The corollary of anti-professionalism is arguably an emphasis on voluntarism. Volunteers have always had an important role in community work, whether as tivists in the tradition of community action or as informal carers and workers ithin state-funded community care (Mundel and Schugurensky, 2008). However, ere are problems with seeing community work as being mainly about commit-d citizens volunteering their time and expertise. In the post-2010 era of neo-peral austerity (see Chapter 5), there are concerns that governments might seek co-opt such activity as part of a wider project of state-shrinkage and cuts to iblic services. Indeed, the UK Conservative Party's key pledge in its 2010 general ection manifesto was to harness the country's tradition of charitable activity by ansferring responsibility for providing welfare services from the public sector to e voluntary sector (Levitas, 2012). Such simplistic notions not only overlook the zable infrastructure necessary to support and supervise the work of volunteers it also fail to engage with wider questions of sustainability and accountability vans, 2011). Voluntarism can also replicate social inequalities in various ways. ne capability to volunteer is unevenly distributed across the population, while vol-ntary roles may reinforce sexist, racist, ageist or disablist assumptions, e.g. about ho gets to do care work, administration, coordination, management, and so on gotnes *et al.*, 2021).

Overall, neither professionalisation nor voluntarism seems likely on its own provide an ideal type of community work. As Pyles (2019) observes, organis-g models should not exclude professional expertise but must ensure that it is ployed under the leadership of the community, not the other way round, in ·der to disrupt the boundary between helper and helped. On this, she quotes ïla Watson, an Indigenous Australian artist, activist and academic:

> If you have come here to help me, you are wasting your time. But if you have come because your liberation is bound up with mine, then let us work together. (Lilla Watson, cited in Pyles, 2019: 183)

road-based Community Organising

road-based community organising (BBCO) is a model of community engage-ent that emphasises the centrality of power and politics in achieving communi-rian goals. The approach was pioneered in the United States by the Industrial rea Foundation (IAF), a national community organising network co-founded y Saul Alinsky in 1940 and subsequently led by Edward Chambers after Alins-cy's death in 1972. Chambers (2003) sets out the key principles and methods of BCO, as practised by the IAF. Among other things, he draws attention to:

> the potential for an organisational network to create capacity to address multiple issues, as opposed to just creating capacity around single-issue projects or campaigns;

- the link between the personal and political, and the need for political objectives to be rooted in what matters to people;
- the need for organisations to be in constant dialogue and conversation (e.g. through 'relational meetings') with people in the community;
- the importance of local organisations, such as churches, schools, unions and community groups, in marshalling a community's resistance to powerful institutions that threaten the wellbeing of its members;
- the value of conflict and direct action in creating a more equal basis for negotiation with established powers.

Bunyan (2010) contrasts these principles with the consensus-based notions of partnership and empowerment commonly employed within community work in the UK, arguing that these concepts have become devalued within an institutional framework dominated by commissioning and managerialism. By way of alternative, he discusses the work of London Citizens, a network of nearly ninety member institutions, each covering a different area of London or different type of London community (e.g. union branches or faith-based organisations). The membership dues pay for running costs, employing paid organisers, leadership training and the operational costs of actions and campaigns. As with the IAF in the United States, London Citizens has used direct action and conflict tactics to force organisations into paying a living wage to low-paid and 'outsourced' workers, as well as running campaigns on issues of concern to local communities, such as affordable housing or the treatment of migrants. Bunyan suggests that such broad-based networks are important because they can bridge the gap between micro-level approaches focusing on the local context (or the issues pertinent to a single community) and macro-level approaches that focus on the structural causes of social injustice. This intermediate or meso-level of social action is challenging because the political work of establishing a power base outside of the apparatus of the state requires a suitable structure and organisation. In BBCO the solution is a sustainable network of organisations, each rooted in the lives and interests of local communities, but willing to agree and pursue joint policy objectives. The combination of a networked structure, independent power base and readiness for conflict can give organisers the political edge to confront social injustice and challenge existing power relations.

Asset-based Community Development

Asset-based community development (ABCD) is another approach that was originally developed in the United States, where it is associated particularly with the work of Frank McKnight (Kretzmann and McKnight, 1996; McKnight, 2011. McKnight argues that it is counterproductive to view communities solely through the lens of poverty and deprivation, as is often the case for inner city eighbourhoods. A deficit-led approach only reinforces people's sense of powerlessness and their dependence on outside help and support. Rather than just responding to perceived problems and deficiencies, urban development projects should instead recognise the abundance of assets and resources that exist within those communities and seek to build on those strengths, helping people to develop their potential and take control of their lives. According to Foot and Hopkins (2010: 7), community assets can include the following:

practical skills, capacity and knowledge of local residents;

passions and interests of local residents that give them energy for change;

the networks and connections ('social capital') in a community, including friendships and neighbourliness;

membership and activity of local community and voluntary associations;

resources provided by public, private and third sector organisations that can support a community;

physical and economic resources that enhance well-being, e.g. parks, libraries.

It follows that a key part of ABCD is 'asset mapping', a process of identifying and documenting the variety of assets in a community. This process should preferably be led by members of the community and might involve a number of techniques such as appreciative enquiry and action research (Blickem et al., 2018). Such techniques seek to enhance people's skills and resilience, develop mutually supportive networks, and encourage collaborative relationships. In the longer term, enhancing people's participation in, and contribution to, community assets and community life is expected to have a beneficial effect on their health and wellbeing (Munford et al., 2017). Indeed, there has been growing interest in ABCD in the field of public health, where it is aligned with 'salutogenic' models of working (Lindström and Eriksson, 2005), i.e. health interventions focusing on factors that have a positive impact on people's health, rather than those that cause disease. It has also been suggested that ABCD is a way of tackling the social determinants of poor health and therefore might help to address health inequalities (Morgan et al., 2010). On the other hand, asset-based approaches have been criticised for downplaying the structural causes of inequality and playing into neo-liberal attacks on public sector provision (Friedli, 2013).

Radical Community Work

Social action undertaken by oppressed and minoritised groups has been a key driver of radical community work, and lies at the heart of social movements such as feminism, anti-racism, disability rights and the LGBTQ+ movement. Yet this contribution has not always been recognised in the field. For example, as Dominelli (1995) points out, while there have been many attempts to define community and community work over the years, many have ignored the centrality of women to both. Feminist approaches rectify this omission and place women and gender inequality at the heart of community action, with a view to transforming patriarchal social relations. Orr (2022) observes that feminist community practice 'relies on engagement with the layers of women's experience' in order to connect individual issues with shared concerns, for example around health, housing and violence against women. Lived experience forms the basis for broader social action, whose scope may be local, national or international. Historical examples in the UK include the Greenham Common Women's Peace Movement, the provision of women's refuges for survivors of domestic abuse, campaigns for women's reproductive rights and women's involvement in the 1984–85 miners' strike (Dominelli, 2019). Feminist practice seeks to avoid hierarchical forms of community organising (e.g. leaders, spokespersons) and to redefine the role of the professional – a recurrent theme in radical community work. Instead, there is a preference for sharing skills, rotating roles, and collectively deciding on priorities for action. Establishing networks and partnerships between feminist groups, in the manner of broad-based organising, can also create a power base for direct action and campaigns for social reform.

Radical community work is increasingly characterised by attention to intersectional issues. Ledwith (2020) reconsiders feminist practice in the context of intersectionality, arguing that 'feminism does not fight its own corner' but should seek to ensure that 'every inequality and injustice, including environmental injustice, is at the heart of women's action' (2020: 224). In support, she cites Eddo-Lodge's challenge to feminists:

> Feminism, at its best, is a movement that works to liberate all people who have been economically, socially and culturally marginalised by an ideological system that has been designed for them to fail. That means disabled people, black people, trans people, women and non-binary people, LGB people and working class people. (Eddo-Lodge, 2018, cited in Ledwith, 2020: 224)

Black feminists have led the development of intersectional approaches to inequality and this work has both underpinned and been inspired by the activism of community organisations. Local examples can be found everywhere that marginalised communities have found mainstream services unwilling to understand or respond to their needs. In north London, for example, Fulani (2019) explains how the brutal murder in 2014 of Valerie Forde and her baby daughter, by Valerie's ex-partner, raised awareness that people of African and Caribbean heritage experiencing domestic abuse were often failed by the police and other agencies, lacked culturally appropriate support, and needed a safe space where they could see themselves reflected. This led to the founding of Sistah Space[1], a

---

1   https://ijelonek.github.io/Sistah_Space/ (last accessed on 19 October 2022)

ommunity-based initiative supporting African heritage women and girls, which
rovides domestic abuse services, delivers training and campaigns for change.

Radical community work has also been pioneered by the disabled people's
10vement, not least in applying the principles of the social model to its own
tructures and organisation. A longstanding principle is to distinguish organisa-
ions *of* disabled people from those run by non-disabled people *for* disabled
eople. For example, the Greater Manchester Coalition for Disabled People is a
1embership organisation whose staff and executive council positions are only
vailable to disabled people. The movement was also an early adopter of broad-
ased community organisation (before the term was coined) in order to enhance
:s political power and capability. An example was the founding in 1981 of the
3ritish Council of Organisations of Disabled People[2], which, unlike most national
harities, sought to represent the interests of disabled people regardless of their
ype of impairment; part of its work was to carry out and commission research
ɔ produce evidence helpful to its campaigning and lobbying efforts (e.g. on
.ousing and independent living). In recent years, internal critiques from femi-
iist, LGBTQ+ and anti-racist perspectives have highlighted the question of dif-
erence and the importance of intersectional inequalities (Söder, 2009; Stienstra,
013; Barnes, 2019; Power and Bartlett, 2019). In turn, such critiques have both
nformed and been inspired by the work of community groups and networks,
iving precedence to a broader range of identities, voices and experiences. For
xample, in November 2020 the UK Stonewall website marked the start of Dis-
bility History Month by featuring a list of five LGBTQ+ disability organisations[3],
Jl of which focused on intersectionally marginalised identities. Among them was
collective called Brownton Abbey[4] – an 'Afro-futuristic performance party' that
rganises events to support QTIBIPOC artists (queer, trans, intersex, black and
ndigenous people of colour). If that seems a long way from what most people
hink social work is about, then perhaps that is the point!

Conclusion

'his chapter has explored various aspects of community social work, taking a
road perspective on the field that points to the potential for social work to
ediscover and renew its historical affiliation with community-based forms of

---

In 1996, the BCODP changed its name to the British Council of Disabled
'eople, and in 2006 to the United Kingdom's Disabled People's Council. It ceased
ɔ employ staff in 2013 and was closed down by the Charity Commission in 2017.
 https://www.stonewall.org.uk/about-us/news/5-lgbt-disability-organisations-you-
hould-support (last accessed on 19 October 2022)
 https://marlboroughproductions.org.uk/our-projects/brownton-abbey/ (last
.ccessed on 19 October 2022)

practice. A brief overview of the field reveals familiar dilemmas, such as the tension between state-sponsored programmes and radical social action, the benefits and pitfalls of professionalism and voluntarism, and the challenge of building broad-based coalitions while respecting difference and giving precedence to marginalised voices. Such debates reveal that community work, like communities themselves, should not be considered as some panacea of equality and social justice. At the same time, its more radical strands demonstrate a tradition of resistance, dissent, resistance and transformation, particularly among marginalised communities, which may act as a source of inspiration for social workers seeking to practice differently. Nonetheless, the dominant neo-liberal ideology of our time creates undeniable barriers to emerging forms of social work that might be closer allied to community work, particularly in its more radical form. The interplay between such possibilities and constraints will be considered in the next, and concluding, chapter of this book.

References

Adams, P. and Krauth, K. (2017) 'Working with families and communities: The patch approach', in Adams, P. and Krauth, K. (eds), *Reinventing human services*, Abingdon, Routledge, pp. 87–108.

Ågotnes, G., Moholt, J.-M. and Blix, B.H. (2021) 'From volunteer work to informal care by stealth: a "new voluntarism" in social democratic health and welfare services for older adults', *Ageing & Society*, Available online, doi:10.1017/S0144686X21001598

Alinsky, S. (1971) *Rules for radicals: A pragmatic primer for realistic radicals*, New York, Random House.

Banks, S., Butcher, H., Henderson, P. and Robertson, J. (2003) *Managing community practice: principles, policies and programmes*, Bristol, Policy Press.

Banks, S. and Carpenter, M. (2017) 'Researching the local politics and practices of radical Community Development Projects in 1970s Britain', *Community Development Journal*, **52**(2), pp. 226–246.

Banks, S. and Westoby, P. (2019) *Ethics, equity and community development*, Bristol Policy Press.

Barnes, C. (2019) 'Understanding the social model of disability: Past, present and future', in Watson, N. and Vehmas, S. (eds), *Routledge handbook of disability studies* (2nd Edition), Abingdon, Routledge, pp. 14–31.

Bernardi, G. (1997) 'The CDEP scheme: A case of welfare colonialism', *Australian Aboriginal Studies (Canberra)*(2), pp. 36–46.

Blickem, C., Dawson, S., Kirk, S., Vassilev, I., Mathieson, A., Harrison, R., Bower, P. and Lamb, J. (2018) 'What is asset-based community development and how might it improve the health of people with long-term conditions? A realist synthesis', *Sage Open*, **8**(3), p. 2158244018787223.

nyan, P. (2010) 'Broad-based organizing in the UK: reasserting the centrality of political activity in community development', *Community Development Journal*, **45**(1), pp. 111–127.

hen, A., Matthew, M., Neville, K.J. and Wrightson, K. (2021) 'Colonialism in community-based monitoring: knowledge systems, finance, and power in Canada', *Annals of the American Association of Geographers*, **111**(7), pp. 1988–2004.

vies, L. (2004) '"The difference between child abuse and child protection could be you": Creating a community network of protective adults', *Child Abuse Review*, **13**(6), pp. 426–432.

vies, L. (2016) *Community work – protecting children*, Available online: https://lizdavies.net/2016/09/11/community-work-protecting-children/.

vies, N. and Evans, K. (2012) 'Perfect storms: An analysis of the operating conditions for the children, young people and families voluntary sector', *London: Children England*.

minelli, L. (1995) 'Women in the community: Feminist principles and organising in community work', *Community Development Journal*, **30**(2), pp. 133–143.

minelli, L. (2019) *Women and community action* (3rd Edition), Bristol, Policy Press.

ans, K. (2011) '"Big Society" in the UK: A policy review', *Children & Society*, **25**(2), pp. 164–171.

ot, J. and Hopkins, T. (2010) 'A glass half-full: How an asset approach can improve community health and well-being', London, Improvement and Development Agency.

iedli, L. (2013) '"What we've tried, hasn't worked": The politics of assets based public health', *Critical Public Health*, **23**(2), pp. 131–145.

lani, N. (2019) *The story of Sistah Space*, Available online: https://safelives.org.uk/story-sistah-space

ll, A. (2012) 'Intersecting inequalities: Implications for addressing forced marriage and "honour" based violence for those working in social work and related professions', in McMillan, L. and Lombard, N. (eds), *Current theory and practice in domestic abuse, sexual violence and exploitation*, London, Jessica Kingsley, pp. 141–158.

enn, C.L. (2015) 'Activism or "slacktivism?": Digital media and organizing for social change', *Communication Teacher*, **29**(2), pp. 81–85.

ntjens, H. (1998) 'Editorial introduction: Community development in the Third World: Continuity and change', *Community Development Journal*, **33**(4), pp. 281–284.

riss, M.M. (2018) 'Key agent and survivor recommendations for intervention in honour-based violence in the UK', *International Journal of Comparative and Applied Criminal Justice*, **42**(4), pp. 321–339.

rpa-Arriagada, C.G. (2020) 'Practices of resistance and community social work: Struggles and tensions in the face of the logics of domination of the colonial and capitalist model', *Revista Eleuthera*, **22**(2), pp. 309–326.

rkwood, G. and Kirkwood, C. (2011) *Living adult education: Freire in Scotland*, Rotterdam, Sense Publishers.

etzmann, J. and McKnight, J.P. (1996) 'Assets-based community development', *National Civic Review*, **85**(4), pp. 23–30.

Kwo, E.M. (1984) 'Community education and community development in Cameroon: The British colonial experience, 1922–1961', *Community Development Journal*, **19**(4), pp. 204–213.

Ledwith, M. (2020) *Community development: A critical approach*, Policy Press.

Levitas, R. (2012) 'The Just's Umbrella: Austerity and the Big Society in Coalition policy and beyond', *Critical Social Policy*, **32**(3), pp. 320–342.

Lindström, B. and Eriksson, M. (2005) 'Salutogenesis', *Journal of Epidemiology & Community Health*, **59**(6), pp. 440–442.

Lister, R. (2001) 'New Labour: a study in ambiguity from a position of ambivalence', *Critical Social Policy*, **21**(4), pp. 425-447.

Martinez-Brawley, E.E. (1988) 'Locality-based social work in four non-metropolitan patches in Norfolk England: Implications for community practice', *Journal of Comparative Social Welfare*, **4**(2), pp. 44–71.

McKnight, J. (2011) The abundant community: Awakening the power of families and neighborhoods, San Francisco, Berrett-Koehler.

Morgan, A., Davies, M. and Ziglio, E. (2010) *Health assets in a global context: Theory, methods, action*, New York, Springer.

Mundel, K. and Schugurensky, D. (2008) 'Community based learning and civic engagement: Informal learning among adult volunteers in community organizations', *New Directions for Adult and Continuing Education*, **118**, pp. 49–60.

Munford, L.A., Sidaway, M., Blakemore, A., Sutton, M. and Bower, P. (2017) 'Associations of participation in community assets with health-related quality of life and healthcare usage: A cross-sectional study of older people in the community', *BMJ Open*, **7**(2), p. e012374.

Nelson, S. (2016) 'Tackling child sexual abuse: Radical approaches to prevention, protection and support', Bristol, Policy Press.

Orr, E. (2022) 'It's like felting: Reflections on feminist social and community practices', in Information Resources Management Editor (ed.), *Research anthology on feminist studies and gender perceptions*, Hershey, PA, IGI Global, pp. 655–670.

Popple, K. (2015) *Analysing community work: Theory and practice*, Maidenhead, Open University Press.

Power, A. and Bartlett, R. (2019) 'Ageing with a learning disability: Care and support in the context of austerity', *Social Science & Medicine*, **231**, pp. 55–61.

Pyles, L. (2019) 'Eight: Relational ethics and transformative community organising in the neo-liberal US context', in Banks, S. and Westoby, P. (eds), *Ethics, Equity and Community Development*, Bristol, Policy Press, pp. 167–188.

Reeves, S. (2020) 'Reflections on 40 Years of ALP (the Adult Learning Project)', *Concept*, **11**(2), pp. 1–12.

Samson, C. and Gigoux, C. (2016) *Indigenous peoples and colonialism: Global perspectives*, Cambridge, Polity Press.

Sliwinski, K.F. (2013) 'Counter-terrorism–a comprehensive approach. Social mobilisation and "civilianization" of security: the case of the United Kingdom', *European Security*, **22**(3), pp. 288–306.

Social Work England (2020) *Professional Standards*, Available online: https://www.socialworkengland.org.uk/media/1640/1227_socialworkengland_standards_prof_standards_final-aw.pdf, Last Accessed: 26/02/2023.

öder, M. (2009) 'Tensions, perspectives and themes in disability studies', *Scandinavian Journal of Disability Research*, **11**(2), pp. 67–81.

tienstra, D. (2013) 'Race/ethnicity and disability studies: Towards an explicitly intersectional approach', in Watson, N., Roulstone, A. and Thomas, C. (eds), *Routledge handbook of disability studies*, Abingdon, Routledge, pp. 384–397.

rolander, J.A. (1982) 'Social change: Settlement houses and Saul Alinsky, 1939–1965', *Social Service Review*, **56**(3), pp. 346–365.

welvetrees, A.C. (2017) *Community development, social action and social planning*, London, Red Globe Press.

Wilson, C., Bates, A. and Völlm, B. (2010) 'Circles of support and accountability: An innovative approach to manage high-risk sex offenders in the community', *The Open Criminology Journal*, **3**(1).

Conclusion
Social Work and Inequality

Chapter overview

....

This final chapter reviews some of the broad themes and implications of focusing on inequality in social work. The pitfalls of professionalisation and ties to the state are discussed, as well as the continuing relevance of national welfare systems in the era of global capitalism. It is argued that resistance to oppression is one of the hallmarks of unequal societies, yet also carries risks for those who resist. It is therefore imperative for the profession to maintain its critical and radical tradition, even as it comes under pressure from neo-liberal approaches and attitudes. The book concludes with a discussion of social work's mediating role, which requires practitioners to align themselves with the powerless at the same time as accommodating the interests of the powerful. Holding such dilemmas may prove untenable in contexts of very high inequality, but in a more equal society could enable the profession's renewal and transformation.

Introduction

This book has focused on inequality as a key area for social work in light of the profession's commitment to social justice. The first five chapters introduced some theoretical definitions and empirical evidence in relation to social inequality, its various forms, and their impact on people's health and wellbeing. The general message in this part of the book was that even if complete equality in all things is unattainable, indeed undesirable, in contemporary societies almost everyone would be better off if social arrangements were more equal. The reason this does not happen is because the interests of rich, powerful groups – and rich, powerful countries – are served by the status quo. Having hopefully made this case, the final three chapters have looked in more detail at how different approaches to social work could be aligned with an equalities agenda. The message in this part of the book is more ambiguous, if indeed there is one. Rather than a clear conclusion, a number of themes and questions have arisen, which this concluding chapter will attempt to summarise and give a tentative response. To begin with, we revisit the thorny question of professionalisation and social work's relationship to the state.

Professionalisation and the State

The IFSW's definition of social work was quoted in the introduction to this book, mainly in order to highlight its commitment to social justice aims. Given the discussion in the last few chapters, it is worth taking another look:

> Social work is a practice-based profession and an academic discipline that promotes social change and development, social cohesion, and the empowerment and liberation of people. Principles of social justice, human rights, collective responsibility and respect for diversities are central to social work. Underpinned by theories of social work, social sciences, humanities and indigenous knowledge, social work engages people and structures to address life challenges and enhance wellbeing. (IFSW, 2014)

Notice that before it gets to the more high-minded content, the definition starts off with a status claim: social work is a *profession*. This might seem obvious, but it raises the question: is being a profession necessary for, or even compatible with, the goal of promoting social justice, empowerment and liberation? After all, as we saw with community work, not every occupation seeks to become a profession, while still being able to develop a knowledge base, ethical code, and standards of practice. In sociological terms, professional closure requires the creation of a protected title that is administered and enforced by a state-sanctioned regulatory body. It has many advantages for members, including monopolistic control over certain types of work, as well as the respect and esteem associated with professionalism. But it also comes at a cost: by regulating social work, the government gets to decide who may, or may not, call themselves a social worker; by employing the majority of social workers (whether directly or via agencies), the government influences what activities fall, and do not fall, within the scope of social work. In England, for example, where 'social worker' became a protected title in 2007, professional education, training and regulation has become increasingly preoccupied with child protection and mental health, and with the activities of assessment and decision-making (Nicholas, 2015). The corollary has been a reduction in social work's role in universal and preventative services, delivering community interventions and providing everyday help and support to individuals and families.

Concerns about social work's professional project and its ties to the state are a legacy of the 1970s radical turn, which have periodically resurfaced. Recently, for example, Maylea (2021) called for the abolition of social work as a profession, arguing that it had proved itself incapable of reform and was unfit to address contemporary challenges. To justify this claim, Maylea pointed to social work's lack of a coherent theory base, the problems caused by professionalism, and its contribution to historical abuses such as settler colonialism. His abolitionist stance echoes arguments for the defunding of police and child welfare services, particularly in the United States, where these institutions have been accused of embodying and implementing racist and oppressive aspects of state power (Fleetwood and Lea, 2022). Responding to Maylea's article, Garrett (2021a) pointed to its evidential flaws as well as problematic tone and positionality; he suggests instead that a longstanding tradition of 'dissenting social work', which include the critical and radical approaches discussed in Chapter 7, provides a crucial counternarrative to the dominant neo-liberal paradigm. Whelan (2022) adopts a similar position while noting that liberal welfare regimes have increasingly confined social work to a repressive role within the state apparatus, which makes it harder to deliver on any 'promise' of social justice. Meanwhile, McGregor (2022) argues that social work has outgrown its anglophone origins and must now focus on 'mediating the social' in diverse cultural contexts worldwide.

If pursuing a professional project inevitably leads social workers to specialise in policing individuals and families, at the expense of the dissenting tradition identified by Garrett and others, then it could be argued that professionalisation is inherently ill-suited to social justice aims. But is professionalism the real culprit here? After all, the nature of social work is primarily shaped by government policy, legislation and statutory guidance. If social work were harnessed within a comprehensive vision of a progressive and generous welfare state, as envisaged in the 1973 Seebohm report that established local authority social work departments in the UK, then professionals would presumably find more opportunities to reduce inequalities than within the more restrictive settings offered by neo-liberal regimes. In some respects – albeit co-opted and compromised – the welfare state can still be seen as a bulwark against the profound inequalities embedded in global capitalism. Without the state, or with a minimal framework of legal rights and protections, market forces would largely decide how resources are allocated, meaning the scope for taxpayer-funded services would be drastically curtailed. Under such circumstances, with social workers (or their equivalent) corralled into specialist investigation units as part of a vestigial 'nightwatchman' state, the paternalist institutions of a Beveridge-style welfare system might well seem appealing, despite their unsuitability for late modern societies (Cottam, 2018). Whether these are indeed the only options, or whether an alternative form of welfare system will proceed to reshape social work in its own image, will likely depend less on its anglophone homelands than on what happens in China, India, and other countries of the Global South.

Conflict and Resistance

Critical and radical approaches to social work share a common idea about inequality, namely that it stems from conflict. People's chances of health, wellbeing

d happiness are determined partly by luck, partly by their own choices and
cisions, and partly by the struggle for power between different social groups.
dical approaches differ in how they define these groups and analyse the com-
ex dynamics of oppression and resistance. Nonetheless, they agree that such
nflict plays a major role in deciding how resources and opportunities, and
erefore also developmental outcomes, are distributed in particular nations or
cieties, or among the world's population. Even in a democratic society in which
ery citizen participates in making the rules, it is likely that any given set of
rangements can be challenged on the basis of fairness. It follows that any
oject to promote social justice requires the possibility of resistance, dissent
d disruption. A professional cadre of social workers dedicated only to the
plementation of government policies will see no need to resist anything – an
likely force for social change.

In his overview of dissenting social work (DSW), Garrett (2021b) identifies a
mber of key themes, many of which are familiar from the radical and critical
rspectives discussed in Chapter 7. DSW encourages practitioners to develop
ays of thinking and understanding society that are both theoretically rich and
bedded in people's everyday experience, with a particular focus on mar-
nalised and exploited groups. Social work's past and present contribution to
ppressive processes must be acknowledged as the first step towards decolo-
sing education and training. As such, dissent is a collective endeavour that is
igned with 'oppositional activity', including that of 'trade unions, activist social
ovements, community organisations, progressive coalitions, "user" networks,
arches and campaigns' (Garrett, 2021b: 5). As well as building bridges with
ch movements, it is hoped that DSW will give rise to 'distinctive forms of criti-
l praxis', helping to generate 'new analytical strategies' for understanding and
ddressing social problems (Garrett, 2021b: 227). Although he does not say this,
arrett's comprehensive and theoretically informed vision of DSW might also be
tended to fashion some coherence to the disparate acts of 'everyday resistance',
ch as those identified by Weinberg and Banks (2019) among social workers.
ch acts have long been the prerogative of the street-level bureaucrat when it
mes to policy implementation (Rice, 2012).

Wilkinson and Pickett (2010) note that as inequalities widen, people's socio-
onomic status becomes (or starts to seem) more precarious; this applies to
eryone below the very top stratum – it does not just affect the most deprived or
cluded groups. By implication, the stakes of resistance might also start to rise.
hile the case for dissent might be more pressing at times of great or growing
justice, it might prove riskier for the dissenter. At the extreme, this is exempli-
d by people who resist the rule of authoritarian regimes, or the invasion and
cupation of their countries. Resistance is a brave and risky endeavour in such
untries, where any such acts can meet with brutal suppression. Those of us
rtunate to live in less draconian circumstances may be minded to dismiss the
alogy, yet we should not be complacent – governments' willingness to tolerate

dissent seems to be waning in many so-called liberal societies (Watts, 2019) while the emergence of populism and the politics of division (see Chapter 4) has stoked intolerance and cultural protectionism. A newly qualified social worker from a working-class background, reliant on the income from her local government job to pay her mortgage and raise her family, might understandably think twice before challenging inequitable policies and procedures, even if she ultimately decides to do so. Practitioners from a global majority background may face other constraints – for example, one study found that that black and minority social workers in England were disproportionately subject to 'fitness to practise' investigations by the professional regulator (Samuel, 2020). The inhibiting effects of state regulation on dissent and resistance is another reason why radical approaches are often at odds with the idea of professionalisation.

Another, more subtle effect of professionalisation lies in the virtues normally associated with it: a field of specialised knowledge and the competence to apply it to real-world situations in a trustworthy and effective way. Ideological considerations, such as the question of which side to take in a perceived conflict between social groups, might be seen as irrelevant or even as a distracting sideshow from acquiring expertise. Debates about whether social workers are agents of the state or champions of the oppressed and vulnerable are therefore beside the point the main issue is training people to do properly the job they are paid to do. An independent, government-commissioned report into the education of children's social workers in England (Narey, 2014) was a case in point; it suggested that university courses were overly preoccupied with teaching students about concepts like anti-oppressive practice, partnership working and empowerment, and that excessive focus on theory was holding back social work trainees from learning the practical skills they needed to protect children from harm. At the time, the report echoed the views of the UK education secretary, who had inveighed against 'left-wing dogma' undermining social work practice (Ramesh, 2013), as well as the then-chair of the Association of Directors of Children's Services, who bemoaned the poor quality of many social workers (Butler, 2014).

Recent years have arguably seen entrenchment of this view, i.e. that social workers should be concerned with efficacy rather than ideology, due partly to the prevailing managerialist ethos and emphasis on performance and accountability (see Chapter 4) but also because of other developments: the impact of information technology, electronic workflow systems and the 'digitisation' of practice (Wastell and White, 2010; Pink et al., 2021); the increasing association of professionalism with evidence-based practice and the 'what works' approach to intervention and evaluation (Ghate and Hood, 2019); a policy agenda of diversification and privatisation of social care provision (Jones, 2018); and the tendency to reframe questions about power and oppression in narrower or reductive terms such as 'protecting children', making them amenable to technocratic solutions. As a result of these shifts, political or moral arguments for ameliorating inequalities

1ust often be combined with economic arguments. For example, Bennett *et al.*
2021) sought to show the cost-effectiveness of expenditure on preventative ser-
ices, such as family support and early help, by demonstrating their effect on
educing demand for out-of-home care. Accumulating and disseminating such
vidence, engaging with policymakers, designing appropriate interventions, and
nplementing them in frontline services, is a complex task; it requires a coor-
inated and coherent set of activities to be undertaken by people with a wide
ange of skills, including practitioners, managers, academics, senior leaders, and
olicymakers. It could be argued that the capacity to plan and link together such
ctivities within a coherent framework of knowledge, skills and values is the
allmark of a profession – a collective project that could underpin social work's
fforts to make good on its social justice claims.

Mediating in the Social

ocial work operates at the interface between the individual and society – seeking,
s the IFSW definition has it, to engage both 'people and structures to address life
hallenges and enhance wellbeing'. Philp (1979) argued that social work applied
 distinctive approach to what he called 'mediating in the social'. The key to this
/as building a bridge of common humanity between established, successful sec-
ons of society (including the 'respectable' working class) and what Philp termed
ne 'residuum' – people who were marginalised and excluded for various reasons,
.g. because they had broken the law, were too ill to work, or were perceived as
eviating from acceptable norms. According to Philp, social workers essentially
/ent about 'persuading the powerful that the others are safe', arguing that people
om marginalised sections of society should be afforded the same dignity and
ecognition to which all citizens were entitled, while at the same time encourag-
ag people to adjust and adapt to social norms (Hyslop, 2018). Philp thought this
nediating role made social workers careful and even ambivalent about the idea
f social structures; after all, people's outcomes in life could not be wholly deter-
nined, e.g. by poverty and inequality, as this would leave little scope for indi-
idual change and empowerment (and no job for social workers to do). Yet social
/orkers often use deterministic theories to help explain and understand why
idividuals find themselves in difficulties, or are posing difficulties to others. The
eason for this ambivalent position is not just to help the individual 'client', e.g.
) overcome specific challenges and problems, but also to serve wider society –
ounteracting the 'othering' of marginalised groups and ensuring that all members
f society are recognised as equal citizens.

Although outdated in many respects, including its lack of attention to gender
nd race, Philp's analysis highlights a key aspect of social work, namely its role
1 mediating between the powerful and powerless. There is a paradoxical sense

that individuals both can and cannot shape their own destiny, that social struc
tures are both all-powerful and able to be transcended. As noted by Hood (2018)
the requirement to hold conflicting ideas in a state of tension, rather than trying
to resolve things in favour of one or the other, or combine them in some sort o
synthesis, seems to be more easily accommodated within 'Eastern' philosophy
than in the more linear traditions of the Eurocentric West. The problems thi
causes for the profession are readily discerned in the negative and often contra
dictory public criticism it attracts, particularly in the anglophone sphere, where
social workers may be condemned, often at the same time and sometimes by the
same people, as do-gooding leftwingers, meddlesome bureaucrats, and draconian
child-snatchers. As Howe (2014) points out, social work is characterised by a bal
ancing act of dualisms: care and control, and prevention, art and science, and se
on. Because these dynamics are part of the messy reality of social work practice
simple or reductive solutions rarely work out. Social work cannot get away from
its core regulatory duties in areas such as public protection and safeguarding
but this does not mean relinquishing its tradition of dissent or commitment to
people's fundamental rights (McGregor, 2022). Social workers are neither social
justice warriors nor professional lackeys of the state – but, by the same token
they appear to be both.

The obvious riposte to such arguments is that they are ill-suited to addres
social inequalities in their current form. Under the influence of postmodern
ism, social work's ambivalence about structural determinism has turned in some
quarters into something more like outright scepticism (Noble, 2004). Traditiona
'grand narratives' of social change, particularly those focusing on class conflict
have been supplanted by a concern with identity and a more contingent and
localised form of critique, emphasising respect for difference and the importance
of dialogue and partnership. As with the 'pluralist' approach to community work
outlined in Chapter 8, the implication is that critical practice should focus on
understanding and contributing to everyday lives in specific social and cultura
contexts, rather than on broad-based organising to achieve political aims. How
ever, as Noble (2004: 302) points out, the postmodern turn towards the local and
specific risks diverting attention from the 'pervasive power of structural forces'
which 'continue to lie at the root of injustice and impoverishment'. It is another
reason why anti-racist social work and the other radical approaches discussed
in Chapter 7 continue to play such a vital role in the profession, shoring up its
ability to challenge the dominant neo-liberal ideology at a time when dissent and
resistance are being curtailed.

A final defence of social work's role in addressing inequality is to adopt a
broader view of its constituent parts. In some ways, this connects to the pattern
of globalisation and internationalisation highlighted in Chapter 5. The emergence
of different forms of social work in the Global South, along with its decolonisa
tion and reconstruction in parts of the Global North, offers some hope of renewa

nd evolution. It is also to acknowledge that the burden of social work's para-
doxes does not rest on the shoulders of frontline practitioners alone. Since struc-
ural problems require structural solutions, it is incumbent on managers, senior
eaders, educators, researchers, professional associations, policymakers, and all
hose participating in social work's professional project, to share the burden. The
direct knowledge and lived experience of inequality, transmitted by individuals,
amilies and communities to social workers who take the trouble to understand
uch things, is not just a matter for social casework. It is also a matter for the planning and design of services, training and education of professionals, evaluation
and dissemination of evidence, organising of campaigns and direct action, and
marshalling the state's resources in favour of the most vulnerable and marginal-
sed. If social workers are in a position to contribute to all of these activities in
. cohesive way, it is because they are connected by what Jones (2014) calls the
golden threads' of the profession's long history: a strong value base, commitment
o relationships, respect for individual autonomy, emphasis on partnerships, and
ecognition that private troubles and public issues are interlinked.

Conclusion

This book has attempted a dual task – first, to examine inequality as a form of
social injustice that speaks to social work's core aims as a profession; and second,
o discuss whether and how social work actually does promote the vision of a
more egalitarian society. The first part is arguably more straightforward than the
second; it is not necessary to believe in a utopian ideal of equality to recognise
hat systematic disparities in opportunities and outcomes are unjust. The second
part – the role of social work – is more challenging. On the one hand, social work
has become embedded in modern welfare systems, giving it a platform to advo-
ate on behalf of vulnerable citizens and at least some influence when it comes
o directing public funds towards deprived and excluded groups. On the other
hand, this statutory role has also made social workers a visible face of inequality –
whether as agents of intervention or bureaucratic gatekeepers of assistance –
n an era of political division and economic retrenchment. Social work's own
story has been tainted by its paternalist origins and acknowledged contribution
o European racist imperialism.

Given these complexities, it is unsurprising that social work finds itself besieged
n many sides: from right-wing critics, for embracing progressive values at the
ost of technical mastery; from left-wing critics, for being co-opted by managerialism and neoliberal institutions; from Indigenous critics, for Eurocentrism
and service to colonial powers; and from the recipients of social work services,
or not listening properly or sticking around for very long. Nonetheless, social
work is one of the few professions that would acknowledge these dilemmas as

a fundamental part of being present: to endorse the radical aims of oppressed groups while administering public services for those groups, to claim sympathy and allegiance with people at the margins while also claiming the status and authority of a profession. In the end, it is possible that social work's mediating role is – or will become – untenable in the face of inequalities that are simply too wide to bridge, that its social justice mission will collapse under its own contradictions. On the other hand, it is also possible that social work will emerge renewed in those jurisdictions where greater equality is viewed as a legitimate social goal. In the end, social work may play only a small part in achieving a more equal society, but we can certainly imagine ways in which a more equal society would transform social work.

References

Bennett, D.L., Webb, C.J.R., Mason K.E., *et al.* (2021) 'Funding for preventative Children's Services and rates of children becoming looked after: A natural experiment using longitudinal area-level data in England', *Children and Youth Services Review* 131, p. 106289.

Butler, P. (2014) *How Alan Wood became the 'go-to fixer' for child protection.* Available at: www.theguardian.com/society/2014/jul/09/alan-wood-go-to-fixer-child-protection-hackney-social-work, Last accessed 6 November 2022.

Cottam, H. (2018) Radical help: How we can remake the relationships between us and revolutionise the welfare state, London, Virago.

Fleetwood, J. and Lea, J. (2022) Defunding the police in the UK: Critical questions and practical suggestions, *The Howard Journal of Crime and Justice*, **61**(2), pp. 167–184.

Michael Garrett, P. (2021a) "A World to Win': In Defence of (Dissenting) Social Work—A Response to Chris Maylea', *The British Journal of Social Work*, **51**(4), pp. 1131–1149.

Garrett, P.M. (2021b) *Dissenting social work: Critical theory, resistance and pandemic*, Abingdon, Routledge.

Ghate, D. and Hood, R. (2019) 'Using evidence in social care', in Boaz, A., Davies, H., Fraser, A., *et al.* (eds) *What works now?* Bristol, Policy Press, pp. 89–110.

Hood, R. (2018) *Complexity in social work*, London, Sage.

Howe, D. (2014) *The compleat social worker*, Basingstoke, Palgrave Macmillan.

Hyslop, I. (2018) "Neoliberalism and social work identity', *European Journal of Social Work*, **21**(1), pp. 20–31.

International Federation of Social Work (IFSW) (2014) *Global Definition of the Social Work Profession*, Available online: http://ifsw.org/policies/definition-of-social-work/, Last Accessed: 01/05/2022.

Jones, R. (2014) 'The best of times, the worst of times: Social work and its moment', *British Journal of Social Work*, 44(3), pp. 485–502.

Jones, R. (2018) In whose interest?: The privatisation of child protection and social work. Bristol, Policy Press.

aylea, C. (2021) 'The end of social work', *The British Journal of Social Work*, **51**(2), pp. 772–789.

cGregor, C. (2022) 'Dissent against "definition debates" about social work', *Aotearoa New Zealand Social Work*, **34**(3), pp. 84–88.

arey, M. (2014) Making the education of social workers consistently effective, London, HMSO.

icholas, J. (2015) Why pretend social work is about social justice? It's not. *Community Care*, 20 October 2015.

oble, C. (2004) 'Postmodern thinking: where is it taking social work?' *Journal of Social Work*, **4**(3), pp. 289–304.

ailp, M. (1979) 'Notes on the form of knowledge in social work', *The Sociological Review*, **27**(1), pp. 83–111.

nk, S., Ferguson, H. and Kelly, L. (2021) 'Digital social work: Conceptualising a hybrid anticipatory practice', *Qualitative Social Work*, 14733250211003647.

amesh, R. (2013) *Michael Gove on a quest to reform social work training*. Available at: www.theguardian.com/society/2013/nov/12/michael-gove-reform-social-work, Last accessed 25 February 2022.

ce, D. (2012) 'Street-level bureaucrats and the welfare state: Toward a micro-institutionalist theory of policy implementation', *Administration & Society*. DOI: 10.1177/0095399712451895

amuel, M. (2020) Black and ethnic minority social workers disproportionately subject to fitness to practise investigations, *Community Care*, 31 July 2020.

astell, D. and White, S. (2010) 'Technology as magic: Fetish and folly in the IT-enabled reform of children's services', in Ayre, P. and Preston-Shoot, M. (eds), *Children's services at the crossroads: A critical evaluation of contemporary policy for practice*, Lyme Regis, Russell House Publishing.

atts, R. (2019) *Criminalizing dissent: The Liberal state and the problem of legitimacy*, Abingdon, Routledge.

einberg, M. and Banks, S. (2019) 'Practising ethically in unethical times: Everyday resistance in social work', *Ethics and Social Welfare*, **13**(4), pp. 361–376.

helan, J. (2022) 'On your Marx...? A world to win or the dismantlement of a profession? On why we need a reckoning', *The British Journal of Social Work*, **52**(2), pp. 1168–1181.

ilkinson, R. and Pickett, K. (2010) *The spirit level: Why equality is better for everyone*, Harmondsworth, Penguin.

Index

Note: Page numbers followed with *f* and *t* refer to figures and tables.